Ruth Ritchie is a very pleasant and attractive freelance writer. After bleeding everybody's expense account dry as an advertising copywriter in the 1980s, she returned to university and play-writing at NIDA (no expense accounts there). For the last 15 years, she has worked as a columnist, feature writer and critic for the *Sydney Morning Herald*, where she regularly savages in print everything from television to bad restaurants.

Ruth lives in Sydney with her husband Jhonnie, their Irish terrier and two/four children. She loves to cook and be cooked for.

waterlemon

Ruth Ritchie

waterlemon

husband in a coma & other setbacks

Ruth Ritchie

MACMILLAN
Pan Macmillan Australia

First published 2006 in Macmillan by Pan Macmillan Australia Pty Ltd
1 Market Street, Sydney

National Library of Australia
Cataloguing-in-Publication data:

Ritchie, Ruth.
Waterlemon: husband in a coma & other setbacks.

ISBN 978 1 40503 755 6.
ISBN 1 40503755 5.

1. Ritchie, Ruth. 2. Journalists – New South Wales –
Biography. 3. Women authors, Australian – New South Wales –
Biography. 4. Mentally handicapped – New South Wales –
Family relationships. I. Title.

070.92

Typeset in 13/15 pt Bembo by Midland Typesetters, Australia
Printed in Australia by McPherson's Printing Group
Cover painting by Eleni Nakopoulos

For Tracey Brown,
for everything.

Day 1

I'D BEEN LOUNGING IN BED, watching TV and eating Haigh's assorted creams for most of the morning. Patrick was asleep in the next room and William was building something prehistoric from Play-doh at preschool. Jhonnie must have been more than halfway through a 20-kilometre bike ride at West Head.

When your husband dons lycra with sudden manic enthusiasm a few months after you have a baby, there's not a lot you can do but sit back and watch. Every time I'm pregnant Jhonnie puts on 10 to 15 sympathy kilos. Then I give birth, step out of my baby suit, and Jhonnie's stuck with his phantom pregnancy gut.

Since Patrick's birth three months earlier, he hadn't hopped, make that lumbered, onto his bike. Hugh and Philip had been training for months, sometimes hundreds of kilometres each week. In spite of his recent departure from the corporate world, giving up smoking, and his fondness for heart monitors and any of the current accoutrements of fitness, Jhonnie was no athlete. All six foot six and 20 years of expense-account lunches went out the door that morning. Fingers crossed they'd go easy on him. Twenty kilometres seemed beyond ambitious, but this was one of those golden, optimistic spring days that Sydney folk are so fond of gloating over –

anything was possible. A day so perfect, it was almost rude not to blow it at an early movie, in the dark. But Haigh's, TV and a sleeping baby were the next best option. While I luxuriated, Jhonnie was pedalling like a fiend somewhere through the eucalypts.

I relish the image of rich ladies lying around eating chocolates, wearing negligees. This is as close as I was ever going to get to Eva Gabor in *Green Acres*. Anyway, the violet creams actually tasted better consumed between Egyptian cotton.

Enjoyment of many foods increases in bed. They are mostly bowl foods. The previous night's goulash or moussaka really improves under the covers. Most cakes, all chocolate, some noodle dishes (not laksa – too sloppy), pea and ham soup, but not chicken soup. Interestingly, tea improves in bed, but coffee really loses something. And if the cup of tea is made by somebody else, and brought to you on a tray, it is better than – well it's nearly as good as a full box of Haigh's creams.

I'd had the chocolates for months. They were my only purchase at the Adelaide Film Festival, my absolutely last hotel/aeroplane hurrah before giving birth. On the same trip I'd organised the freight of chocolates from our boys for Mum's birthday. It was the most practical way to deliver her grandson and chocolates on the same day. Months later, the plunder from Haigh's was still spreading joy. Mum's milk chocolate double-dipped ginger was long gone, and I'd polished off one small box of creams just before the caesarian, in case I died on the table. But this stash I'd buried for just such an occasion.

These Wednesdays were perfect. In hospital or on holiday, I always managed to file my weekly newspaper column on Tuesday night, meaning that the rest of the week was a spring picnic. Today, for a blissful change, the house was virtually empty. Nothing to do but count Patrick's toes, play in the bath, and watch video-tapes for next week's column. The absolute bonus of this whole dreamy picture of assorted creams in bed, complete with pink marabou mules, was that I was actually working.

If all new mothers could be paid to watch TV and then share their unsolicited opinions with thousands of people in print, there'd be a lot less post-natal depression. Perhaps heavy exposure to TV criticism isn't healthy for small children, but they'll all need something to complain about in therapy, eventually. Once, when William was about three and I asked him to turn off the *Bob the Builder* tape and have his bath, he declined my invitation. He was working.

And so, while Patrick slept, I usually hung washing, jumped on the computer, made lists, or chicken stock, but on Wednesday 3 September 2003, I decided to plan my next column. My 9/11 column. There were plenty of how-the-tower-fell documentaries, and a lot of very paranoid tapes about terrorist cells in Pakistan, or Nowra. But I decided to write about *Six Feet Under*. Yet another episode began with some poor unsuspecting fool going about his business until – poof – dead, another body finds its way to the Fisher family funeral parlour. *Six Feet Under* might actually be the first truly 9/11 drama, in that every week it acknowledges the sudden, random nature of tragedy. The way anyone's life can change – just like that. That seemed like an excellent way in to the column, without being cynical about our filthy government, and losing too many readers in the first paragraph, as I so often did. A very viable theory, I thought, as the phone rang. Don't wake Patrick. Don't wake Patrick. I want to finish this episode.

I answered the phone with a mouthful of strawberry cream, and I could see from the number and hear from the terrible reception that it was Hugh. He was riding with Jhonnie. And Jhonnie's new ridiculous phone didn't work anywhere, let alone West Head. So it was either Hugh or Jhonnie.

Hugh was out of breath and the reception was bad.

'What have you done with my husband?'

The silence was unnerving, and I could hear Hugh bracing himself.

'Hugh, Hugh? Are you okay?'

'There's been an accident. You have to go straight to Emergency at Royal North Shore. They're expecting you. He'll be there.'

'What kind of accident? Are you with him? How will he get to hospital?'

'He's in a helicopter.'

'A helicopter, Hugh, did you say? What happened to him? Hugh –'

And the line went dead.

I ran up and down on the spot, shaking my hands. How does this phone return numbers? No, Hugh will ring back. He'll move to somewhere with better reception . . . Helicopter? The phone rang.

'So what happened?'

'I don't know. I couldn't ring before. They said not to ring until we knew where he was going or if . . .'

'If what? Hugh, is he going to die? Is he dead?'

'I don't know.'

The phone went again.

I tapped my fingers on my lips. The temperature in the room plummeted. I couldn't feel my lips. My fingers moved very quickly, and I couldn't feel them either.

Emergency.

I dialled my sister. Wednesday. She'd be at the racetrack. She could be here in minutes.

'Julia. Jhonnie's in a helicopter on his way to hospital. Are you at Randwick?'

In situations such as these (all right, we'd never been in anything like this) Julia and I become very calm and organised. I can't remember the rest of that phone call, but it was pure logistics. Julia to come here. Julia to ring Esther. Esther to get William from preschool. Me to ring Mum. Me to ring cab. Don't drive to your husband's corpse. A no-brainer. Some things are stupidly clear in an emergency. I rang my mother.

'Mum . . . Jhonnie's on his way to Royal North Shore. Are you busy?'

Checked Patrick. Cleaned teeth. Put on shoes. Bottle of water. My husband was in a helicopter and I didn't know if he was alive. I rang Hugh's phone and it went straight to voice mail. Out of range. I checked Patrick. I made Patrick a bottle. Checked I had money for the taxi. I put the remote control back on the stand and the chocolates on the high shelf above my bed. I turned the TV off.

Standing in total silence, waiting for my sister and a taxi, I could feel all the blood coursing through my veins, and electricity in every nerve ending. My hands were damp. My mouth dry. Where was Julia? It'd only been 11 minutes. If Jhonnie was dead, these few minutes of me standing silently in our bedroom, trying not to sway, these minutes weren't going to make any difference. Cleaned my teeth again. Chocolate and Colgate – terrible. But it wasn't that. I already had the most wretched taste in my mouth. It might have been fear.

As soon as Julia arrived I felt better. Julia can fix anything. Nearly every member of my family has some reassuring talent, not all of them useful in an emergency. Julia's 'take charge' manner, her cool eye, fooled me that this was just another day, any day, when she was taking care of the kids so that I could trip out the door – to go shopping, at David Jones perhaps.

The taxi hooted outside. I went over Patrick's routine, again.

'Just go. Give him a big kiss for me.'

Julia and Jhonnie hadn't been doing much kissing of late. They were barely speaking. Julia had read him the riot act a few days after I came home with Pat and he'd told her to fuck off.

Months and many Sunday yum chas had passed since the blow-up. What would it take for them to move on? She never backed down. He couldn't bear confrontation. Give him a kiss? It took a helicopter. Apparently, it was a helicopter-sized family fight.

I thought about that fight and Jhonnie's bike as the taxi zoomed down the expressway to the Royal North Shore Hospital. Jhonnie hadn't exactly taken to freelance life since leaving work in February. He'd managed to busy himself with coffee, the odd meeting, golf, and (of course) reorganising his electronic address book. The agency had given him a very flash racing bike as a farewell present. While I, groaning theatrically in the last stages of pregnancy, painted baby furniture and rewashed William's baby clothes, Jhonnie kitted out the new bike with gadgets. In that tough first week home from hospital, Jhonnie wasn't making himself too useful. My bossy older sister had told him so. Then he told her to fuck off . . . Now, how would I get his bike home in a cab?

A blue hospital sign appeared. They had their own exit. How handy. There were three, maybe four traffic lights between our house and this hospital. And the traffic moved brilliantly. How handy. This was really going well. That's what I thought as the driver tried to drop me on a back street by a boom gate.

'I'm not getting out of this taxi until you pull up next to an Emergency sign. Keep going,' I said. 'Keep going.'

I was shouting at a man who wanted me out of his car.

'Go through this boom gate and take me to Emergency. NOW.'

And he did. This was going well.

As the doors parted I could see the waiting room was busy. I hate waiting in Emergency. The anxiety of the injured and unwell as they jostle for position nearly matches the unrest of a Chinatown crowd on Sunday morning waiting for yum cha. I had to find my mother. I had to push right to the front, because I really didn't care if some pensioner or some drunk had been waiting for two hours. I had a three-month-old baby at home, and this was all a bit frightening.

None of the nurses at the desk looked up. Expert at avoiding eye contact, their charts captivated them. I took a few breaths, and spoke to the tops of their heads.

'Excuse me, my name's Ruth Ritchie and I think my husband was brought here by helicopter from West Head.'

All three looked up. Two stood. Maybe all of them spoke. The service here was excellent.

'Come this way, Mrs Ritchie. The doctors will see you.'

Escorted down a corridor, away from the people who had to wait. I went in, further in, deep in the middle of the hospital. They opened the door to a small, dimly lit room. An ugly purpose-built cell. Table, chairs, jugs of water, telephones, boxes of tissues and my mother.

'Fuck. This is worse than I thought.'

Mum hugged me. She was purple in the face, and looked completely rattled. My mother had obviously just been told very bad news.

'Is he dead?'

The nurse didn't want to answer. My mother couldn't.

'The doctors are with him now. We'll come in and keep you updated as soon as we know anything. Is there anything else you need?'

'Can I see him? When can I see him?'

'The doctors will tell you. I couldn't say.'

'Have you seen him?'

She'd seen him all right, and she didn't want to tell his wife what she'd seen. This was definitely worse than I'd thought. How I longed for my opportunity to barge in front of a toddler out in Emergency. Instead I was standing in a room that I never knew existed, a room that was made for widows.

You have a choice, at this point, of how you will behave as the drama unfolds. I wondered if howling like a dog would achieve anything. I checked out my facilities – all the toiletries and snacks in my bathroom and bar fridge. This was an absolute first. I was being handled like eggshells in a Sydney hospital. I'd nearly bled to death giving birth, and nobody raised an eyebrow. Now I had my own hideous little office and a lot of people offering me tissues. I would behave graciously, and drink their water, and possibly use their phone.

'Judy Prisk, please . . . Jude, it's Ruth. I'm at RNS. My husband has been in an accident, so I won't be able to get home to proof my copy.'

Silence. I could hear Judy, my sub-editor at the *Herald*, computing this news.

'Is he okay? Are you okay? Don't worry about your copy. Is there anything I can do?'

'I haven't seen the doctors yet. I think it might be incredibly serious. So maybe we should line up Michael for my column next week, in case he . . . This is a bit surreal, isn't it?'

'Are you alone there?'

'No, I'm with my mother. My sister is with the baby. Yeah, I'm sorry about my column. I might go now, okay?'

Another nurse entered quietly with a clipboard and a wad of forms. How marvellous. Something to do. She even had a pen. This just kept getting more serious.

The words were meaningless on the page. Weight, hospital of birth, mother's maiden name. Allergy to penicillin? History of surgery. Childhood diseases. Perhaps some other wife should have filled in these forms because I clearly had no idea whom I had married. I didn't think, under these circumstances, that I could remember any of these details about my own medical history. And if I got Jhonnie's wrong there wasn't another soul alive who'd have the right answers. Jhonnie's medical history, as of that moment, was a guesstimate. I handed back the forms. The quiet nurse disappeared. Mum looked really terrible.

'Can I get you a wet face cloth?'

She drank more water and waved away my fuss.

'At least if I have a stroke we're already in Emergency.'

'Damn, but you're thoughtful.'

We both laughed a little, and I remembered something that might have been important. Outside the door two nurses stopped speaking suddenly. How awkward.

'It might be nothing, but Jhonnie's allergic to scallops. Really allergic. I guess they're not giving him any scallops in there. But in case there's something in them that –'

'Thanks. That should be fine. Is there anything else you'd like us to know?'

'We have a three-month-old baby.'

They both looked at me and I think I heard a little gasp of exhalation. A tiny shock. Damn. I've shocked a nurse in Emergency.

'I guess that's a bit like the scallops. Not really a factor. But we have a little baby, and three other children.'

We stood in that corridor in silence for a while. In a thought bubble hung the father of four, and his problem with scallops, and his missus above a couple of very uncomfortable nurses. That hideous little room existed as much for the staff as for people like me.

'The doctors shouldn't be too much longer.'

I got back in my box. And I waited for that door to open, and wondered what else I could tell them that would make Jhonnie just walk out and get his stupid bike into a cab and home.

A little man hovered by the door. He introduced himself. 'Hello. I'm Blah Blah Blah.' The name went in one head and out the other. His hushed tones were creepy. He was whispering, at church volume. Not church: funeral parlour. It seemed only minutes ago I'd been watching those attractive undertaking brothers on *Six Feet Under*. This was no Fisher brother.

Sure, he said he was a social worker, but I knew he was an undertaker, without any TV charm. This little man was damp.

'And you're the wife, yes? And his mother?'

'No. Her mother,' Mum's voice boomed back at him. Without conferring, I knew this guy was giving us both the creeps. Get out. Get out. Get out.

'Well, Mrs Blam-pied . . .'

'Blom-pee-ay. Common mistake – everyone gets it wrong. But my name is Ritchie.'

'Okay, then. Mrs Blompee . . .'

'No. *Blom-pee-ay*. Could we stick with Ritchie?'

The little undertaker started to whisper about the gravity of our situation. 'I'm here as a conduit between you and the doctors. They'll take care of [check clipboard for husband's name] John, and I'll take care of you.'

'His name is Jhonnie, and I don't require . . . His name is Jhonnie.'

Undertaker blinked at me. I blanked back.

'Is it hot in here?' My mother was completely purple now.

'Could you perhaps find some ice for my mother? You could take care of that.'

Clearly he couldn't. Miffed undertaker wandered away. Mum and I looked at each other, mystified, and the door opened again, just like the pacy antics in a restoration comedy.

'Hugh.' And my eyes filled with tears when we hugged. Poor Hugh.

'I'm so sorry. I'm so sorry.'

'Why? Did you push him off the bike?' We both nearly smiled.

What to do with Hugh? He was still shaking, hours later. Tall, dark and shaky. Completely silly-looking in lycra. Top covered in logos, shorts, shoes. All the accoutrements of racing bike riders scream fetish to me, and look as improbable as whip, suspenders and stockings might in an Emergency ward.

So what happened? It tumbled out in chunks, some clear, some mysterious.

The conditions had been perfect. Road clear. No traffic. Jhonnie had been struggling with the hills. He had to dismount near the top of the previous hill, out of condition. Philip had gone ahead. Hugh had waited for him. Jhonnie raced down the hill, probably trying to build up speed for the next steep climb. But there were no more hills, just a quick dead end. How could Jhonnie have known that? He'd never been to West Head before. They shouldn't have taken him on such a demanding ride. He wasn't fit enough. He wasn't fit at all.

There was no car. He was going downhill very fast. They didn't see what happened. Philip heard Jhonnie shout, 'Fuck.' Hugh heard the thud of metal. When he rounded the corner Jhonnie was lying 40 feet from the bike, breathing hard. Struggling to breathe. And the phone worked there, but not anywhere else. Lucky, huh? The ambulance, no two, no three, were there in minutes. And they called the helicopter. And Hugh thought Jhonnie was just unconscious, but the doctor on the helicopter said that the head injury was the main thing.

The head injury.

'Is his head in one piece?'

'I don't know. I didn't take the helmet off. Yes, it is. I mean, I couldn't see once they put the tubes in.'

The floor and my knees seemed to fall away. It made no material difference, what Hugh was saying. I knew for certain that this was beyond my comprehension, beyond my control. A house in Kansas can be whisked up by a tornado. And I'd always said, why would anyone live in the path of a tornado, in Kansas? But clearly, you don't have to.

I was really struck by this inevitability as Hugh filled in the gaps. Short of breath, his heart still pounding, unable to sit still for long. His conscience kept meeting my eye for absolution.

I kept gripping his arm, occasionally in a pang of fresh fear, and as often as I could in consolation.

'This is that day, isn't it? The day in the songs. *This is the day your life will surely change . . .* It's today. It's not the day you fall in love, or write a poem or get a degree. It's today. I'm living in a fucking The The song.'

My mother managed to comfort Hugh with more focus than I could muster. I didn't blame him, and I made that clear, but I had too many notions spinning in the air to focus on his absolution, so really, she did well.

'Shit just happens, Hugh.'

Scores of years as a devout Catholic and she dredges up 'Shit happens'?

As we waited in silence my mother prayed, and did the next best thing. She got on the phone and rang some power nuns, and the odd Jesuit. Shit happens, and when it does the Catholic network swings into commando-style action. Why wasn't I praying? Was I praying and I just didn't know it?

'What else?' I grilled Hugh to pass the time, to picture the scene. 'So he never spoke? Never regained consciousness?'

'No. The ambos and police rescue arrived and we started to clear the road for the helicopter to land, and it was covered in branches. Only three cars passed, the whole time. Only one slowed down to offer help. So we cleared the road, and one of the ambos runs down and tells everybody to stop. There's a heli-pad about 30 feet away. So we go there, and try to use our mobiles, and the reception was terrible, so I had to keep going back. They said I couldn't call you until we knew where they were taking him.'

'How long was that?'

'It seemed very fucking long. Sorry, Mrs Ritchie. Maybe half an hour. And I rang you, and it kept dropping out. And there was no signal, fuck-all signal from the heli-pad. Sorry, Mrs Ritchie. And after all that, Philip pointed at this public phone, right there in the middle of the field. You just get so used to grabbing the mobile, you don't even see public phones for what they are . . .'

'Misleading organs of public utility that rarely work?' My mother's blood pressure had come down with the water and the ice and the phone calls to prominent clergy, and maybe the prayers. This was going as well as could be expected, without any new input or any visits from damp undertakers in nearly 20 minutes; and then the door opened.

A young man in fluorescent weather gear filled the room. He was dirty, maybe muddy, and unshaven. The Emergency outfit made him seem tall, but as he crouched down on his haunches before me, I could see that he was slight, nearly translucent, exhausted, but his clear pale gaze never dodged mine.

'I'm Rob Turner. I'm the doctor with Careflight.'

I didn't really know what that meant, so I introduced myself, polite, wondering.

'I intubated your husband – John, is it? – at the site. Has anyone spoken to you about his injuries?'

'Just Hugh.' They acknowledged each other, and Rob in fluoro orange continued. His manner was practised, a routine. There's a protocol, but this guy looked straight at me, not wasting words, trying to give me something.

'The scans will indicate if there's broken bones and organ damage, but that head injury is very serious.'

'I guess I don't understand what that means.'

'He scored a 3 on the Glasgow Coma Scale. That's low, okay? That's the priority. I wouldn't expect them to treat any of his other injuries until that score is higher. I'd say they'll operate, and then they'll know more, but that fixed dilated pupil is a very bad sign.'

'A bad sign of . . . ?'

'Brain damage. His youth and fitness are on his side. That's quite a bike. He's a regular cyclist then, is he?'

'Hasn't been off his arse in three months. We've just had a baby. So he's not fit. He's . . .' I ran out of words and this frank young doctor didn't dodge me.

'Well, youth is a big factor in brain injury. I'd say he's about 50–50, without knowing the extent of the brain damage. That's why he's here, not Gosford. This is the place for a brain injury.'

'Fifty–fifty chance of . . . surviving this?'

'They'll know more when they operate. They'll be getting him stable, probably checking for internal injuries beyond the punctured lung.'

The punctured lung? Jhonnie's uncatalogued treasure trove of injuries wouldn't be addressed until . . . They might never be addressed. He might die before they got his arm in a cast. Made sense – what would be the point? This really wasn't like any episode any of us had known in Emergency, where you wait, with a bleeding knee or a twisted ankle. Jhonnie might have died waiting for a bandage.

The young doctor said more about how he rode bikes, and he'd got young kids and he'd like to be here, in this hospital, if he was in Jhonnie's wildly expensive preposterous cycling shoes. He apologised for his appearance, to me and to my mum. He'd been on duty for 36 hours, but he just wanted to speak to me. I was grateful that he did. I felt like Jhonnie had been in good hands. Before he left he took my Filofax and opened it on 3 September, and wrote his name and phone number. He wanted to know if, how, Jhonnie made out. And he was gone.

'What an impressive young man,' noted my mother. Remarkably impressive, confidence-building. That can't be easy to do, tell people that sort of news. He did it very well. And there, in his wake, was our social-working undertaker, wringing his hands once more at the door. Had he been standing behind that doctor, blocked by the size and brightness of his Emergency wardrobe?

'So, what's going to happen now . . . the doctors will assess the extent of the brain injury, and probably operate. His injuries are very, very serious. You need to prepare yourself for the possibility that he has only a 50–50 chance of survival.'

I struggled to hear this new news. Maybe old news? Maybe no news. This guy was stealing material, and making it worse. It hadn't sounded so bad out of that young TV doctor's mouth.

'What are you telling me? Were you just listening to what he said, that guy who just left? I was right here in the room. Are you telling me anything different?'

'Only that you need to be prepared for . . . the severity of the situation.'

Hugh, Mum and I leaned in, concentrating – sceptics at a séance – and this guy had nothing new, not a scintilla of news from the front. He shuffled from foot to foot and then he was gone. We said nothing and finally shook our heads.

'Is it just me, or is that guy totally fucked?'

'Ruth. Language!'

'Mum, two different characters right out of *Twin Peaks* have just given my husband two-to-one odds of survival. "Fuck" is really just a starting point.'

Hugh was confused. 'Was that guy a social worker? Is he supposed to be making you feel better?'

My mother did her best imitation of the 'doctors-take-care-of-him, I'll-take-care-of-you' exchange for Hugh, and we all laughed. Quite loud. We talked about getting him fired. And then we talked about the young doctor again, and I could tell that Mum and Hugh were dodging that 50–50 factor. It was out there, the elephant in the room, and neither of them was going to raise it.

'If the Melbourne Cup favourite was two to one, you couldn't possibly bet against it, could you? Not real money. You couldn't hope to win real money by betting against a two to one favourite?'

Mum and Hugh looked worried, and reluctantly agreed.

'Well then, that's good. Jhonnie is a very short price for the Melbourne Cup. If this injury could kill 50 per cent of blokes, none of them would be Jhonnie, right?'

Mum and Hugh didn't exactly rally behind this perverse logic. We sat in silence for a while before my mother reminded us, 'Shit happens.'

And then the door opened, again.

'The doctors say you can see him now.'

Off to see Jhonnie, in the saddling enclosure.

Jhonnie is a big man standing up. Lying down, inert, on life support, he was a giant, much greater than his six foot six inches. Much heavier and oddly lighter than his 120 kilos.

Jhonnie's head, a swollen purple veiny pumpkin, looked like a special effect, but not a particularly convincing one. His brow was beaded with sweat, although the room was cold. The colour I recognised instantly. Years earlier I'd helped a man who'd had a heart attack at Newcastle pool. My towel was under his head as my boyfriend of the day gave him CPR. He revived him twice while we waited for the ambulance. We could see the hospital on the hill above the pool, but the ambulance had taken forever. I lost my towel when paramedics descended on him. We backed away. Before he died his forehead and neck had turned an angry meaty purple.

The colour and the breathing were the things I noticed most. Intubated breathing is nothing like sleep. Mechanical, gurgling, a metronome that bears no resemblance to the nearly comic, vulnerable sound of a big man when he sleeps. An unrecognisably still purple giant, naked under a sheet, covered in machines.

What could I touch? Where did it hurt? What could I break? His hand, arm, legs were deeply lacerated. One eye was swollen shut like a punch-drunk heavyweight; what was I looking at? I can't remember now anything anybody said by his side in those moments. I got the gist. I got the sense of occasion. Have a good look, because this may be goodbye.

'Hey babe. I'm here.'

The skin on his good hand was baby-smooth familiar. I was worried he was cold, and suggested as much to the nurses, who found some polite way of telling me that Jhonnie knew absolutely nothing of this, and never would. A doctor lifted the blackened eyelid to reveal a fixed dilated pupil, opened out sideways, glaring at nothing. An eye like a dead snapper's. Not a flicker of life.

I didn't manage to do anything but hold his hand. My mum planted a kiss on his forehead. Funny that I didn't. The purple. I didn't know if it was okay to go so near the purple. A nurse handed me his wallet – the one we'd bought in Florence when I was pregnant with William. His watch, the Rolex Mariner I'd given him for his thirty-eighth birthday. And his wedding ring. My mother grabbed the bag of torn, bloody lycra clothes, and the helmet, the life-saving helmet. She whisked them away, rightly sensing that I never ever needed to see them, wash them or dispose of them.

Staff waited, I presumed, for me to say that I was done.

'Okay.' I kissed his hand. 'Come back to us, Jhonnie, okay?'

They looked at each other, and the undertaker and yet another nurse shepherded us back into our box. A doctor and nurse trailed into the room, so that it was nearly crowded. The doctor explained that they were about to cut a hole in Jhonnie's skull and insert some kind of shunt, an EVD, to drain the bleeding. The Careflight doctors had saved Jhonnie's life by intubating him at the site and administering a drug that had reduced the swelling of the brain as it haemorrhaged. He had remained haemodynamically stable throughout the resuscitation. He would be Dr Small's patient, and Dr Small was really the best neurosurgeon there was. But he wasn't exactly in the building, so the surgery would be performed by somebody called Saleh, a young doctor on Small's team, and also a great practitioner. (They managed to make all these guys sound like concert pianists.) And so the main issue would be the EVD, but because of the collapsed lung and the broken ribs, a small incision to include a tube to drain the blood and fluid from Jhonnie's lung would certainly help him rest more comfortably.

I couldn't think of any questions before they disappeared. I might not have listened to everything they said, as it occurred to me that total strangers could well have just told me they were about to stick a McHappy Meal toy inside Jhonnie's brain and I would still have thanked them politely. When they left we sat in silence for an uncharacteristically long time. Nothing to say about it really. If Mum and Hugh muttered anything about him being okay it was so half-hearted as to be barely audible. Seeing him had made it no more real, but it was finally clear that Jhonnie and the bike and I weren't hailing a cab back home any time soon.

And so, I poured another glass of water and sat down at the phone. 'Hello Chris. It's Ruth Ritchie. Can you talk at the moment? If you're driving, pull over.'

This phone call wasn't ever going to go well. Jhonnie's ex-wife had to be told. Even though they were at each other's throats and engaging lawyers for another round of battle after all these years, she had to be told. The children had to be told. Jhonnie had dropped Madison at school that morning and put her on a bus for a three-day camp. Connar was supposed to be staying with us so that Chris could go away on some grown-up camp. That wasn't going to happen. I didn't know when I would get home to my own children, let alone hers.

'Chris, it's very bad news. I'm ringing from RNS. Jhonnie's been in a bad accident.'

Don't tell her he might die. I'll know more after they operate.

'Is he okay?'

'No. They're operating now. I guess I'll know more tonight, or tomorrow. So, Connar won't be able to come to us, but I guess you'll be cancelling your plans anyway.'

'Why?'

'Because Jhonnie is about to undergo brain surgery, and Connar and Madi will need their mother?'

Silence.

'Well, there's no point in ruining Madison's camp. Can't Connar just come to yours after school? I have to run a conference in the Hunter Valley.'

'So? Get out of it. Connar's father may not live through the night.' Damn, I told her.

'Well, what I do at the Hunter Valley conference nobody else can do. Don't you see? I can't be replaced there.'

'What are you doing, Chris, brain surgery? Maybe I haven't made myself clear. I might be at this hospital around the clock, so I can't take care of Connar.'

'Well somebody is going to be with William and Patrick, or are they there?'

'Wow. So, you're saying that you're going to leave for the Hunter Valley to teach people how to use a flip chart and a white board, and leave your son with . . . who?'

'He'll have to stay with Nigel.'

'I have no idea what to say about that.' Nigel was Chris's ex-boyfriend. She'd left Jhonnie for Nigel; they had a child and broke up. Nigel had been out of Connar's life for more than half his life.

'I don't care what you have to say about that. Ring me when you know how the surgery goes. I hope he's better.'

Click. She hoped that her husband of eight years, the father of two of her three children, would be 'better'. And toodle-oo, she was gone, like Mayzie the lazy bird in *Horton Hatches the Egg*.

I rang Meera. We'd recently hired her to mind Patrick four days a week, so that I could go back to work full-time. It would be the first time in five years. The day she started I began to think of Meera as a lifeline. I couldn't have known then how much we would all need her. I had to tell her what to expect, or not to expect, when she arrived for work in the morning. I rang Julia. William was safely back and bathed. Patrick was fine. Would I be home for dinner? Dinner seemed like a gorgeous remote tropical island. Thick organic lamb cutlets with rosemary polenta and baked eggplant. I should have been standing at my kitchen sink, pressing all the buttons of domestic comfort and familial joy. If he died, any time now, on the table, would I ever make dinner again?

Finally it was time for Hugh to go – hopefully to Esther, and a bar full of strong martinis and nice friends. It's wrong to always imagine Esther holding up a bar, but she does it so well. We'd all managed spectacular bar behaviour in our time, before kids. Esther managed to keep one foot in the camp of irresponsible youth and the other grounded in her business, her fruit salad, AFL-mania and her great friends. Esther had been the obvious one to pick William up from preschool, and all these hours later, hopefully pick Hugh up, post-emergency.

And then it was time for us to leave our luxurious little box, and make what seemed like a very long journey for my mother to another building, another foyer, past horrible floral arrangements made even more hideous by the inclusion of bears and balloons on sticks. Carnations and gerberas and a lot of ugly, bossy, brightly coloured goodwill filled the brown-brick foyer. Banners shouted 'GET WELL' at other people. Nobody was shouting at us. We were told, by a quietly spoken nurse, to use the toilet on the ground floor. In a 10-storey building the public was only allowed to use the toilets on the ground floor. In some misguided prescriptive act of 1960s town planning, it was decided that people right on the verge of losing a loved one could use the exercise.

'There's not a bathroom in the Intensive Care Unit?'

'There's a staff loo.' The nurse looked embarrassed. 'That's why I'm telling you now. Use the staff elevators if you want. They're not as crowded.'

I was worried about my mother walking much further. In this maze it was impossible to guess where we were going, or if we were close. Another scuffed corner, another shiny linoleum corridor.

And finally we were taken to a sitting room on the sixth floor. Big as a classroom, a few badly art-directed posters about emergency procedures, but otherwise not a coffee table, not an outdated magazine. Bad mismatched chairs lined the walls. Everybody staring inwards, at each other, at nothing. (Couldn't be good feng shui, surely?) Just two phones hanging on the wall, which I came to learn were the direct lines to ICU. When they rang, the waiting entourage, the silent family members, picked up. Anybody could pick up. Everybody here was in the same boat. Nobody spoke to each other. Maybe they just weren't speaking to us because we had 50–50 written all over our faces. Maybe their odds were better than ours.

There was no news, it seemed for hours. Perhaps I simply lost track of time. Friendly faces bobbed up. Sister Claire Koch, a friend of Mum's and a heavy hitter with the Sisters of St Joseph, appeared. My mother must really have pull. Claire said such comforting things – I can't remember a single one now – and like the nice helicopter doctor, tone and manner seemed just right. These people could really be rated on how their performance affected the temperature of panic in a woman trying to gauge the seriousness of a medical situation.

I thought about that, sitting there. How composed yet stupid I was. If everybody had cracked jokes and eaten choco-late bars and told me Jhonnie would be fine, I would have been happy. Instead nuns and priests and social workers were flocking and speaking in hushed tones. The social worker on this floor wore nice pearls. She was a friend of Claire Koch's (these clergy must spend some terrible nights with the faithful in rooms such as these). She took me aside and showed me the staff toilet. I entered, grateful, and looked around the least glamorous en suite I'd ever visited. I didn't even need to go. Was some hard-working sister crossing her legs outside, waiting for the vacant sign?

I looked in the mirror at this slightly rattled woman, her grubby loose blue jeans, vaguely milky sweatshirt and dirty hair. What about that hair! Long blonde faded ends, three inches of grey roots, all gathered together in a knotty ponytail – hair beyond redemption.

Everything is just a little out of kilter after you've had a baby. And Patrick was, what, three months old that very day? I looked like shit. No wonder I rated entry to the staff loo. Everybody in that waiting room of doom looked better than I did, and some of those people were nearly dead themselves.

Back out there, in our terrible room, Sister Claire said she could arrange for me to sleep at the hospital. I'd done that when William had been stricken with asthma, sat up all night in a chair, listening to him breathe. Would I sit next to Jhonnie's bed? Would I sit in this room? Was there a disgusting dorm for people like us? If he died in the night, would there be any advantage in me being here? What to do.

Eight hours had passed. Sipping water, pacing, making calls. How was that young doctor going in there, microchipping Jhonnie's head? Part of me just wanted to get home. To get home while William was still awake so that I could give him a cuddle. Give Patrick his next feed. Something normal. I'd had enough of this already. Back to the real world, and we'd all be fine, surely.

Maybe another hour passed and finally Saleh emerged.

Young, Indian, inscrutable. Good news. Jhonnie was alive. Really?

The EVD would stay in until the bleeding stopped. Perhaps a few days. Saleh seemed pleased. He relayed details of a procedure that I didn't understand, and said they were still going to do more X-rays, but he didn't expect any more major internal injuries to present themselves. I asked if Jhonnie would be able to walk; the huge stiff collar that pressed from his ears to his shoulders had looked ominous. An image of it digging into his cheek had stuck with me as we whiled away the time with various supportive clergy. Not his department. Saleh did heads. And so now we were just going to have to wait.

The real consequences of a bilateral frontal lobe contusion and an interthalmic haemorrhage are not easy to quantify. Ten different patients could endure the exact same injuries, be treated with identical surgery and drugs, and achieve ten completely different outcomes. Frontal lobe damage is never good, but the brain is a mysterious organ. Were they telling me this to prepare me for bad news? Because they had no idea what they were doing? Because Jhonnie was going to die anyway, so why was I wasting their time?

I'm almost certain that I didn't see Jhonnie again that night. I didn't see him covered in iodine paint, coughing and struggling to breathe. Details, tiny terrible paper-towel details are so clear, but I can't remember seeing him after surgery. I can't have. Or if I did, the overload of the day just cut a few of my circuits. Sister Claire offered to drive Mum home. She offered to drive me after. No. No. I'll just get in that cab and be home in minutes.

I could be home by nine. This wasn't so bad after all. A weird detour in a normal Wednesday. I hugged them both. I took a card with ICU direct phone numbers, and instructions to ring as often and whenever I liked. ICU is a casino that never closes. I could ring and tell the nurses to give Jhonnie messages (what, like 'Get-the-fuck-up you, you Bicycle Idiot'?). I would be up in the night feeding Patrick. I would ring.

Then I was back in that broken bruised elevator, back past the flower vendor, closed now, those lurid balloons peaking from behind metal security blinds, back into a temporary tunnel of a construction site, and out into the cold evening spring air.

The relief of fresh air. The rush of oxygen. I was filled with the positive spin of optimistic nuns and survivalist's delusion. I reached for my phone and rang Tracey. My cousin Tracey and I were very close, like sisters, like best friends, like disaster confidantes. Her qualifications as a psychologist, nurse, mother and conspiracy theorist whose notions nearly always agreed with mine, made her *the* person to ring in a crisis. I'd been trying not to ring her with too many crises of late. Her breast cancer diagnosis had coincided with my miscarriage the previous year. A lot of other strange, unpleasant family planets had lined up since then. Weeks later, when Tracey and I had taken Mum for a routine skin-cancer procedure, Mum had suffered a shocking episode that scared the pants off us. The next day, Jhonnie's sister Vivvy, who was living in Australia at the time, was scheduled at Manly psych ward. And days after that, Jhonnie hopped on a plane for Turkey. One particular day, I'd toured three hospitals between preschool drop-off and pick-up. It was a time of unprecedented incident for a couple of cousins who mostly drank coffee, shopped and gossiped. After a long, strange year, Tracey was finally recovering from the mastectomy and months of chemo as I delivered Patrick. We'd decided Trace would be one of Patrick's godmothers – a brash, positive leap of faith.

So, I thought it was a good idea to tell Tracey about Jhonnie, and tell her while I felt I could get through the call without sobbing.

And I did. And she was great. And I could tell, from her

professional control and completely neutral silences, that the true picture was even worse than the one I was trying to cover up.

'It sounds like they're doing everything right. Nothing about what you've told me sounds fishy. Are you happy with the way they're informing you?'

'I don't know, Trace. I don't know what to ask. Not much point holding a Portuguese phrase book if they're going to answer in Portuguese. Do you know about a Scottish Coma Chart?'

'Glasgow Coma Scale?'

'Maybe. What's it out of? I mean, is it out of 10 or 100?'

'It's out of 15. It's a universally accepted interpretation of various vital signs, scored 1 to 5. The total is a number out of 15.'

'So 3 is low?'

'Three is dead. Are you sure they said 3?'

'Three. I was too embarrassed to ask the helicopter doctor what that meant.'

'That was at the scene. That fixed dilated pupil might not be a sign of –'

'Fuck, *what*? Brain death?'

'He's not brain dead – they wouldn't operate if he was. That fixed pupil could be the eye itself, not brain activity, that's all. Did they mention nerve lesions, in the eye?'

'No. I don't think they're bothering with his eye, or his ribs, or . . . I'm home now. I'll go. Thanks . . . Trace, will you tell me if I'm fucking up?'

'You won't fuck up.'

Tracey's not a pessimist, but she does know hospitals. I really had no idea what was going on, and part of me was certain I was too dull to ever work it out. There's that moment when you must face the fact that no matter how many newspapers you read, you'll never get to the bottom of the situation in the Middle East. You can know more, but you can never really *know*. Where the fuck was that bike?

I'd probably never been so happy to see Julia. William was still awake, and keen for a hug, and a book, and bed. Julia offered me a Scotch, but I was too lost in the Middle East to drink. We talked about lamb cutlets, and eventually I grilled some. Not too many accoutrements. No red wine. We made plans. Julia's organisational savvy would shore up a freefalling situation. Ring friends. Get help. Make a rosti. A rosti? No, a roster, you idiot. Julia agreed to stay, in case the phone rang, in case.

Oddly enough, I went to sleep. Maybe it was 11. The day had been tiring. Alone in our bed and without even thinking about crying, I drifted off. Patrick's tiny insistent voice woke me three hours later, firmly demanding his bottle. I knew the moment my feet hit the carpet that nothing was right. I knew Jhonnie was gone, and the baby was oblivious. How lucky. I shuffled barefoot downstairs as his little voice kept barking. Back in bed with the bottle, the baby and David Letterman, I decided this was probably the best part of the day, possibly any day to come. Just his little hand gripping his muslin, gulping, smiling with trust up at me. His soft little blond head, perfect. This is still joy, I thought – just the two of us in a cosy capsule of darkness. I let Pat snuggle in the doona as I reached for the card next to the bed.

'Hello. This is Ruth, Jhonnie Blampied's wife, and, I'm awake feeding the baby, so . . .'

'This is Sharon. There's no change, Ruth. He's serious but stable. Nothing to report. Is there anything you'd like us to tell him?'

'Just tell him Ruth loves him. Can I come in any time?'

'Do you want to come in now?'

'No, I'm at home with a baby and a little boy. Shall I just ring in the morning?'

'You ring anytime.'

And that was that.

'Dad's serious but stable, Patrick.'

Day 2

WILLIAM WAS NEXT TO ME, sleeping diagonally, in his Cowboy and Indian pyjamas. Plenty of room in that big empty bed this morning.

'Where's Dad?'

'He fell off his bike, and he's having a big sleep in the hospital.'

Enough for William. He rolled over back onto his father's pillows. It was barely light. I couldn't remember him wandering in. His face and arms were sleepy warm. I kissed his long blond hair. On top of everything else, this kid needed a haircut.

'Do you want to go to karate today?'

'Okay.' And up he hopped. Julia was standing at the door holding Patrick, enchanting William.

'Doody! Mum, Doody stayed!'

'Swap ya.'

Julia passed me the baby and disappeared with William. Jhonnie's accident had turned into a spontaneous midweek sleep-over, and within minutes time-honoured early morning routines were in motion. One of the great things about having family over at the early stages of a near-death crisis is that you still get exactly the cup of tea you need first thing in the morning. Julia, William and I sat at the breakfast table: sliced fruit, lemon tea, hot chocolate, toast and Vegemite, laughing

Patrick. And we made plans. In her perfect architect's hand-writing Julia had already listed the friends and family who warranted a phone call immediately. She'd brought the same vim to the seating arrangements at our wedding. Excel spread-sheets of little tables with tiny colour-coded initials. She could make anything look reasonable.

Julia wrote down the names of friends in their pecking/ringing order. She was moving too fast for me.

'What about his parents?' she asked. 'What about Julian, Justin and Vivs?'

I had thought about Jhonnie's parents in the night – perhaps gardening, pottering around their farmhouse in Umbria. I thought about Vivvy, his younger sister, still in Italy, probably picking up a bargain in a market. Pictured his older brother, Julian, stuck somewhere in London traffic, multi-tasking on his newest, latest, zippiest mobile phone – would I even get through? I could see Justin smoking in front of a computer screen in a film studio in LA. Everybody, as I had so recently learned, is always in the middle of doing something very normal when they get those calls. When I made them, what would I be saying? 'Please sit down. Your son/brother is dead.' Or: 'It could be worse. Your son/brother is recovering – which is lucky, because he was *nearly* dead.' That would be better.

'How about I leave them until I've seen him today? I might have some good news.'

'What time is it in Italy?'

'You know what, it's just the wrong time. William, eat your pineapple.'

'I'm off pineapple.'

'You don't get to go off pineapple. Jules, have a baby. I'll call the cavalry.'

For not the first and most certainly not the last time, smiling Patrick was handballed into another loving pair of arms, while

I got busy. Like the family members with the tacit understanding of a correct cup of tea, old friends communicate in shorthand, invaluable in an emergency. A few clipped calls to friends who were busily packing their kids up for school secured a barrage of help.

Nobody ever wants to find out how their nearest and dearest might respond to a call that goes something like 'My husband's in a coma, and I was wondering if you could come with me to the hospital/pick my kid up from preschool/watch the baby while I curl up in the foetal position'. My friends were coming through with flying colours.

When I sat back at the table and retrieved the smiling baby, William had dealt with his fruit (aunts can always relieve you of offending pineapple in a pinch), and hot crumpets had magically trailed honey all over the table.

'Jo's coming. I might try Justin. This is an okay time to ring LA.'

Julia seemed happy with the compromise. Justin, Jhonnie's youngest brother, was the easiest, lightest Blampied of the bunch. He and Jhonnie were the most alike, and devoted to each other. Thirty, going on nine, Justin's nearly nerdy obsession with computer animation had taken him to Hollywood and a job animating credits for DreamWorks and other heavy hitters. Justin could never have 'gone Hollywood'. A chain-smoking, take-away-eating creature of the night, he couldn't even drive a car, and now he lived in LA. You could take the boy out of London, but you could never put Hollywood into the boy. All his numbers went to voice mail. So, I had made my first family contact with the news – just that it was serious and very important that he call back.

I made more calls to Mum, to Eleni, to Jhonnie's best friend, Pete. Mostly voice mails – quite handy, really, at seven in the morning.

I called another friend to cancel our dinner on Saturday.

She had spent months in ICU with her baby daughter. She told me not to bother taking a book to hospital. She seemed to be speaking in code. Cool, kind of in-the-know information. She didn't sound shocked. Hers was the voice of tired and awful experience. This is the kind of thing that changes you forever, I thought, and I picked up a novel and put it in my bag.

I left more messages. I realised I knew none of Jhonnie's friends' phone numbers. I would have to ask him. I could ring him. I could always ring him. Anywhere in the world, at a conference in Istanbul, or Florida, with clients, in the middle of the night, at a bar, at the rugby, on the golf course, Jhonnie was a guy you could always get on the end of a phone. But not today.

As I showered and dressed William for preschool, and charged my mobile phone and made lists, I made a fairly stupid assumption. It was muddle-headed housewife thinking, I knew, even then. Jhonnie had been given a 50 per cent chance of survival. He hadn't died in the night, so he was going to make it. You didn't have to be a rocket scientist or, hell, a brain surgeon to work out that Jhonnie was in the lucky, coming-home-when-he-wakes-up 50 per cent. And now William would like to wear his Bob the Builder sweatshirt, again, and was it washed? Who knew?

Meera arrived at eight. Meera had only been working with us for a month, taking care of Patrick, opening the mail, helping Jhonnie with his terrible tangled mountain of admin. Already her presence had changed our lives. She'd stayed at her last job for nine years. That family became her family. Hopefully this little hiccup wouldn't scare her away. The sound of her big old Volvo in the driveway was always music to my ears. On that particular Thursday morning I realised she might be the most valuable human being in the house, if I was going to wade through this with my sanity.

And so Meera took Patrick to his bath, and Julia took William to preschool, and I rang the hospital, and Esther turned up with take-away coffees, and we called Hugh and filled him in, and finally Jo arrived and we jumped in her car and went back up the expressway to the exit with the blue sign, and found ourselves a good parking space, and made our way back through the makeshift tunnel, into the broken-brown brick foyer, past the lurid gerberas and baby's breath, into the elevator, and pressed Six: the floor of neuro and cardiac Intensive Care units.

I glanced at Jo in the elevator and thought she looked beautiful. Her lipstick was perfect.

'You look nice.'

'Are you right? Get fucked.'

Jo and I had been at school together. I was a few years ahead of her, but with Catholic girls' schools full of big families, everybody's little sister would eventually become your brother's girlfriend and by university the years blurred. Jo and I had been close, on and off, for more than 20 years. We'd given birth to our first kids at the same time and the shock of losing our cherished selfish independence so suddenly had probably bonded us for life. That, and our husbands got on. On this particular morning Jo had managed to look much nicer for my husband-in-a-coma than I had.

'Do you wear lipstick every day?'

'Duh! Yes. Don't you?'

'No, really only when I'm going out, then I just drink and eat it off, which is pointless, huh.'

Eventually that very big slow elevator landed. We approached a desk and began, like kids on the first day of school, a process that was to become old-hand, automatic, nothing-to-it tedium far too quickly. It seemed so shocking and tentative on that first morning, as we were escorted back to the waiting room with no magazines or coffee tables.

The ICU routine shares territory with the rock 'n roll VIP backstage entourage and the popular shows at Fashion Week.

Identification and credibility are key. To get a front-row seat at this show, blood relationship, marriage or best friend status must be verified. Less than 24 hours into this ordeal and I was already 'the wife' – an archetype dripping with stoic yet sniffling pathos and, in my case, several supposedly crying babies. Jo opted for an 'I'm with the band' tone, which seemed lighter and more approachable. And so, if anybody needed to share the news that Jhonnie's head had rolled off his shoulders during the night, I had the feeling they might approach Jo first. That was fine by me.

We were told to sit and wait for that phone on the wall to ring, and answer, and go in, and wash our hands thoroughly at the entrance, and perhaps go one at a time. Oh, and be prepared for a shock.

We waited for a while, staring at nothing.

'Should we go for a coffee?'

'Joanne! You go for coffee. I might stay here and wait to see my nearly dead husband.'

'Are we going to get coffee after?'

'If you're very good.'

And when the phone on the wall rang nobody knew who should pick up. A defeated-looking elderly couple looked up, but didn't move. I jumped.

'Hello?' Was there a password? What to say.

A disembodied voice instructed Jhonnie's family to come through. And we were on.

I know my hands weren't shaking when I washed them under that tall elegant surgical tap. Jo was so reassuringly calm I figured we really had nothing new to fear. New nurses. A new room. New machines. What if it was a new Jhonnie?

ICU 6C, the neuro ward, was another small and awful classroom with some high windowed daylight and a light industrial view. Most of the windows in the ward were covered with photographs. Nobody, not the nurses, doctors or patients, nobody here was looking out the window.

There were only six patients in the ward, and it struck me on entering that none of them appeared to be alive. That is not to say that they appeared to be dying. Nobody moved or even breathed for themselves. In a blackout, they'd be gone. A little shop of life support horror. And at first I couldn't see Jhonnie. I saw a boy, a teenager, who looked the size of a jockey, but withered, and another man, next to him, bald, forty-something, covered in machines, alone. The pictures around their beds might as well have been clippings from *Who* magazine. It was days before I realised that the happy snaps attached to the ceilings above their bodies were actually pictures of them – healthy, in life – taken innocently sometime before the moment that had suddenly catapulted them to 6C. These photographs, cheaply printed at home on A4 paper, were the dark opposites of Dorian Gray's portrait. These people lay shrivelling in their beds as the joyous surfing/barbecue/Christmas tree pictures remained brilliantly colourful and unchanged.

A sunny open-faced girl greeted us and introduced herself as she sauntered over to Jhonnie.

'I'm Carlie. I've only been on since five. He's had a pretty steady night. No change. His surgeon is in at about 11. Hey Jhonnie – Ruth's here.'

Silent and clean, wearing nothing but a sheet and a lot of heavy machinery, my husband lay still, with a purple shaved head as big as a watermelon held together by staples. When he breathed, his chest moved artificially, like a robot on special in a bin at Toys 'R' Us. The hand and arm were strapped and bandaged. That dangerous right eye was a hideous ripe plum resting on his otherwise unmarked perfect smooth face. He needed a shave, and his feet, in fact his shins and ankles, hung off the gurney. If a nurse rushed to another patient's side she might snap off his foot. Well, at least he was already in Intensive Care.

The proliferation of tubes resembled one of William's books of mazes and puzzles. Follow the tube to the machine.

Can you find a match? The tube in his mouth connected to the machine that handled his breathing. The tube in the side of his chest drained pale Ribena fluid away from his lung. A catheter in his good hand supplied saline, nutrients, and a sublime cocktail of drugs. Catheters and tubes from his nether regions connected to bags that looked as if they too would hit the deck if Jhonnie's feet were accidentally knocked off. He really wasn't doing anything for himself. Where was Jhonnie under all those tubes and machines?

'He looks good.' Jo broke the silence.

'Do you think?'

I asked the lovely Carlie about ICU etiquette. During this, our first visit, Jo and I were the only non-essential people in the room. There were six patients in the ward – and maybe six nurses. Maybe there were more. Maybe there were fewer, and they moved quickly. Every patient's progress, or lack thereof, was checked every 10 minutes. Carlie smiled as she took Jhonnie's vital signs, again.

'This is the best care they'll ever receive in a hospital, and they'll never remember it.'

'I will.'

We pulled up chairs either side of the sleeping giant.

'Look at his beautiful skin.' Jo stroked Jhonnie's shoulder.

'Bloody Poms. Wouldn't you kill to have skin like that at 40? He's like an eyelid. Hope the boys get his skin not mine. Darling, you look fine, and your skin is really, really . . . nice.'

I was definitely struggling. But it was true; Jhonnie had a healthy, freshly fallen look, much more like a man than a corpse. I wanted to whisper that he looked better than the other guys. Was there any point in whispering? Was there any point in speaking?

'Darling, Jo's here, and we were just talking about Yahoo's birthday party, and how much fun it was, and how Jo sat on a coffee table and broke it.'

'Did Jhonnie tell you that?'

'Jhonnie doesn't retain gossip, do you, babe? There's no point telling him anything. He got a lift home all the way from Whale Beach that night with Billy Thorpe, and he had no idea who he was.'

'Fair enough. He isn't anybody anymore, and he was barely a pop star when we were kids and Jhonnie was stuck in a boarding school in England.'

'I'm sorry, Jo, but it is frustrating when one's husband cares naught for trivial trash. Send him off to a flashy party and he just comes home saying he had great fun and how much he loves you all.'

'And we love you, Jhonnie.'

That last month had been strange. Two of our closest friends had celebrated their fiftieth birthdays on the same Saturday night. In post-partum enthusiasm I had RSVPed to both. And they were furious with us. Our Solomon-like solution was to send Jhonnie to Yahoo's big fun party up on the Peninsula while I went to Eleni's civilised dinner party at Longrain. Jhonnie and the rest of the gang had whooped it up wildly. Weeks later stories from the party were still emerging. Only the previous Wednesday, Jhonnie, Jo and I had taken Patrick to Red Lantern for a mountain of salt and pepper mud crab and those amazing little spicy cubes of Wagyu beef they do so well, and we'd been post-morteming wild parties; now, we were making small talk in 6C. And Jo managed to keep up a breezy line in patter.

'Jhonnie, when we leave here, we're going to Red Lantern. If you put in your order now, we can bring you something. I don't think they get a lot of mud crab around here.'

One of the nurses laughed.

'So he likes his food, does he?'

'What do you think?'

Next to the tiny teenage boy, Jhonnie was a different

species. I told the nurses what he liked, and who he was. How else would they know? He could be anybody, just lying there. I told them about his kids, and the baby, and the bike, and how he'd only quit work a few months earlier, and how before that he ran a big advertising agency. And now he was trying to get a life. The irony!

Were they just polite, or interested? After about half an hour they asked us to leave, because Jhonnie was to be turned. (This involved importing strong male staff from the other ICU.)

'How big is he, exactly?'

'Six foot six in the old money. Two metres? Sorry. He's worth the effort. I promise.'

I held his good hand and whispered close to his head. 'I'll be back, darling. I love you. Don't run off with any of the pretty nurses. Some of them are nude. Some of them are just wearing Benny Hill underwear and nametags on their enormous breasts that all say "Pat". You've got to open your eyes and have a look. It's a riot.'

Jhonnie stirred. Probably involuntary. But a slight flicker of movement nonetheless. The nurses were unmoved. Jo and I took it as a welcome, no matter how fictional, sign of recovery.

I kissed his face. I had to find a doctor. I had no idea what to do next.

'He's going to be fine,' said Jo in the elevator, going down, still with perfect lipstick.

'Thanks, Dr Corrigan. What a relief. On what do you base this prognosis?'

'He's still in there. I can feel it. He's still Jhonnie. He knew you were there. He's not like the others. He's Jhonnie. He's going to be fine.'

We talked about our kids, over milky sorry coffee in the café of the considerably more glamorous private hospital. The sunny café in this new and salubrious development, which sat cheek by jowl with our own gruesome accommodation, somehow added insult to injury. It was like the bistro of a cheerful Gold Coast resort. Why weren't we on the Gold Coast? Why were we in Canberra, sometime in the late '60s, in winter? Not fair. Jo and I still managed to bitch about the coffee while we discussed our kids. And five trained professionals turned Jhonnie.

When we returned, we checked in. They weren't ready for us yet. That nice social worker had offered to organise parking. We saw her. We couldn't find a doctor. We saw Jhonnie again. We kissed him goodbye. We went back down to the hideous brown foyer, with the toilets and the parking office, and I came away with an official pass and a new appreciation of our desperate situation. Jhonnie's healthy, smooth skin and the absence of serious nods from men in white coats hadn't saved us. The man in the booth in the foyer had given me unlimited free parking at Royal North Shore Hospital for three months.

Day 3

I COULDN'T REALLY SAY WHEN the days began and ended. Did they begin with those moonlit calls to 6C as Patrick lay rocking in my lap? Nothing to report again in the night. Actually – a spiked fever. They didn't fear infection. Just standard stuff after brain surgery. Sure, I knew that. Patrick knew as much about brain surgery as his mother, and there we were in the dark, with the infomercials and a direct line to Daddy's bedside.

Dinner the night before with Julia and William had been punctuated with plans, and a few phone calls. Messages left on his parents' answering machine in Umbria satisfied my sense of duty. More messages on Justin's various voice mails in LA elicited no reply. How much more serious could a voice mail message be? Perhaps Justin too lay in a coma somewhere, unable to receive his messages.

I had spoken to Julian, Jhonnie's older brother, at length. I could picture Julian, his neat, business-like wife, Claire, and their two pretty children in their wonderful tumbledown old house outside London – the huge yard, and storybook fields beyond. I could picture Julian trying to take control of the situation, and alert the troops, and not frighten the horses, and do that eldest kid in the family, bossy thing. Julian would be our key man in Europe for this operation. Whatever. He had been very frightened by the news, and apparently even more frightened by how it would affect his ailing father.

The Blampieds could handle this any way they liked. I assumed they would be descending, in some numbers, when we had more news, for a funeral or a dramatic hospital vigil. I hadn't thought far beyond telling them the news. When the beloved golden boy is felled in another hemisphere, what does one do? I thought about that, sitting up in bed, waiting for Patrick to wake, and I began to get really angry at Justin. I stomped downstairs in the cold dark dawn and punched in all those long ridiculous numbers to leave my angry message.

'Justin, it's Ruth. Again. I cannot comprehend what is happening over there. I've been leaving messages for days. Your brother is in serious trouble, in an Intensive Care ward. I hope whatever you're working on, whatever piece of shit Hollywood film you're working on, is more important than that. Call here, any time. I need to speak to you.'

Smack. Where the hell did that come from? I'd been simply too afraid to get angry, but now, with my face red and hot and tears dripping from my chin as I stood by the fridge, I realised I was holding back a fury that would silence barking dogs. And then Patrick woke upstairs and needed an urgent change of pants.

With another call to Pete, Jhonnie's oldest friend, I reached Nicole, his girlfriend. He'd already left for work, and she reeled with the news. As she took in tiny details I knew that this pair would be valuable assets, not just people to inform. Pete would call me. They would help.

I finally reached Sam, an old work mate, at breakfast, with his kids. Again more substance. Sam would check out the brain surgeon. Sam and I had been at school together. The time-honoured Catholic professional network would swing into action. Sam was on the case.

Setting off for hospital again, with my fancy parking pass

tucked into my bra, a bottle of water and a lot of useful phone numbers in my handbag, I felt quite in command. I took the unopened novel out and threw it on the floor before I left the house. I drove across the bridge and picked up my dear friend Eleni, my company for today's journey into the unknown.

Eleni and I had worked together for years in advertising. She had hired Jhonnie, and imported him all the way from Baker Street in London, and we'd often joked that she'd really cast a wide net to find me a suitable husband. Jhonnie went on to be chairman and CEO of the agency for which we'd all worked. She had left the business for full-time motherhood more than a decade ago. I'd gone back to university. Now, finally, none of us worked in advertising, but we were all still close friends, godparents to each other's kids.

Eleni is one of those sensible yet rather dramatic Greek girls. Histrionic at times, but always baking and practical in a crisis. On the way to hospital I filled her in on what to expect and what we were doing – meeting with doctors, nurses and the social worker for our first family conference. Everybody handles the macabre curiosity that is Intensive Care in his or her own special way. Jo had appeared to be warming up for a game of netball. Eleni became strong and silent. And while I know that if I'd pulled out her fingernails she wouldn't have cried, it was clear that the sudden random nature of our situation was particularly confronting to her.

The swelling and bruising were more pronounced. His huge purple face tipped out from the top of that hard plastic collar like the lip of a soufflé. The purple itself was a recognisable lively purple, not the one I'd seen the first day, in Emergency. We washed our hands and looked around at the still, silent ward.

'So, I just talk to him about normal stuff. I don't think he can hear shit, but if he can, if he can hear anything, it would be very frightening to hear us wailing, "Come back, Jhonnie, we need you." If I heard that, in some dark cloud, and I had no idea what was going on, panicked sobbing would give me a few ugly clues. So . . . if you've marinated any quails lately, I suggest you share the recipe.'

Eleni took my lead, and took his hand. I had to take it back.

'That's the broken one. Do you want to squeeze the other one?'

'Shit.'

We both laughed. We talked about food, and the kids, and nearly dead advertising people she'd seen recently. Eleni went out for a drink of water, and maybe a breath of stale air. I pulled out the *Herald* and started to read Peter FitzSimons' column. I really didn't know enough about rugby to keep Jhonnie informed, so Brendan Cannon's progress after an injury must have come as welcome news if it made its way into Jhonnie's subconcious. Reading the paper aloud made a refreshing change from keeping up both sides of a rather tense and artificial conversation. It was like first-date small talk – only we weren't in a darkened bar, or drinking vodka, or smoking cigarettes. No, it was nothing like a date, but reading Peter Fitz's column made light relief.

As Eleni returned, I peeked at Jhonnie's charts. The nurses who had made themselves scarce for the rugby update returned. I was sprung.

'You know you're not supposed to read those.'

'Well, I was told three broken ribs, but it says here five. How else would I know, huh?' I was already getting cheeky with the nurses. With very rare exception they were an amazing bunch of women. The older ones were gruffer, more knowledgeable. The younger ones were less serious, more party. Their combined approach was reassuring, with the occasional breath of much-welcomed levity thrown in for good measure. Every shift there were new nurses, but the same faces were beginning to appear in rotation and my level of comfort in this twilight zone was already much increased from day one.

'What's a "right pneumothorax with associated fractures of the second to seventh ribs"? And what's a "comminuted fracture involving the superior wall of the right orbit with moderate inferior depression – no treatment at this point?" Is that his arm?'

The nurses didn't want to play. An older nurse snapped the chart from my hand and tried not to dismiss me, but she didn't want to get down on her medical hands and knees to come down to my level.

'Head. Not hand. Bump on *head*. Eye socket. No treatment at this point . . . Okay?'

'Mrs Blampied has been ringing and wants to bring her son in. I didn't know what to say.'

'Mrs Blampied? I'm Mrs Blampied. That's his *ex*-wife. At the moment they're only speaking through lawyers. And that little boy is 11, and in no way prepared to see his father like this.'

'What do you want me to say? She says she's next of kin. And he *is* next of kin.'

'Until six months ago, I used to turn on the taps in his shower because he was wary of the water temperature. Do you think he sounds like a candidate for 6C?'

Carlie was taking Jhonnie's vitals, and laughing under her breath. I stomped out in search of the social worker. I couldn't stand guard at the elevator night and day, but I could certainly get a professional to speak to Chris and explain the situation. It was time to turn Jhonnie over again. They sent for reinforcements as we headed back to the waiting room, and off down the wide, highly polished old corridors, past the lone staff toilet. We went knocking on all the narrow, numbered doors of pokey little nooks that housed the various specialists and ancillary staff who kept the wheels of Intensive Care in motion.

The social worker's door was open, and sitting at the desk was not the lovely sensible Liz but the undertaker from Emergency. He hadn't remembered me. Perhaps he'd frightened the pants off hundreds of potential widows in the last three days.

'I've spoken to Jonathan's wife and she assures me it is very important for their son to see Jonathan on Father's Day.'

'I'm the wife.'

He checked his notes. 'No, really, Mrs Blampied and I have had a long talk and she thinks it's —'

'She's not his wife. That kid is not going to celebrate this Sunday with his father the eggplant. You don't know any of the individuals involved here. I know what Jhonnie would want, and what's suitable, and she's not setting foot in this place until Jhonnie can smack her with his good arm if needs be. Get it?'

'You're very upset.'

'You're not listening to me.'

'With the right preparation, I can help the boy so that a visit with his father, if it's a comfort to Mrs Blampied and Jhonnie's son, will be a constructive thing. I can help him.'

I didn't say 'You're creepy and you'll freak him out, you sick self-important midget', because with the last dregs of self-preservation still in my grasp I had decided that the truth, in this particular situation, would not set me free. Instead, I said, 'Could you please have another conversation with . . . Mrs Blampied, and say that perhaps when Jhonnie opens his eyes, and can recognise his son, perhaps when he can speak, perhaps when he doesn't look quite so much like Frankenstein's latest model, Connar might be reassured by a visit with his father. But quite frankly, if Jhonnie wakes for the first time to find her at the end of his bed, it might just finish him off.'

Undertaker made a few short notes, didn't look up as Eleni and I turned on our heels to walk away. Those were charts at which I would never sneak a peek. 'Wife mad. May carry gun. Must warn the *real* Mrs Blampied.'

Eleni said nothing until we made it to the elevator. 'Under no circumstances can Connar go in there.'

In the daylight of the window by the gigantic staff lifts I could see for the first time that all the blood had run out of her face.

'So, I'm right, aren't I?'

'He should never go in there. I'll tell her that. Connar can come and spend Father's Day with us. We don't celebrate it. We'll just go kick a football around or something. Father's Day? What is she thinking?'

Back in the optimistic café of the private hospital, Eleni and I got practical. Jhonnie needed pictures of everybody above the bed, in case he opened his eyes. Eleni could print them at home. Nice and big. All the kids.

'I've got a picture of him with John Eales.'

'Who's John Eales?'

'Ex-captain of the Wallabies. Jhonnie's hero. The World Cup starts in, what, two and a half months, and Jhonnie has tickets, all over the country. It's the only thing he's actually followed through on since he left work. He's got enough tickets to the Rugby World Cup to trade for a brand-new Korean car.'

'But it's months away, right? He'll be fine by then.'

'Have you been talking to Jo? He's in a coma. He has more tubes than the London Underground. When is he going to wake up and hop in the car and come home? I have a free parking pass that's good for *three months*.'

'This coffee is really terrible. We're going to have to start bringing it from home.'

Back upstairs for the medical conference.

The sixth floor must have been larger than it had first appeared, because nearly every day new and increasingly awful rooms unfolded and opened their doors to us, and in each one some memorable if somewhat surreal revelation occurred. This little conference room was full, yet not quite full enough, of nearly broken vinyl-padded chairs. Torn brown vinyl, and some dove-grey, and some hard chairs, that weren't broken, but they were dirty. I haven't caught public transport since school. I haven't enjoyed the tatty vandalised furniture of the under-funded university campus in years, so I don't see a lot of miserable government-issue public spaces on a regular basis. But the sadness of the broken furniture as it barely supported the shaky families of patients in Intensive Care could nearly redefine the word 'poignant'.

I didn't feel particularly poignant. I felt bewildered as Eleni and I sat in a circle with three nurses, two doctors, a nutrition-ist and, thank God, Liz, the real live human social worker. She convened the meeting. Eleni and I hadn't worked together for years, but we had spent what seemed like thousands of hours together in meetings, presentations and pitches – usually in the plushest agency meeting rooms or most imposing clients' boardrooms. We'd told people they had no idea what they were talking about in the wood-panelled halls of banks, the tinny training rooms of McDonald's, the hideous corporate caverns of every toilet cleaner manufacturer, tampon plugger and frozen fish-finger purveyor in the land. But we'd never been in a meeting quite like this.

For 48 hours we had all been waiting for some kind of pronouncement. Expressions that pad the drivel dialogue of daytime TV soap come into play here. Life hanging in the balance. Hanging on by a thread. Clinging to life with all his might. Touch and go.

If the EVD did its job, there'd be no more haemorrhaging. Could anything else kill Jhonnie at this point? Who knew?

Everybody was really waiting for someone to tell us what I already knew, that Jhonnie was going to live. That would be something, a chance to exhale, and the details we'd work out when everybody got their new scripts.

It's odd that I cannot recall who spoke, or the exact words used when the meeting began. Was it 'nearly out of the woods'? Nobody said anything as obvious as 'defied death', surely. Neither Eleni nor I could recall how they broke the news – or were they just fairly confident that, based on current vitals, Jhonnie was not going to die?

That should have been it. On a daytime soap the rest of the meeting would've taken place in an ad break. At no stage did we hoot and holler with relief.

The nurses and nutritionist gave a brief summary of Jhonnie's status and progress. The ophthalmic surgeon had visited but it was too early to tell if the nerves in Jhonnie's eye had been severed. He might have had a third nerve palsy, or he could even have severed the third, fourth and fifth nerves around the eye – both of which could've accounted for the fixed dilated pupil. On the other hand, perhaps it was simply a temporary condition resulting from the swelling involved in the orbital fracture in the skull around his eye.

Okay, if you say so.

The complete fracture through the right transverse process of L1 displays minimal displacement. Neurosurgeons do not indicate treatment.

'Hang on. I've had physiotherapy – L1 is in your back. Did I just hear "fractured back"? Can that be right?'

Again I was assured that the rest of Jhonnie's injuries were not life threatening, and consequently they could wait. I would have the rest of my life to wonder about Jhonnie's fractured L1.

I tried to ask brainy questions about what was going into the various drips and tubes. Was Jhonnie so heavily sedated that he couldn't wake up? No, he had in fact been stirring, and when pain relief was reduced, he became distressed and attempted to move, though with great difficulty. Premature uncontrolled movement could threaten his recovery from his other injuries.

'But when is he going to wake up? Is he drugged, or is he . . . ?'

A cool-eyed young doctor stepped up to the plate. I didn't know which of Jhonnie's limbs or organs were his responsibility. He could have been an intern.

'He won't wake up because he is not asleep. The coma is not drug induced, but as Jhonnie has stirred and coughed he might return to consciousness, momentarily, in a matter of days, or weeks. Even when he does come to, the patient will remain in REM sleep for most of the day. A damaged brain requires a lot of rest.'

I raised my meeting with the undertaker, and my concerns that the ex and the kids should not appear in some scene from a Movie of the Week. Could they stop her, please? Eleni voiced a concern that if Jhonnie should wake up when Chris was there, he might be confused and forget he was married to me. Even as she said it, she knew it didn't sound smart.

'That sort of amnesia really is more the stuff of fiction.' That clipped young doctor managed to be dismissive, patronising and humourless in just one breath. What was his role, was he the junior mini-boss of Intensive Care? I'd only seen him once before and he wouldn't stand still long enough to answer questions, but I gathered this was my time. His expression was at once neutral and grave as he asked me, 'What do you understand Jhonnie's injuries to be?'

I had been listening, and if this was a quiz I should be okay.

'Well – the brain injury. Orbital fracture to the skull. Three, five or seven broken ribs, depending on who you ask. Broken hand. Collapsed lung. And the eye – to use technical language – is fucked.'

'But what do you understand about the injury itself?'

'I really think I've told you what I know. What do you know? Is there stuff you haven't told me?'

'There's a difference between brain injury and brain

damage. Your husband's brain injury is severe, and until he regains consciousness we don't know the severity of the brain damage. And even when he does come to, he may improve and then plateau after five days, or five weeks, or five years. We simply don't know.'

'But his spine isn't damaged. And if he can walk and talk . . .' I clearly had no idea how to finish the sentence.

'Patients who survive an injury as serious as that which Jhonnie has sustained have around a 50 per cent chance of a good recovery.'

'They told me that in Emergency; but Jhonnie's in that 50 per cent, isn't he?'

'A good recovery includes patients who return home to modified houses with full-time care.'

'And the other fifty?'

'Never leave an institution.'

'Do you think . . . Do you have any reason to believe that's Jhonnie? Or would you just say this to anybody sitting in this chair – like, reading me my – I dunno – rights?'

'Brain injury is a very mysterious and unpredictable field. We won't know anymore until he wakes up – but you need to know he isn't going to get up and walk out of here.'

'Ever?'

'We just don't know.'

I looked at Eleni. Our eyes filled with tears. We thanked everybody involved. The lovely social worker thanked Eleni for driving me today; as this information might be very difficult for me to absorb, I really shouldn't be behind the wheel.

'Ruth drove me. I can't even drive her home. It's a manual.'

'My stupid car.'

I kissed Jhonnie again. So he'd been stirring. He had attempted to squeeze a nurse's hand; feebly, but a squeeze . . . They were underwhelmed by my response.

It should have been cause for jubilation, apparently. He was going to live. Jhonnie was going to come out of the coma – but come out to what? I think I liked it better when I just thought he had a bung eye and a few broken ribs. Hooray. He would be able to squeeze a stranger's hand. What news. I bowed my head onto his good arm and cried.

When the 'lucky' victims of those home renovation TV shows return from a weekend away to discover that their perfectly ordinary backyard has been transformed into a small but hideous Balinese resort, they often respond by repeating the same pointless plea: 'Oh my god! Oh my god! Oh my god!'

'And here's your new tool shed . . .'

'Oh my god!'

I walked through the hospital grounds to my stupid convertible manual impractical car repeating the word 'fuck'.

The fresh air had me wailing.

'He has three sons. What am I going to do? How are they ever going to know their father if he's drooling in a broken vinyl chair? Oh fuck. Oh fuck. Eleni, what the fuck am I going to do?' (God knows why I thought Madison would fare better with a vegetable for a father – perhaps images of rugby fields were fuelling my bathos.)

I threw my arms around. People in hospital car parks must do this all the time. I simply didn't care. Eleni went with it. Greeks have no problem throwing their arms around.

'You know he just has to say that. He shouldn't have said it quite that way. That's just the wrong way to – the other people in that room didn't seem to think Jhonnie wasn't ever going to be okay. They just have to say that, because for some tiny, tiny percentage of people it might, just might, be true.'

'Tiny, what, like 50 per cent? Fuck.'

We sat in the car until I could collect my thoughts. Stupid car. I'd bought the black convertible in a last desperate attempt to fall pregnant. After several 'procedures', a miscarriage and my forty-second birthday I was becoming reconciled to life as a stepmother to Connar and Madison, and mother to William. Some people are never *that* lucky. And the relief of letting go of all that hope had already begun to pay dividends. We'd put plenty of positive spin on the idea of 'moving on' . . . Go back to work full-time. Take adventurous holidays with William. Buy a convertible again.

I'd driven convertibles since my mid-twenties, and something about the navy-blue four-door sedan with sensible interior that arrived with William had never really suited.

Jhonnie, William and I had spent hilarious Saturdays on Parramatta Road playing in fast cars. William had been inconsolable when the British racing green Jag 'invertible' was left at the showroom. He'd never thrown a tantrum in a supermarket. He'd never really thrown a tantrum anywhere before, but I hadn't ever taken him 'invertible' shopping before.

Just test driving these cars seemed to have knocked 10 years and some unpleasant drudgery off me. Invoking Murphy's Law, Jhonnie was sure that if I bought a convertible I would most certainly fall pregnant, and if not, we could have fun christening the back seat. (I imagine it would be quite difficult for any six-foot-six man to make out in the tiny back seat of any convertible, so I figured this, like Jhonnie's desire to have sex with Charlotte Rampling sometime in the mid-'70s, was just another impossible fantasy.) But he was right, and I was knocked up by the time I took delivery of the European two-door fertility machine. And now look where it had brought us – to a car park, in tears, with a friend who could only drive an automatic. Stupid car.

'Don't take me home. I'll go home with you. Just concentrate on the road. I'll come home and see William and Pat.'

'Thanks. Are you sure? Okay.'

As I headed onto the expressway, still shaking, I knew she was right. Focus. Concentrate. We'll be home before we know it. Mobile phone. I answered, and put the wired piece in my ear. It could be the hospital, or Jhonnie's family, or the baby. I'd never been away from Patrick for more than a few hours in all of his three short months of life.

'Ruth, it's Chris. How is he today?'

'Not so good, Chris. I've just come from the hospital, and they are painting a pretty gruesome picture. He has moved his feet though, and that's good.'

'Great. Well Connar has made him a Father's Day present. He's going to take it in to see him. Jhonnie's got two full days to get better.'

'No, Chris. He hasn't. He's in a very frightening place. He's next to a little boy who has been in a coma for months. The kid isn't much older than Connar.'

'He just wants to put the present by the bed so it will be there when he wakes up.'

'There is no bed. He's on a bench, naked, with tubes in every orifice, breathing on a respirator. There's no bed. Just a lot of machines. He can't go in there.'

'You don't seem to understand what Father's Day means to Connar . . .'

Eleni looked at me, horrified by my end of this bizarre exchange. (My driving may also have frightened her.) Her face of shock returned. I'd already seen it so many times that day.

'Fuck Father's Day. There is no Father's Day this year.'

'There's no need for that. I am not going to deny my son's wishes. He feels very strongly about this –'

'I'm happy to talk to Connar and describe the situation. I feel fairly certain that he won't want to see his father's head full of staples. It would be great if they both did some drawings, and even a tape, on a dictaphone, and I'll play it to him.'

'Well, if you're going to play him a tape, what's the difference? Connar could be there for him.'

'We don't know if he's brain dead. We don't know if he's hearing anything.' That wasn't strictly true. Jhonnie had feebly squeezed a hand in response to instructions, but we didn't know if he would ever recognise any of us. I figured that would be even more frightening to his vulnerable little boy than the machines and the staples. 'Seriously, a tape, and some drawings we could put on the ceiling above him would be a great start. Does Connar want to speak to me? When does Madi get back from camp? – Hang on, I'm going into the tunnel, so I might lose you.'

Click. I didn't call back. Too dangerous on so many levels.

And then we were home, where Patrick was stirring.

'He's going to live, after a fashion,' I announced.

Esther went mad with the mobile phone, texting the good news to one and all. I can't SMS at all. I don't know if there's a happy-face symbol or some modified abomination that lights up a mobile phone screen in an appropriate way to spread this sort of news. 'Heel liv!' Perhaps.

There was a mountain of calls to return. Sam had checked out Jhonnie's surgeon. Rave reviews – what a relief. Julian, Jhonnie's older brother, had called back, and I was to call him in London, any time. Gabriella, Jhonnie's stepmother, had called, but I was to call Julian, not their house in Umbria. Nothing from Justin in LA and Peter and Nicole were taking me to the hospital on Saturday.

Saturday. What was I going to do on the weekend? Julia had printed out Excel spreadsheets of the volunteers booked in to watch the kids over the weekend. Offers had flooded in to whisk William away for a festival of football finals that had begun to grip every tiny sporting field all over the country.

Footy finals. Spring. Swimming lessons. Spring racing. The World Cup Rugby. What to do with Jhonnie's tickets? Esther and Pete were going to handle the tickets.

Thank god Esther was such a sports fanatic. She and Jhonnie had pawed over the rugby fixtures for months, sending off applications at every opportunity, for as many tickets as they could get. Oddly enough, their success in this department never cropped up over gossip when Esther and I went for leg-waxes together. I would have had no idea, nor any interest in sorting out the World Cup tickets. Pete and Esther would unload them sensibly, over a few beers. But first, I had to find them. That doesn't sound like such a challenge, but Jhonnie's 'office' was a mysterious web of disorganisation. Like an archeological dig, the mountain of paperwork that teetered on Jhonnie's desk was sorted according to a system known only to him. It looked more like a movie set than a real functioning office. We had no idea how to get into his computer, operate or charge his stupid new phone, find his contact lists or even a diary. A forensic team with magic dust and special blue torches would be required to find the rugby tickets, and everything else that we needed. Insurance? Medical records? Money? Car rego? Jhonnie didn't even use a bank that any of us recognised.

I'd always kept my finances separate because I was 36 years old and master of my own portfolio when Jhonnie and I got together. Jhonnie still wasn't divorced, and all his investments and admin were bound up with the kids, child support, and his own mysterious snake-oil schemes. As CEO of a big company he had a lot of rather confusing financial advice, all of which sounded like speculative nonsense to me. Advertising people loved the sound of a get-rich-quick scheme. I'd made certain none of my hard-earned, conservatively gained fortune would get messed up with his.

I had wrongly assumed that his personal assistant had some organised system for him at the office. Now there was no office. Just archive boxes and piles of prospectuses, unopened mail and reminder bills on the desk and the floor and the couch, downstairs. In there, somewhere, was a goldmine in tickets.

We all sat around the big white table over another cup of tea. Julia, Eleni, Patrick, Meera and Esther. We pulled out photos for Eleni to print. Eleni called Chris to invite Connar for Father's Day. We made lists, and crossed out old lists.

'Does anyone feel like John Dory for dinner?'

Julia never felt like fish.

'Come on, it's Friday. Every fucking Catholic in Christendom is praying for Jhonnie; the least we can do is eat a little pan-fried fish with almond beans.'

'Can we have lyonnaise potatoes?' And just like that, she was in.

I roamed around the shops, peering at fish, and making a new melon selection now that pineapple had officially fallen out with William. The fennel and celeriac both looked good. Baby chat potatoes or kipflers would be fine for lyonnaise. I could decide at home. I found a fluffy, floury white loaf of bread for Julia and William to share. Together they made up one rather particular and naughty child who refused to chew or eat crusts. How lovely for William to already have an adult with whom to misbehave. Did anybody else buying bread at Edgecliff shops have a husband in Intensive Care? Would I recognise her if she passed me in the nappy aisle?

When I walked into William's preschool none of the teachers or other parents could look me in the eye. Some close mothers had called and kindly offered car-pooling and play dates. But the people I barely knew were embarrassed. Suddenly, from being the happy people with the new baby, we were the family with the terrible tragedy. I made other wives feel awkward.

The lovely teacher who ran our little school took me aside, without prying or really asking about Jhonnie at all. He said it would be fine for William to come to school five days a week instead of three. Only then I thought that I might cry. I swept up William, who was still happy and busy with his friends. It was the first time I'd picked him up all week.

At home Julia and William played loudly upstairs while I returned calls. Jo had offered her services in the morning. Pete and Nicole would be around at lunchtime. Jhonnie's old agency had called, offering to send a technician to unlock the mysteries of the computer, and perhaps the phone.

I dredged the Dory in flour and called London. I felt reassured to finally have a long conversation with Julian. I told him the whole story from the hospital that day. I didn't want to create a panic, and I looked to him for guidance, but perhaps three days into this strange adventure, the time for diplomacy had passed.

'I don't think Dad can take news like that. He's not well himself. Neither of them can take it.' Jhonnie's father had been treated for prostate cancer the year before, and as far as I knew all had gone well.

'The cancer isn't back, is it?'

'No, but he has an ulcer on his leg. If he's upset, it will make things more difficult for Mum. I think if you just tell him that Jhonnie's had a fall, and he's in hospital for a few days . . .'

'I can't keep on top of a lie like that.'

'It's not a lie. He *has* fallen off his bike. He *is* in hospital. I'll keep them informed, and when they ring you just try to sound positive.'

'I've got a three-month-old baby and a husband in a coma. I just won't be able to do it, so they'd better not ring here.'

'You know what they're like, Ruth. This could kill them, and as for Vivvy, she worships Jhonnie. She's not strong enough for this.'

I hadn't thought about Vivvy's reaction. Jhonnie's sister had spent the last two and a half years in Australia. It had not always been an easy or happy stay, and Julian was probably unaware, as the family rarely told each other the truth, that Vivvy had returned home, while Jhonnie was in Turkey, full of unresolved anger and resentment for her brother. I should speak to her. Julian didn't have her number in Umbria.

'Have you spoken to Justin? I'm getting really worried because he hasn't returned any of my calls.'

'You know Justin is hopeless. You've got enough to worry about there. I don't want to make this any worse for you. What else can I do at this end?'

I racked my brain, still reeling from the poorly laid plan to lie to the folks.

'Well, you could make a tape of your voice. Just tell him anything, maybe childhood stuff. We don't know what he can hear or understand. And pictures of you as kids, maybe? I'm going to start an email update, and send it to you, so if you could forward it to the London friends. Yes, track down the old school friends. I'm trying to pull his contact list from the computer. So – that way I can keep people in the loop, and maybe not talk so much.'

'I'm sorry, are you all right talking to me?'

'Of course, but email me, tonight, and I'll send something probably tomorrow. So, you've really spoken to Justin, and he knows what's happened.'

'He's very worried. I'll start contacting those school friends, but don't send that email to Mum and Dad. Trust me on this; if it feels like chaos now, it will be much worse when they panic.'

Maybe he was right. I opened some wine. Julia had a tumbler of Johnnie Walker Blue Label and Diet Coke with her dinner. People can be so unpredictable. Julia hardly ever drank at all. A glass of champagne at the racetrack. A bourbon and Coke with country people. She always drove to a restaurant. I always caught a cab. Neither of our parents were big drinkers. There was a bottle of scotch, and ice and black olives, on the kitchen table before dinner for the day's post-mortem. We Ritchies did some of our best work standing around with icy glasses of good scotch in our hands.

Recently Mum had discovered Johnnie Walker Blue – a

drop so smooth, so rarefied, so flash that it was too expensive for mere mortals to purchase even duty-free. Jhonnie used to bring a bottle back after every trip. He travelled a lot.

We rarely drank spirits together, so there was a solid cellar of Blue in place for this drama. Julia might have felt that she was stepping into Dad's shoes as she poured the whisky, then stepping back into her own when she poured the Diet Coke.

Day 4

I PIECED TOGETHER A CONTACT LIST of family and friends, about 20 names initially, and called the group Jhonnie's List. I typed quickly and didn't bother to check what I'd written before pressing SEND. Esther arrived with take-away coffees, and we were gone.

EMAIL FROM RUTH TO JHONNIE'S LIST

To everyone concerned with Jhonnie's recovery – hope this doesn't seem impersonal, but it's the best way to keep you up to speed with his progress.

I'll be brief. If any of you don't know that Jhonnie Blampied was in a serious bike accident on Wednesday 3 September, this is a terrible way to get the news. Sorry. I won't give the story so far here, because I'm on my way to the hospital.

My plan is send an update by email, hopefully daily, because I know you're all very concerned, and keen for news. Speaking of which, the news is all good at the moment. Jhonnie is stable, in Intensive Care at RNS.

In terms of head injuries, his is very serious. In terms of recovery, his is remarkable. Yesterday Jhonnie opened his eyes, squeezed hands, moved feet and responded with what I can only hope was enthusiasm when I read him the Wallaby World Cup selection. He dozed off again when I read Peter Fitz's column, but for Jhonnie that's probably a lullaby.

Jhonnie has pictures of the kids above his head – and a rather large print of himself standing with John Eales. If Jhonnie comes to and thinks he's John Eales for a while, I suggest we indulge him.

Don't mean to be flippant, but as of yesterday, things are really looking up. His other injuries – eye, ribs, lung, hand and chipped vertebrae – are progressing well. I'm passing on all your messages of love and concern. Thank you all for rallying so much. The kids and I are very, very lucky to have all your support, and Jhonnie will need every one of you in the weeks and months to come. This boy has a Rugby World Cup to get well for.

Thank you, love

Ruth

Weekends don't exist in Intensive Care, but the parking is less challenging. What a change from that first morning. Esther was clearly overwhelmed by the ward, or the machines, or maybe Jhonnie. She couldn't look at him. The bad eye, completely black, and swollen so badly that it distorted the shape as well as the size of his head, might have really been off-putting. She couldn't speak to him, and I could tell she just didn't know if he was there. He did stir when he heard my voice. He squeezed my hand when I talked about the kids. The lovely Carlie said that he was very sweet, and most head injuries weren't.

A sweet head injury. What would Jhonnie make of that? A father. A son. A husband. A CEO. A rugby fan. And now he was a sweet head injury. We had to step outside for a few minutes. In the waiting room the mother of the boy by Jhonnie's bed sat with a thermos. We finally introduced ourselves and swapped stories. I simply couldn't before, and she must have intuitively known that. Tim, her 17-year-old son, had been suddenly stricken with an aneurism three months earlier, and she'd been camping in 6C ever since. She washed, dried and rubbed cream into the hands and feet of her boy every day. I'd seen the pictures of Tim laughing with his friends. I'd seen the friends visit. The boy in the bed was now half their size.

'Your husband is doing really well. He made a lot of noise last night. He really did.'

I felt far too guilty to respond. Her son had been completely comatose for months. How could she keep up hope? How could she stand the sound of this newcomer growling with a mouth full of tubes, oblivious to his company, to her silent son. I had no idea what this meant for us. Because he growls, does that mean he can no longer speak? I couldn't think what part of the brain controlled speech. The frontal lobes? Surely not. In any case, Jhonnie had been making noise.

The phone on the wall rang and Esther and I went back inside. Not a doctor to be seen this morning. There would be no more harsh realities to face over the weekend; that seemed certain.

More newspaper recitals, a foot-rub for Jhonnie, sneaked peeks at the charts and some jokes with the nurses. They were all fascinated by the photo of Jhonnie and John Eales.

'They look alike. Are they friends?'

'Only in Jhonnie's dreams. They met at some corporate function. Jhonnie used to spend a lot of time at corporate functions.'

'What did . . . does he do?'

'He ran a big fat advertising agency – short answer. Long answer is probably just too long without a drink in your hand.'

'Well, he's a very patient patient – aren't you, Jhonnie?'

They all tended to shout a little at the patients in comas. They shouted as people do to the deaf, elderly and lost Japanese tourists. This was not so much for the patients' benefit, but so everybody else who was awake in the ward knew not to reply by mistake. Was it patronising, talking to these corpses, or was it polite? I could speak to Jhonnie. I didn't think I could talk to the others, but from that day forward I said, 'Morning Tim,' when I entered the ward.

Outside, Esther was busy with text messages. As an advertising headhunter, AFL fiend and single party girl around town, Esther's whole life relied on text messages. It always infuriated her that I wouldn't play. My argument that I spent my whole life typing, I didn't want to type on the phone, just infuriated her. She'd managed to text everyone Jhonnie had ever met about the accident, about rugby tickets. Her skills complemented mine perfectly. Esther was lost in her phone, and slightly green. It had been Esther who'd picked up William that first day from pre-school, Esther who I'd called any time I was robbed, lost, drunk, dropped, in need of a shopping excursion. Esther had all the guts and gusto to move mountains and change moods when times were tough. Esther had just seen Jhonnie and she looked terrible. Was it the staples? I wanted to offer her a martini, but as she was minding the kids for the rest of the day, that particular line of relief was going to have to wait.

Pete and Jhonnie had worked together in the UK. They had swum on the same backstroke team. Pete was Madison's god-father and had been one of Jhonnie's best men at our wedding. Nicole, Pete's lovely partner of many years, was a shy willowy sylph-like creature who had been working on her PhD forever. In spite of our closeness I had never asked why they weren't married or having kids, or what would happen if she continued to work on that PhD for another decade. I never asked, because they were really Jhonnie's friends, not mine. My level of nosiness and bossiness knew no bounds with my own crew, but Jhonnie's friends seemed to 'do things' together. My friends were always more inclined to sit around a table and eat, drink and talk themselves into a frenzy.

Pete was Jhonnie's best friend, and one of the most thoroughly decent and substantial people I'd ever known. Years before he and Nicole had met, Pete and I had bungy-jumped together on a ski-ing holiday. Pete's a fishing, mountain-climbing, hiking adventure guy. I'm just a nutter who jumps off things. But the two of us were bonded by that icy nerve-wracking experience all those years back. Nicole had endeared herself thoroughly over the years by listening patiently as Pete recounted, blow by blow, the fateful bungy day on a windy bridge in Queenstown. Is there anything more boring than other people's tales of derring-do?

While my family had already supplied the infrastructure that was making this hospital vigil possible, Jhonnie's family were nowhere to been seen. Any decision to be made on his behalf was made by me. Jhonnie needed a brother here for conference, for consultation. Pete was that brother, and Nicole was his steadfast sidekick.

My second shift at Royal North Shore that rainy Saturday began in the front seat of Pete's car. *Groundhog Day* – I pulled the parking pass out of my bra for the second time, the boom gate rose too slowly, and I scoped out the nearest parking spot. The waiting room routine, the ringing phone, the hand-washing, the low-lit buzzing machines of 6C were already second nature to me, but I could see on Pete and Nicole's faces the efforts to suppress awkward discomfort.

I greeted the nurses, and Tim, and Jhonnie, and noticed that two of the elderly stroke victims on the 'good' side of the ward had gone. Dead? Home? None of their families were lurking in the waiting room. The 'good' side of the ward consisted of three beds where patients with flailing arms were restrained with straps. They drooled and gurgled and screamed. They were in much better shape than the bodies that rested on the 'bad' side – the side that was home to Jhonnie, Tim and the silent guy with no visitors.

Pete had managed to swallow the lump in his throat. He was talking to Jhonnie, struggling at first, and full of blokey bravado. Pete called Jhonnie 'Pretty Boy' and accused him of malingering. Nicole excused herself. I walked her back to the waiting room. Not far enough – she had to get out of the building. Father Kelly, a racing man and uncle of one of my old crew from school, appeared, doing his rounds. If the Catholic network is tight, the racing network is tighter. In these situations a racing priest is a sensational man to have in your corner. Royal North Shore is not a Catholic hospital, and Jhonnie is at best a crappy Anglican, yet his accident had transformed 6C into a mini Lourdes on the lower north shore. Father Kelly had already seen Jhonnie, and thought he looked better for a few days' 'rest'. We talked about rugby and racing, out by the lift, and old schools and old teachers and old nuns. He had a great touch for this sort of business. He could have handled his own talk show – a sort of holy Parkinson. He came back into the ward and chatted with Pete and talked directly to Jhonnie.

'This could be a great way to nail converts. They can't talk back.'

'He is a captive audience.'

I wanted to know if he'd given Jhonnie his last rites. I had the feeling, from his admission that he'd slipped in during the first 48 hours, that he might have. I was too squeamish to ask. I thought about all those babies in limbo, the ones who'd died before they'd been christened. They needed the prayers of devout Catholic kiddies to send them to heaven. Did they still teach such punitive nonsense? I knew that classrooms of bony-kneed Catholic children were praying for Jhonnie now every morning, but there was no talk of limbo.

Nicole could barely speak for the rest of the day. Back home, around the big white table with the rest of the family, I offered her a Scotch, but she declined. Mum accepted the Scotch. Pete accepted a Guinness. We reviewed the day and I peeled the veggies for a little roast beef dinner. Pete had spoken directly to the ICU nurses about how to behave. He asked me if it would be okay for him to visit every evening after work. ICU is a strictly next-of-kin gig. So far, that meant me and whoever accompanied me, in case of bad news, flood and general unpleasantness.

There was no room in that tightly packed mechanised unit for well-wishers. There were no chairs. No bedside tables. Not a superfluous soul found its way into ICU. I wasn't sure what I was achieving when I went. Was I proving to myself that he was alive, or was I talking to my husband, who, although inert, might somehow sense my presence and benefit from it? I had no idea. It's not something I would ever ask another person to do. Nobody could take on such a burden. Pete told me that it would be a privilege. After he left I cried, and sat down to type while I seared a neat, nicely aged piece of rump.

EMAIL FROM RUTH TO JHONNIE'S LIST

Nothing much to report. Jhonnie is still mostly asleep, but impressing doctors with his progress. The two other guys in 6C do absolutely nothing, and while I would hate for their families to hear this, Jhonnie is definitely winning Intensive Care. Aside from some ugly injuries, and more gadgets than even Jhonnie would fancy, he looks very robust.

Broken ribs (five, not three, I glean from illegally snooping his charts) are giving him so much trouble breathing, they're keeping him on the respirator, but that is only a matter of days.

Father Michael Kelly and Sister Claire Koch have been visiting. I've told Jhonnie that he has gone in brain injured but he might come out Catholic. Both Kelly and Koch have agreed that the two are not mutually exclusive.

Pete came in with me today, and when Jhonnie heard his voice he made huge effort to open eye and squeeze his hand. Pete was rather annoyed that even after all this Jhonnie was still a bit of a pretty boy. I threw around the 'metrosexual' tag. Pete opted for megasexual. The outfit and the haircut could use some work, but Jhonnie doesn't have a mirror, so what Pete says goes.

His waiting room – a special little piece of hell from *Beetlejuice*, looks like a transit lounge in Dubai Airport, but in style, more like a badly wiped ashtray. Families sit there, waiting for the phone on the wall to ring, with good or bad news. This room is so shitful, they don't even bother to glorify it with old magazines. Every family sits around with unopened novels.

Day one, a friend told me not to bother with a novel. I thought it was odd advice at the time, but after lugging *Running With Scissors* to no effect for two days, I realised it was pointless going in with anything but a bottle of water.

Everything at home is running like clockwork. The great Ritchie chick network, and all our very good friends, are just stepping in and taking charge. (I'm still cooking dinner at night, partly because I'm a control freak, partly because it is good to do something not so Intensive Care, and partly because if William saw anybody else cook in my kitchen he would know something was beyond seriously wrong. We know that things are seriously wrong, but I'm trying to strike a balance. All very tiring.) Thanks again for all your good stuff. Hope to go in tomorrow to find him sitting up reading Faulkner (which really would be a miracle as he's never read anything longer than Tintin).

More later

RR

Day 5

ONE OF THE MOST SHOCKING things about having a baby is that you're never alone. Maybe in the shower, for a few minutes. But that singular independence of life before motherhood fades like an old fax until the idea of walking aimlessly in any direction for an uncalculated amount of time seems impossible.

The never-alone factor increases exponentially when you have a new baby *and* a husband in a coma. Waking up on Sunday morning, the suffocating notion that I had not been alone since the cab ride from the hospital on Wednesday night propelled me from bed. It was barely dawn but I hurried from the house with dog, phone and water into the crispy dew of Rushcutters Bay Park.

There were nearly always necking couples on benches, barely wearing the outfits of Saturday night conquest. The dregs of the drugs often drove them to the waterfront for romance. It was the drugs, or perhaps a skerrick of sense that told them they were in no shape to face their mothers.

Rushcutters embodied every incongruity of our neighbourhood. Luxury yachts snuggled together, millions of dollars of proud white achievement, only metres from homeless men, junkies, canoodling party people, tiny urban families who had stubbornly refused to move to the suburbs just because of 'the baby'. But the least likely tenants of Elizabeth Bay were always the dogs. Who knew that so many dogs were hiding in all those apartment buildings, just waiting for dawn and dusk when we'd take them walking?

Technically I wasn't alone. I was with Devlin. There was no question of me walking aimlessly in any direction never knowing if I would return. I could breathe. I could walk. I started to run but the caesarian scars didn't feel right.

Devlin disappeared with his friends. At the end of Darling Point I stretched my back and legs on the low sandstone wall as I had done so many times before, and on this perfect spring morning the harbour, the park, the whole world looked different. I thought my heart might explode in my chest. I slumped on the bench and phoned Tracey and told her what the doctors had said.

'I'm really, really scared.'

'I know. I can't believe you have to do this.'

'Trace, I don't know what I'm doing. Is he ever coming home?'

'Nobody can answer that. You're doing everything right. He's in the right place. RNS is the only place to be with a head injury. Is he still on the respirator?'

'Um, I don't know. He's covered in tubes.'

'Is a machine breathing for him?'

I could picture his bare chest going up down up down, like pumping air into a balloon. I stopped crying so that I could answer.

'Yes. They tried to get him to breathe on his own but he couldn't.'

'Well, that could just be the broken ribs. Have they taken the drain from his chest? Is there a tube coming out from a hole in the side of his chest?'

'Yes.'

'Is it running clear or blood?'

'I don't know.'

'Little face, I can't go in there. I have the flu. They won't let me into ICU until I'm better.'

'Okay. They say the tubes will come out in a few days.'

'Well, that's amazing. That's off the charts. Great, that means they're keeping him intubated for the ribs.'

'Intubated — is that the stuff down the throat? I'm such an idiot. What else do I need to ask them?'

'I'd want them to hazard a guess at brain damage. They won't want to. Is the eye nerve damage or brain damage? Get the eye specialist in. If that eye is still fixed dilated they should know why. He's not in ER anymore.'

'Okay. Sorry Trace. Sorry to ring you.'

'Never apologise for ringing me.'

If my beloved cousin Tracey was too sick to go near a hospital, something might really be wrong. Maybe she was still run down from the chemo. It couldn't be anything worse, surely.

I've never understood people who catastrophise. It's an exercise more pointless than the jealous rage. Unfortunately, in the middle of a catastrophe it's hard to resist. If you can face death on a bicycle on a sunny Wednesday, then lightning, flying pigs, reckless buses and even the flu can present a real threat.

I drove alone. I went to Chris's house to pick up the dicta-phone and some pictures she'd put out on the front verandah. They weren't home and I was relieved. I didn't want to speak to Chris or hug the children in front of her.

My conversation with Connar on the phone the night before had gone well. I had described his father as if he were a special effect in a movie, trying to keep all the fear out of my voice, yet still paint an accurately ugly picture. I described Jhonnie's side of ICU as a slum, and told him when Dad moved to a better neighbourhood he'd be in a better position to entertain. I told him that some of the adults found the place so scary that they wanted to vomit. I talked for a long time and I could hear him nodding on the other end. Did he have any questions?

'Are they staples like in an exercise book?'

'Bigger.'

'Okay, then maybe I'll wait until he can talk to me.'

'I think that's a great plan. Connar, I can't think of anyone he'll want to speak to more.'

The children's voices sounded tiny and light, humming from the dictaphone by Jhonnie's head. I put up their drawings, along with William's art – a rather special firework affair he'd titled 'A Beautiful Thing'. Jhonnie didn't stir. My throat was hoarse from talking. It was a relief to let Madi chatter to her father about the tiny details of her camp. 6C was empty on Sunday morning. Families and visiting clergy are all busy elsewhere. I read Jhonnie the paper. An old lady on the good side of the ward howled occasionally, like a wolf. I upped the volume on Peter Fitz's column. The nurses filled in paperwork. For long periods nobody whispered or coma-shouted. Every machine in the place whirred in sorry electronic proof of industry. I held my husband's hand and stroked his face. This was almost like being alone.

EMAIL FROM RUTH TO JHONNIE'S LIST

Awake morning and afternoon, but still too groggy to breathe without assistance. Tubes out by Wednesday if he keeps progressing this well.

You can spend your life watching *The Bold and the Beautiful*, but nothing can really prepare you for Intensive Care. Right now

Jhonnie's not too aware of his surroundings, but frankly they have nothing to recommend them but the nurses. Jhonnie's main nurse (my particular favourite), Carlie, says that he has a fantastic temperament for Intensive Care (that'll look good on the CV). She says that he definitely knows where he is now and is really co-operating – very patient, very focused.

I show him family pictures all day long and cards from the kids, and I am completely sure that he recognises all the faces. I keep him informed of the kids' movements: Madi's camp, Connar playing over at Kosta's, William at a bowling party; Patrick doubling in size. They've made voice tapes to play; so far he's been asleep – but maybe those familiar voices are working their way into his dreams.

Rugby continues to figure in his recovery. William Petley forwarded my first email to Peter Fitz, who rang me last night and offered to pay Jhonnie a visit, and even deliver a call from John Eales. I sat on the floor and sobbed – that would be a yes. Definitely Starlight Foundation Moment of the Day. When I conveyed this generosity to Jhonnie today he opened his eye widely and gave me a definite 'Don't shit me' look.

Jhonnie is a bit of a Dory just now (Ellen DeGeneres' forgetful fish in *Finding Nemo*). So I can give him good news over and over again, and he comprehends it as if for the first time. Good news is at a premium these days, so the amnesia has its up sides.

I keep telling Jhonnie that he is not hideously disfigured, he can move his arms and legs, and just before the accident he promised to buy me a string of enormous Broome pearls. Of course the latter is fiction, but if I keep sliding it in with the truth I might get lucky. Seriously thinking of tidying his office and doing six years' back admin, and when he gets out I'll tell him he's the most organised man in the world. He would need more than a life-threatening bump on the head to believe that.

We are holding up well at home. Walked Devlin first thing this morning and avoided eye contact with all the other dog walkers – but great to get out at dawn. Therese and her bevy of beautiful blonde daughters entertained my boys all afternoon, and I can hear screeches of bath-time laughter upstairs as I write. Scallopine and silverbeet for dinner.

In just five days the unspeakably strange is becoming a new normal. Nothing I see or hear shocks me anymore. On day two the social worker offered to organise my parking, and issued me with a three-month pass. Nothing the doctors have said has shocked me more.

more later rr

Sitting down to write after returning from the hospital every day was becoming very therapeutic. Every time I turned on the computer the email In box was full of messages in reply to my updates, old friends and work colleagues sending best wishes and asking respectfully to be added to the list. Sympathy cards covered with doves never seem enough. Nobody who writes them ever feels their words are making any difference. But I started to feel that the emails that rolled in every day were like prayers. Strange intangible slips of hope and humour, flying through the ether, around the world. Where was Jhonnie, after all? His body was lying in that ward covered in machines, but he may well have been out there somewhere on the internet, absorbing all the electronic hope. Crap. He was fast asleep in the ugliest hospital ward in Australia, and contact, however electronic, with the people who loved him most made him feel more present, and gave me strength.

As I steamed the silverbeet, Jhonnie's stepmother, Gabriella, rang. Julia kept the kids out of the way but craned to hear the conversation anyway. Was Jhonnie's dad in earshot? What was I to say? Gabriella's thick elegant Italian accent could make a discussion about weeding the garden sound theatrical, so this was always going to be opera.

She's an amazing woman, my mother-in-law. Tiny, groomed, imperious, energetic, controlling, funny, a lioness and a damsel in distress, all rolled into one occasionally fierce woman who sounds not unlike Gina Lollobrigida on the phone. She's easy to impersonate. She's an Italian character in a Peter Sellers movie. She makes the most gorgeous bookend to my father-in-law, the white-haired tall English gent. They lived in England until all the children left home. Ten years ago they moved to Umbria to restore a dilapidated farmhouse. They kicked the cattle out of the kitchen and moved in a year later. There they live and work, building and renovating, fighting and cooking, playing cards with their odd coterie of friends, expats and Italians – all the fine folk of a tiny walled town called Todi.

Early September still held the last whiff of the long Italian summer. I could picture them at the table under the olive tree a little way from the house. I could see her at the kitchen sink washing the last of the homegrown radicchio and some field mushrooms for a risotto. I could remember us all lying around the pool reading *Hello!* magazine and eating bread and cheese in the August afternoon sun, and William, just turned three, running nude and peeing on the cherry trees, a gardening cupid.

Gabriella's voice, so quick to swing from enthusiasm to anger, from self-pity to pride, sounded very vulnerable and far away. She was full of fear for her Jonathan and love for us. She sounded as if she couldn't bear to hear one word of bad news, so I played it down, but I didn't lie. She was stunned and shocked, a victim on a home renovation show: 'Oh my god. Oh my god.' She didn't want to tell Michael any of this. It would kill him.

'This has been the most terrible time for Michael and myself. So many trips to the apartment in Rome, in the heat, to see the doctors. And then, on this last trip, did you know that we were robbed?'

'Um, no. I didn't.'

'And now, it is so terrible, now, of the medical records of Michael and myself for the last 35 years, I have nothing!

Explain who would take such a thing. And now this! Jonathan, with a head injury!'

It fleetingly occurred to me to sympathise with her loss. I mixed up a bowl of roast beef leftovers for Devlin and poured a jug of fresh water, the phone tucked under my chin, as Gabriella went on to tell me the woes of life in Umbria these many months we'd not spoken. Had she even asked if Patrick was well, fat, stupid, hideous, alive? I couldn't recall. But the ulcer on Michael's leg simply wasn't getting better. After a while I made my apologies. The veal was ready, the wine was open, Julia was desperate to hear the other side of the single most bizarre conversation to have taken place in the house all week.

Jhonnie's family, like my own, punctuated any and every occasion with food. I could see Gabriella standing in her sunny Italian kitchen at breakfast the day after our long flight from Sydney. With a sleepy look and a tiny coffee, she asked Jhonnie, in her world-weary way, which risotto he would like – radicchio or zucchini. Zucchini. And which pasta sauce? Carbonara. Meat or chicken? Veal. Okay then . . . And she proceeded to make lunch for 40 that very day, with produce from the garden. We drank a lot of local wine and William ran around the grounds with cups of blood orange juice and mad little Italian lollies. A lot of locals and oddball British expats turned up to inspect the prodigal son. My mother-in-law was in her element. The risotto was sensational.

In bed that night I thought about the fatted calves of my own homecomings over the years. Even if I'd been away for a month, my dad liked to make a pilgrimage to the fish markets for mud crabs, plenty of chili and garlic. To Chinatown for a duck; and Bondi for some Jewish deli treats, and enormous nutmeat tortes from the Gelato Bar. Mum knew all my favourite dishes and the order in which I would most like to consume them in those first few days back home. Saturday night was roast beef, after the races. Sometime in his sixties Dad measured out the rest of his life in roast beef dinners. A disappointing cut of meat marked a Saturday he would never get back.

I could picture the way our dining table was set on Saturday nights – the pepper mills – a selection. Dad couldn't stand it when a pepper mill didn't work. Julia or I would make up the Keens mustard, fresh so it was hot. Depending on the season, we'd have white asparagus or broad beans. The quest for fresh horseradish nearly always ended in disappointment, as did Dad's various attempts at pickling olives or making his own pastrami.

He once smuggled live sourdough culture in from a famous San Francisco bakery so that we could make our own. Highly illegal, and the results were terrible, but we only ever ate sourdough in America, and deprivation for years at a time made this a grail worth pursuing. In the square white-bread Australia of the 1960s and 1970s, my father's obsession with baked goods must have been unusual. Every single day, a different bread – fresh bread. And salty butter, plenty of it.

All those meals we shared, for 40 years. I often joked that William was made of lamb loin chops and spinach, because he had consumed so much already. In that case, I might be a green salad with Mum's vinaigrette, which was uncopiable, even in the best kitchens in town. Salads and roast beef sandwiches after the beach. Lambs-fry breakfasts and pancake stacks after swimming on Saturday mornings. Hot Akta-Vite when we were cold. Flat lemonade when we were sick. Now, after a lifetime of landmarks and their associated meals, I found myself searching for the quintessential flat lemonade that would heal a brain injury, and keep us all happy, and keep me busy, steady in the process. I lay awake and wondered what my mother-in-law was cooking. That would have been a better conversation. Maybe if we stuck to the menu we'd get on better.

I was shaken from a very deep sleep by the telephone. It rang into my dreams before I stirred. Awake and terrified – this could only be bad news.

'Hello, doll. You poor thing. My love, how is he?'

'What? Who is this? Who are you?'

'Doll, it's me, and I'm so worried. What can I do? Tell me what to do!'

It was midnight, the caller was drunk, and I was furious.

'Send him a card and get off the phone.'

'But I'm so worried. And how are you?'

'Asleep. I'm asleep. Now fuck off.'

People were taking the news of Jhonnie's accident in strange ways. They were getting drunk and checking their own pulse. They were sending flowers, but crossing the street to avoid me.

A man who had been one of Jhonnie's closest colleagues rang as I was serving dinner. They had fallen out when Jhonnie left the agency. I decided it was more important to eat veal with my family than humour his need to take centre stage in the Jhonnie saga. Fifteen minutes later his girlfriend rang from the same mobile phone number, and I decided not to speak to her either. Jhonnie had never liked her, and we both felt sorry for his wife. No way that pair were going to ruin my dinner.

Now there were drunken calls in the night, and stepmothers mourning the loss of their medical records, and a brother in LA who still hadn't returned a call.

I stomped downstairs in the dark and dialled.

'Justin?'

'Ruthie, is that you?'

'Tell me you haven't received all my messages . . . '

'I got one –'

'Tell me you didn't know that your brother has been lying in a coma for five days. What the fuck is wrong with you people?

Are you wolves? How much more serious does this need to get before you pick up the phone, you lazy sack of shit?'

'I spoke to Julian. He said not to ring. I did return the call. I rang Jhonnie, and left a message.'

'He's not checking his voice mail just now. He's in a COMA! Don't you get it?'

'I do. I'm beside myself. I just love him to bits. I've asked Julian what to do, and he said to do nothing until we know more.'

'But you don't know *anything*. Jesus, and you're the *good* brother. You're supposed to be the close one. And I leave you five messages to call and you do what? Draw another cartoon, and order a pizza. Grow up, Justin. Your brother needs you. I need you.'

'I'm so sorry.'

'You don't get off the fucking hook with sorry. You just stand there and take it while I fucking tell you what a useless prick you are. And of your whole useless prick family I thought, maybe, just maybe, you'd behave like a human being, but that is far too great a stretch. That's species away, you amoebic piece of shit. I don't care what you do now. And I'm not telling any more lies for any of your fucking relatives. Jhonnie may be a vegetable for the rest of his life and we have four small children. If that news is going to give any of you indigestion, well boo-fucking-hoo. Thank Christ you're not here. I'd physically fucking hurt you, you childish piece of shit. That's about it. Any response?'

There was a long silence.

'Are you dead? I hope you're dead.'

'No. I am so sorry. You're right. I just followed Julian's lead, and I should have called, but the only number I had must have been Jhonnie's mobile.'

'I kept leaving you all the numbers.'

'I'm sorry. What can I do now? I'm sorry.'

'Oh nothing really, I just had to get it off my chest. I feel much better for screaming at you. I hope I woke you up.'

'No.'

'Damn, some drunk fucker just woke me up, so I decided to share. I don't think there's much you can do. Any plans to see him at all?'

'Not really, I've got a wedding in Corfu in a few weeks, and that's all the holidays I have left. Mum doesn't know I'm going to Corfu, and not going there, if you see what I mean.'

'Justin, I don't care if your mother finds out that you've chosen a wedding over a weekend with Mummy – or a deathbed visit to your brother. Fuck, you're seriously another breed.'

'Ruthie, he's my oldest friend. I'm the best man. I've had the tickets for months.'

'Yeah. Jhonnie's scheduled this little exercise rather badly. You've got a wedding and I've got a three-month-old baby and a five year old who wants to know when his father's going to wake up.'

'I'm so sorry.'

'It seems there's "sorry" and then there's "Blampied sorry". And in my experience, Blampied sorry doesn't butter any turnips.'

'Sorry? What do you –'

'I'm not sure any of you are capable of doing any better. I've been thinking, how awful for Jhonnie, with none of his family here. And really it wouldn't make the slightest bit of difference.'

'That is so unfair. We all love Jhonnie so much.'

Justin was crying, and I was finally tired of swearing.

'You've picked the wrong person to cry on, Justin. I'm just the wrong person. Why don't you call me once a week, in between weddings, and I'll tell you if he ever wakes up and remembers who the fuck you are.'

Day 6

Some people hate Monday mornings. I've always seen them as another opportunity to have a fresh crack at it. By Wednesday, inevitable disorganised mediocrity has always taken hold again, but Mondays can begin with fresh sheets, an organised diary, an ironed shirt. I got up on Monday morning, walked my dog and wondered if my tirade at Justin may have been a little too much for such a delicately raised boy. Nobody in Jhonnie's family ever says anything unpleasant, which strikes me as odd, because they don't like each other much. My family, on the other hand, all scream like banshees, and then we get on with it. People of action, and shouting, but at least we know where we stand.

I felt surprisingly light, despite having dumped on the baby brother with the bad head for phone numbers. I thought about my father's wild justification for shouting at all and sundry: 'I give ulcers, I don't get them.' Maybe it was genetic. I had no qualms about ripping the lining out of my brother-in-law's stomach. It was the least I could do. By the time I returned to a plate of fruit – no pineapple, plenty of kiwi – and a mug of hot tea, I'd formulated a plan. Julia was keen to take notes for the spreadsheet.

'Meera has to track down that guy from the agency to

come here and get us into Jhonnie's computer. I don't have his password. His desk is an archaeological dig. He's probably got unpaid bills, and lapsing insurance, and God knows . . .'

'He'd be insured for injury . . . wouldn't he? Everybody with their own business carries key man insurance, don't they?'

And there it was. Jhonnie wasn't everybody. He had planned his escape from the coalmine of multinational advertising for nearly a year: if he resigned, appointed the managing director as chairman and CEO, technically he would make himself redundant, and so get a big fat payout; he would then stay on a few days a month for client continuity, to iron out the bumps as the reins of power changed hands. But his cunning plan stopped about there.

Jhonnie had left the agency in February and still 'consulted' for them two days a week. His busy days consisted of odd coffees with other 'consultants' or a serendipitous game of golf with still more freewheeling consultants.

I was nervous about Jhonnie drifting into Consultant Land. He had an Aquarian tendency to float around in the breeze, even when he was anchored down by a hugely demanding job where the livelihoods of hundreds of people depended on him. With the loose but tempting parameters of consultancy luring him from the straight and narrow, I was already worried. Consultants, like life coaches, computer viruses, antioxidants, low GIs and free radicals, seemed to be a recent development, one that we all once lived happily without. Now I was married to one.

Jhonnie had enjoyed the support of a personal assistant for 14 long years. There was a good chance he didn't know how to open mail or pick up dry-cleaning. He never banked, or filed. I paid all the bills on the home front. Jhonnie was something of a fiscal lily of the field. Without access to his computer, I couldn't even guess at his accountant's name. I thought I knew that guy in a coma, but his life was a messy mystery.

'I'm getting rid of my car. I can't drive two cars at once. The convertible has to go anyway, and we need the room, and maybe the money.'

'What are you doing about Jhonnie's commitments?' asked Julia.

Along with facility to give ulcers to others, we anticipate financial tidal waves long before others sense a change in the weather. The children's school fees had arrived. There would be child support to pay.

'I'm putting them in an envelope and sending them back to Chris.'

'Do you think you can sell her a car?'

Nothing about this was going to be easy. She was not going to like this at all. How to avoid a fight with the ex-wife about money? I rang the lawyer. I rang the accountant. I rang a car yard. I rang another friend of Jhonnie's to drive me to the hospital that afternoon, then I rang the acupuncturist. An electric fence of pain ran up and down my spine. If I didn't do something about it soon I might accidentally self-immolate. We'd already gotten this week off to a good start.

Jo picked me up from acupuncture, and we made bad jokes all the way to the hospital. Parking ticket out of bra, plum parking position under a tree, two terrible coffees and another week was under way.

Tim's mother and father were waiting by the phone.

'How is he this morning? Have you been in yet?'

'Same. John is making plenty of noise. I think he's keeping them busy.'

'I hope he's ordering a vodka and lime.'

'I brought my camera.' Jo's eyes narrowed, the pirate smuggler.

'Joanne, that's weird, even for you.'

'If it were me, I'd want to know what I looked like, later. He's never going to remember any of this. They won't mind.'

I looked at Tim's mother, and felt that perhaps she would. She wasn't in any position to take happy snaps of her son for later. But Jo was right. I wanted the pictures, even if I never showed anyone.

Jhonnie was certainly more awake. Never for more than a minute, and he had no control over his drifting state. The nurses would shake him quite hard and shout in his ear, then apologise, saying he'd been wide-eyed (make that one wide eye) for nearly five minutes only an hour before. Bad timing. For most of our visit he only stirred when shaken. Jo whipped out the camera and started flashing. Most of the machines and the neck brace were already gone. The tube from the side of his chest was gone. Hair was even beginning to grow on his scalp around the staples. They had shaved him every few days, but already, in less than a week, his appearance had taken on the strange characteristics of somebody groomed by another. Nose hair. Sponge bath. No shampoo. Blunt razor. How long before a captain of industry begins to look like a homeless victim? No time at all.

Jo and I both spoke to him with total confidence, as if he were just passed out, with a broken leg. When his eyes were open he recognised us. That's all we knew.

If he could hear us he would never remember. If he could hear but was unable to open his eyes or communicate, it would be lonely, frightening and disheartening, and he would never remember. While he slept, his brain rebooted. Sleeping was good. But it didn't do much for the cheer squad who sat bedside every day, talking about children he might never recognise.

'Babe, Patrick hasn't pooed for anybody but me. He's a genius of poo. We've got this passing parade of family and friends, all feeding him and dressing him up in little outfits. He doesn't cry. He doesn't poo. He just gurgles and charms. He's a people pleaser – a bit like you, huh?'

And then he'd squeeze my hand. So he remembered Patrick? Nobody knew. Jo and I decided that he did. His grip was weak. I'd never held a hand so large with such little strength. His three-month-old son would pack a more convincing punch than Jhonnie.

'William has completely grown out of those Cowboy and Indian pyjamas. They don't even reach his ankles, but he won't part with them. So he's a bit like Jethro Clampett. Did you get the *Beverly Hillbillies* in the UK? I suppose you were in boarding school. Speaking of Beverly Hills, I spoke to Justin in LA. He sends you all his love. The whole family is sending, you know . . . love.'

Still no doctors to see. As Jo drove over to Eleni's we reviewed the situation and decided that no doctors must have meant he didn't need a doctor. Second-guessing and reading between the lines were beginning to drive us all bonkers.

Eleni had printed more big pictures to decorate Jhonnie's environs. We'd all spent summer holidays with Jhonnie's parents in Umbria the year before, and pictures of our families together in those blindingly bright hot villages seemed impossibly pretty and sad. Derutia, Todi, Norcia. Our boys had run up and down cobbled lanes in the midday sun. We'd driven for miles and navigated the Umbrian region for wild boar prosciutto and truffles. Now pictures of a long lazy truffle lunch would be Blu-taced to the window of 6C – Neurosurgical Intensive Care, Royal North Shore Hospital.

Eleni started to sob as we looked at the pictures. She made strong coffee. Jo had never been to Eleni's house. She looked at her paintings – enormous pumpkins and oranges and dark walls full of huge bright intense canvases. Jo boiled over with genuine enthusiasm for Eleni's work. Eleni settled down with the coffee and stopped crying.

During these days, huge waves of emotion could rise from apparently nowhere and drain just as quickly. Eleni sniffled over a print of us together, sitting on an ancient Umbrian wall, smiling; then, suddenly calm, like a toddler after a tantrum, she apologised for her outbreak. That was nothing. I told them about my tirade at Justin. They loved it. And then the in-laws' robbery. I confessed to berating Chris over the unimportance of Father's Day.

'People are fucked, aren't they?' For a Greek migrant with an unreliable grasp of the English language, my friend Eleni had a marvellous turn of phrase.

I shared the afternoon shift with Sam, an old colleague of Jhonnie's, who, coincidentally, I'd known since ballroom dancing classes at the age of 14. I'd once, long ago, thrown Sam out of my parents' house for gate-crashing a party. We'd never been close as kids, but somehow, he'd ended up as one of Jhonnie's pals and William's godparents. He hadn't seen the boy since the altar at St Cannice's, but I knew he loved Jhonnie and the whole incident had rattled him.

'I've been too upset to drink, seriously, Ruthie. None of us can believe this.'

'I think it's that it could be any of us. It's random, don't you think?'

'No, it's Jhonnie. Nobody can believe this can happen to a bloke like Jhonnie. He's about the only decent man in advertising. What the fuck's in store for the rest of us?'

'There's nothing very CEO about Intensive Care. It's one of life's levellers, like groin strain.'

'Dr Small checks out well. He was at Sydney with three of ours, and he comes up trumps. Not a bad word.'

Sam was also part of the great Catholic professional network. All of our families had been at Riverview, the official Jesuit breeding ground for doctors, dentists, lawyers, vets, Supreme Court judges and annoying conservative politicians. Within hours of the news breaking, the network had galvanised, and every aspect of the hospital, ward, staff and treatment had been filtered through the system. Jhonnie couldn't be in better hands.

Sam was very jolly in the car, very positive. Although he'd been a serious family man for years, there was something very adolescent about Sam, especially when he was in a group. There was a crew of mildly bad boys, mostly from advertising, who used to go off for lads' weekends, play golf, and burn large volumes of meat on homemade barbies. When Jhonnie and Sam were with the boys, they behaved as if they were 11, an immature 11 at that. The boys had none of the details of the accident. They thought he must have collided with a car. Sam wanted to see what was left of any car hit by a speeding Blampied. This is what guys should do. They should drive the nearly widowed to and from hospital and crack jokes. They should help, and Sam was helping, right up until we walked into Intensive Care.

When men turn 40 they become as vulnerable as little boys on their first day of school. Midlife crises make sense to me now. Their tenuous grasp on the meaning of life can be undone by the birth of a baby, the death of a dog, or the failing fortunes of a football team. Men who have turned 40 are no longer the bulletproof buffoons that propelled themselves from carefree childhood to torturous middle-aged responsibility. When the wind changes direction they are lost.

Sam's hands were shaking as he washed them in the basin inside those flapping plastic doors of 6C. As he approached Jhonnie, he lost the power of speech and tears welled. He grabbed Jhonnie's hand, the bad one, and Jhonnie opened his eyes. Jhonnie's happy recognition of his friend undid Sam completely.

Our timing had been momentous. Jhonnie was breathing well, on his own. The tubes were coming out, right now. We were politely requested to retire to the waiting room, as the process wasn't going to be a pretty one.

Outside, in the very bad place with the phones on the wall and tape on the carpet, Sam spluttered and sobbed, overcome. 'Oh Ruthie, he's going to be okay. Don't you think? I mean, that's really Jhonnie. He's bloody amazing, isn't he?'

Was Sam's reaction relief or shock? He'd come over completely Irish all of a sudden. At least if Sam's performance had been frightening, Jhonnie wouldn't remember it in years to come. Back inside, Sam was more composed but speechless. The bed was tilted up for the first time, Jhonnie strapped in place. His mouth looked twisted and swollen from the tubes. Exhausted, shaven, battered but not beaten, Jhonnie sat propped up in bed and smiled as we entered the room. I kissed his face. He couldn't lift his hands around me but he tried. He tried equally unsuccessfully to speak. I looked nervously to the nurse.

'His throat will be bad from the tubes for a few days, but he'll be right.' Then she shouted, 'You'll be right, won't you, Jhonnie?'

Jhonnie raised one feeble thumb, a punch-drunk fighter staggering with delusion. Sam covered his own red bulging eyes and looked away.

'Well, there you go. Amazing. Ruth, he's amazing.'

Amazing. Perhaps this was one of those rare moments to correctly use the ubiquitous 'awesome'. Sam had done my emoting for me. This was great news, and yet it was hard to rejoice. I knew how to cope with the completely horizontal intubated Jhonnie, and that was all I knew. Sam had seen Lazarus rise up, and that was a great snapshot of recovery. I knew Jhonnie wasn't taking up his bed and walking anywhere. When he could finally speak, what would he say?

In the car we talked business. Bad investments. Bad agencies. Lawyers. And then there was all the money the old ad agency still owed Jhonnie. Would I have to put in an invoice? I should, anyway. It's his payout. And Sam wanted to know, immediately, if the bastards gave me any trouble.

It's very reassuring having a man around at moments such as these, even if he blubbers like a baby and can't remember his godson's name. I was pleased to have Sam on our side in case things got ugly. Uglier.

EMAIL FROM RUTH TO JHONNIE'S LIST

Unbelievable. The tube came out half an hour ago. Jhonnie is propped up, wearing an oxygen mask, a sheet and a determined look on his face. He is very confused, trying to speak, get out of bed and make sense of his surroundings. Sleeping giants, *Gulliver's Travels* and Herman Munster are all fairly good clues to this phenomenon. The staff – all so fond of Inert Jhonnie – won't know what's hitting them when he throws his full 100+ kilos of confusion into his recovery.

Sam was with me for the great untubing visit and was speechless, struggling to be tearless, with glee at Jhonnie's performance.

Earlier this morning we had very few tricks. Jo reminded him of Yahoo's birthday party and we were both sure he could recall it – nodded in accordance anyway.

The kids' tape continued to soothe him, but never fails to amuse the ICU staff. Connar's earnest and accurate details of the Spring Fair activities, which had escaped his father, put a smile on otherwise serious faces. But nobody is prepared for Madison's performance on the recorder. Tuneful and focused, really note-perfect, small-girl-playing-recorder could become a new tool of recovery in ICU units worldwide. With all the silence and low humming machines, no one is expecting the recorder, and everyone bursts out laughing within seconds. The camp song, complete with clapping, that follows is an encore that no nurse can resist.

Back to the present. Jhonnie has moved from the intubated silent creepy seriously unpleasant side of the ward to the more awake, thrashing around from strokes side of the ward, where everyone speaks in relatively loud voices. All his pictures are stuck on the nearby window. His toiletries are by the bed. It's the goddamn Plaza Hotel compared to the last six days. I told him he was moving from a terrace to a semi and we were shooting for a triple-fronted brick-veneer home within days. And as Sam and I left, Jhonnie waved.

Thank you for all the emails. Can't believe I'm actually going to be printing them out and reading them to him – more or less awake (him, not me). Still no visitors, but it is just a matter of time.

This truly disgusting experience has only been improved by the realisation that our family and friends are a seemingly bound-less source of love and support. Not something that I ever want to test again, but you are helping us in ways too numerous to ever properly acknowledge.

Thanks

It's all good news

love rr

Julia finally went home. She scheduled the oddest assortment of family and dear friends to keep me company at night. It was unlikely that I'd be suddenly called to his deathbed. In truth, the parade of people provided a little help with the kids, and somebody for whom I could cook.

I'd hardly seen Simon since Pat was born. We'd know each other since we were 20. (Somehow, an entire lifetime later, Simon had become very much younger than me, but I'm certain he wasn't when we met. Actors!) Over the years Simon had made that tough transition from single party friend to loving family friend. Jhonnie adored him and he was William's other godfather. The days of staying up late and both lying about our age in bars were behind us.

The great thing about having a *Playschool* presenter as a godparent is the tuneful renditions of 'Put on Your Hat' that fill the home during those toddler years. The other great thing about having an actor in the house is that a certain amount of any evening must be devoted to discussing the status/crisis/dazzling success of the acting career. What a relief.

Simon wasn't much of a baby expert. He didn't know how to drive a nappy, or a microwave. I didn't care, and neither did the delighted William. (Patrick, like his father these days, would never remember one inept nappy change.)

After the babies went to bed, Simon and I sat down to some excellent lamb racks, baked desirees full of sour cream and chives, and a bucket of my mother's homegrown green beans. We talked about his career, and projects we would work on together one day, in another time-space continuum. We left Intensive Care outside for the night. Some time after midnight, when Simon was gurgling at the baby, I made us hot Akta-Vite milk and we sat up in bed watching David Letterman until Pat went back to sleep. I hadn't realised just how lonely and silent our bedroom had become.

Day 7

THE LITTLE SCREEN ON THE phone read: OUT OF AREA. I presumed it was Julian or Justin. That was my first mistake. Jhonnie's father could smell a rat.

'What kind of hospital is this that I can't even ring?'

'Well, Michael, there are no phones in the ward. I think they affect the machines. No mobile phones allowed.'

'Can't he use the phone by his bed? He's in a private room presumably.'

'Not exactly.'

'Is this a good hospital? What's going on? He's been in there for, what, three days? How long do they plan to keep him under observation?'

'Under observation?'

I couldn't think. I was making William's breakfast, and coffee for Simon, and filling up the dog's bowl, and lying to my father-in-law.

'Julian said he'd taken a bad fall off his bike and they were just keeping him under observation.'

'Well, it's a bit more serious than that. He's been badly hurt, Michael.'

And then I heard him reeling in catastrophe. Too much. Time to lie.

'He has a lot of broken ribs, and a broken hand, and
. . . well, he's too banged up to come home.'

'But he's fine, Ruth – he's okay, isn't he?'

'He's getting better every day. The doctors are really
pleased.'

'Well tell those doctors that his father wants to speak to
him.'

'I'll do that, Michael. Send all our love to Gabri and Vivvy.
If you could send Jhonnie an email, I'll read it to him.'

'No. I can't use that email. I type so slowly. Before I've
finished a sentence it cuts out.'

'Why don't you write it first, before you connect to the
net? When it's finished just press –'

'I'll ring him.'

'Whatever you think. I've got to get these kids ready now.
Bye-bye.'

For my second mistake, I called Julian, who told me not to
scare his father. I rang Pete, Pete who had visited Jhonnie every
evening after work since his first visit. I told him the story. He
took all the Blampied phone numbers and said, 'Leave them to
me.'

Jhonnie's lawyer returned my call. He told me that they
were in the middle of renegotiating the settlement based on
Jhonnie's change in income. Given that he might never earn
another cent, and he'd left no power of attorney, I wasn't to pay
Chris anything. Nothing. Direct all her demands for money
to him.

My bridesmaid, Sarah, accompanied me to hospital for the
first time and we inspected the new ward, the next stop after
Intensive Care. A floor up, and much more recognisably a floor
of wards, full of beds, nurses' stations, physios, social workers,
microwave ovens. There were signs of life, everywhere. And
then, in nearly every bed, patients, unconscious, unattended,
alone and hopeless. This layperson's diagnosis would prove to

be incorrect. Many of them would go home. None that I saw died. And many more were there awaiting a berth at an institution of care or rehabilitation that would become their new home.

'This doesn't seem too bad,' said Sarah, full of optimism. 'Big windows, almost sunny. Four to a room.'

'You make it sound like a bungalow in Sumatra. It's a real hospital ward, which is, well, progress. Just wait 'til you see 6C.'

As it turned out, we visited 6C that morning for the last time in a long time. The nurses were excited for us. They all insisted that Jhonnie walk back in there one day. They'd never seen him standing up, or heard his voice. They'd calculated and catalogued his every medical statistic. Every sleeping moment for the last week one of them had been by his side, and yet they had never met.

EMAIL FROM RUTH TO JHONNIE'S LIST

He's out of Intensive Care. He speaks – with a rather more Pommy accent than he had last week. Still, he knows he's married to me, has four children and lives in Sydney. He's very confused and drifts in and out of consciousness.

He's still wearing the oxygen mask and has considerable trouble breathing. He seems to be worried about the bad eye. I've told him the bad eye will have to wait, and eventually there might be surgery to make the lid open and close and give him some focus – too much information too soon.

He seems outrageously polite. Sarah came with me to Intensive Care this morning. We checked out his new home – the neurological ward upstairs, much more human than ICU – and came back to tell him about it. Sarah was very positive: 'Your new room is much better, Jhonnie. Nice view, plenty of light.'

Jhonnie considered this then politely inquired of her, 'Do you like it?'

'Yes, very much!'

I asked him if he wanted to see the kids. Yes. If he wanted to see them today. Yes. Did he want to hear the tape of Madi playing the recorder again? NO. See, he's really back.

Jhonnie has some understanding of what's happening to him, but struggles to hold a pen, and his frustration at being unable to do anything, even sit up, is constant. When he's with us he wants to know what's going to happen next. I've told him he's going to the ward, then into rehab. I told him it was a pity to enter rehab without enjoying any of the traditional drugs and alcohol, to which he replied 'Go figure.'

Simon stayed here last night to keep me company, demonstrate some *Playschool* skills with his godson, William, and take over the night feeds with Pat. Pat distinguished himself by sleeping through until 3.30, feeding and going straight back to sleep. I'm quite sure Simon can't see what new parents whinge about. Babies are a piece of cake. Well, Patrick is anyway.

Now that I know Jhonnie is going to live, and come home, and eventually recover, I'm just getting angry. Why did a prick of a thing like this have to happen to him, to us? Are all those years of happily singing along with 'Girlfriend in a Coma' coming back to haunt me? We had no medical insurance to speak of until a month ago. If I hadn't taken out top cover with Medibank Private, would we ever have needed physio, speech therapy or ophthalmology? No. Never! And Jhonnie said, only last Monday, 'I don't think I've ever seen you happier.' And I told him that most certainly I had never been happier. What was I thinking? Never, never admit to being happy, or somebody will come and throw your husband into hospital.

Esther and I are off to see him again now. Esther rang Hugh with the great news. Hugh was with Jhonnie when he had his accident, and in Emergency with me immediately after. I took him into ICU on the weekend, which I know was hard. Hugh has been shocked and relieved by Jhonnie's progress. But when Esther told Hugh, 'He's out!' he replied: 'Of hospital?' Oh Hugh. Not yet, but it's only a matter of time.

More later. Still, no visitors please. Will let you know how and when. Don't ring the ward. They made a point of saying that they don't have a private line or any time to answer it. So there. Hope he fares well with the kids.

xrr

Offers of help flooded in from everywhere. Mostly practical, viable offers. I spoke to Julian and his wife, Claire, several times a day, and mostly, Julian made a lot of sense. In his world-view every other member of the Blampied family was mad and hopeless, and there was plenty of evidence to support his theory. When I spoke to the others they sounded vulnerable and afraid, and I felt their helplessness, so many miles away. But days and calls had passed, and as school friends and distant relatives of mine had started turning up with the tools and goodwill to erect a Shaker's barn, it became clear that Jhonnie wasn't the only Blampied incapable of moving a muscle. They weren't hopping on a plane or calling their grandchildren or making a tape or sending an email.

EMAIL FROM RUTH TO THE BLAMPIED FAMILY
Dear Blampieds,
As of yesterday I feel confident that your son/brother is not going to die.

I have been asking for a week now for you to send emails or tapes that I can read or play to him.

So far nothing. Not exactly sure what else you are doing on the other side of the world while I juggle four children, insane ex-wife and husband in coma. I have just dumped a bucket of bile on Justin, without remorse. He hasn't rung or acknowledged one of my emails. I don't know still, having spoken to him, that he has read them. They ask one and all to write to Jhonnie, and hundreds of his friends are doing so.

Perhaps my calm demeanour to date has led you all to believe that this is a walk in the park. I understand from Claire that making tapes is not really Julian's thing. Boo-hoo.

I am too angry to speak to any of you – a good sign: I haven't been game to feel anything other than concern for Jhonnie so far. But now that we are hopefully at the beginning of what will be months but might be years of slow rehabilitation, you lot leave me gobsmacked.

Sit down right now and write that man something I can read to him so that he knows you care.

Ruth Ritchie.

I sent it to all of them. I imagined they kept it from Michael, or perhaps gave him the 'gist'. Something along the lines of 'Ruth would like you to send Jhonnie a get-well card.' And that advice, completely out of context, might have made no sense at all. My missive certainly stirred the rest of them into action of some kind.

EMAIL FROM VIVVY BLAMPIED TO RUTH

Ruth

We've all been waiting with bated breath for the breakthrough news when Jhonnie was untubed and sitting up – I can assure you that at this end while waiting we were frantic with worry, tearful, upset, you name it, and frustrated that we were on the other side of the world and seemingly totally powerless to do anything – to be that far away while this was going on has its own particular type of torture. I haven't rung 'cos the message I got was that you didn't want calls – I haven't hopped on a plane (which was my first instinct) because I was told I would be in the way – however, you are right. I haven't sent Jhonnie an email or made a tape for him – I'm sorry. I'm concerned that you say it might be years of rehab? And I also confess to a certain amount of denial in that the minute I heard he was untubed and sitting up I thought, well it's all going to be okay then – again probably another feature of being on the other side of the world. I am glad that you have a lot of support around you – I'm glad you're married to him because I know how much you love him and I think that love will carry him far in his recovery. Love Vivvyx

Pog – I am calling you that because I'm reminded of the times you used to go to Robot Land, where they had exceptionally large ice-creams and you would be replaced by Robot Jhonnie and I would be a bit scared and keep demanding that the real Jhonnie come back – this time you have given us all a bit of a scare – but tell me were the ice-creams still as good? I'm glad you have got all your robotic powers to help you get well quickly – I wish I could be there – can't wait to see you again and to meet Patrick for the first time – not only are you a wonderful brother but also a great robot-being – love you more than I can say – Poo (only signing off with that because you're in hospital, so making special allowances).

Esther did very well in the new ward. Jhonnie was delighted to see her. He seemed to be cheering.

'Are we going to the football, Es? I haven't got my jacket.'

'You won't need your jacket yet.'

'They've taken my jacket. She put it in the dorm. Make her give it back.'

'Who Jhonnie? Who took –'

'The woman with the vinyl. That's her! No it's not. She got some . . .'

And then he'd drift off. His voice was light, and childlike, without awareness of his surroundings. Jhonnie sounded carefree. Esther looked at William's art, taped up to the windows, and pictures of Jhonnie with his children.

'Hey, Es, are we going to the football?'

'Not yet, Jhonnie.'

And it went on like that for hours. Still, mostly Jhonnie was asleep.

Chris Blampied was so thrilled by the shift of ward she decided to bring the kids for a visit. I suggested she meet the social worker, Liz, who would prepare Chris and the kids. Chris decided not to wait.

When Pete called me as he left the hospital that evening, we sat on the phone for what seemed like hours. He'd had no luck talking sense into any of the Euro-Blampieds, and he was there when Chris and the kids came to visit. A lucky thing really, because Chris and Connar passed out. Madi had to get them a red drink and find the nurse. Connar spent most of the visit in the bathroom (Not for visitors! Use the Foyer!). Only Madi could bring herself to touch Jhonnie. Poor Jhonnie. Poor kids. Poor Chris.

As Pete recounted the strange developments from his side of Jhonnie's recovery, Esther made loud noises with ice and olives. Virtually any situation, in Esther's book, can be improved by a martini. She kept my sister-in-law, Anna Ritchie, amused while I roamed around the house on the phone.

Esther, Anna and I sat up reviewing the events of the week. Anna had taken much of her holiday to muck in with us. She'd be away next week, but this week, she put herself at our disposal.

Jhonnie didn't know what day it was, how many children he had or if he was on his way to the football. He'd frightened his ex-wife and one son unconscious. His father wanted him to answer the phone, and his entire family was telling each other lies. Somewhere in there we became a one-car family. Esther made another martini. Anna and I sorted ourselves out with healthy tumblers of Scotch and ice, the flashy Blue Label that Julia enjoyed so much with Diet Coke.

Day 8

EMAIL FROM RUTH TO JHONNIE'S LIST

Jhonnie is settled in new ward. No visitors please. Can't stress this enough. Jhonnie won't be himself for a very long time, so it is still family only and Pete at night.

Chris and the kids visited him for the first time last night, and were understandably shocked. Jhonnie recognised them all, and I know they will be an invaluable part of his recovery. But this is not the great big capable Dad they know and love. I might wait a few days before taking William. The ward is peppered with surprising and occasionally inappropriate behaviour from various patients. Don't think we need the addition of a five-year-old boy trying to take the staples out of his father's head.

I explained to Jhonnie that he has eight staples in his head and he looked perplexed. 'Why?' Told him the doctors had to get into his brain, and after some consideration he remarked: 'I'm surprised.' Not half as much as we were while it was happening. He's very groggy, running a high temperature and has started to ask for his jacket so he can leave. He would also like to go to a meeting in Adelaide, and is 'pushing Patrick's buttons'. I asked him if he was changing Patrick in the night. 'Yes – pushing the buttons on his suit.' So he remembers Patrick, but if he comes out of this and thinks he's been doing 3.00 am feeds for months I'll kill him.

Red meat continues to figure in Jhonnie's recovery. The more we eat, the better he gets. Last night Anna Ritchie and I ate some fat-boy aged Angus steaks (roast leeks, pumpkin and snow peas). Esther stayed for dinner and demonstrated enormous vegetarian tolerance of all that rare beef, and kept her filthy capsicum risotto to herself.

The home front is ticking along with the help of Anna, Esther and my amazing sister, Julia. (Julia has done Excel spreadsheet schedules so that we all know who is coming and going. Fantastic, as my brain is mush.) And, for those who have been inquiring, Patrick is mostly in the capable care of Meera, an amazing woman who started working with us a month ago. She already has a tight relationship with both the boys and can clearly do a better job running the household than moi. (See, if we didn't have any help with the children, this never would have happened.)

My car went yesterday. We won't be needing a two-door convertible any time soon. So I'm driving Jhonnie's new Audi. This is the first new car Jhonnie has ever owned – ever. It arrived around the same time as Patrick, and he loves it nearly as much. Chock full of very Jhonnie toys, seven seats, great stereo and a chassis that goes up and down – presumably for the change in terrain between Cremorne and Elizabeth Bay. His favourite toy is the sat nav (the voice of an annoying nagging English woman constantly telling you where to go. Some people just can't get enough of that, I guess). So now I'm blaming the satellite navigation unit. You see, you wouldn't need sat nav if you remembered where you live. So, I'm thinking of suing Audi. Somebody is going to pay!

Off to the hospital with Hugh. Meanwhile my mother is making Jhonnie chicken soup. Stand aside surgeons, Pat Ritchie is coming through.

Your emails are starting to roll in and they are brilliant. I'm taking a pile today to read him – so keep them coming. Any amusing shit that comes to mind is good. I'll keep a file for him to read when he is fully recovered.

Really, the only person out of the loop now is Jhonnie.

more later

xrr

Jhonnie had remained close to a small group of friends from his boarding school days in England. In spite of being the worst correspondent in the world, he had managed to follow their progress, husbands, wives and children from the other side of the world, seeing them on occasional business trips to London.

We'd hooked up with his favourite girlfriend, Katri, when she was living in New York. For the long years of our friendship before we got together, Jhonnie had described Katri as his 'High School Ruth'. Funny, naughty, good sport, a writer. We could have safely assumed that we would hate each other on that recommendation. But the instant we met, at a bar in SoHo, I could tell that Katri and I would have made great friends, with or without Jhonnie. In fact, we had many Sydney/London friends in common that Jhonnie had never met.

The sight of her emails coming in was heartwarming. I could hear her voice. It felt like a real live connection with Jhonnie.

EMAIL FROM KATRI TO RUTH AND JHONNIE

Dear Ruth

Jules called me earlier this morning with the awful news of Jhonnie's accident; and also able to deliver the better news of his astonishing progress. And he's just forwarded to me your bulletins of the past several days. God – I wish I believed in Him because I would certainly be praying to Him now – how bloody fucking horrible, and unfair, and just plain shocking. You sound as if you are coping with admirable strength and honesty. And also, congratulations on the birth of Patrick; his arrival must have felt like such a gift. And as you say, fucking sod's law that just as everything finally seems to be steadying, wham bam, if the gods don't decide to play a funny trick and put Jhonnie into hospital. Even though I live on the other side of the world, and see him rarely (and you even less, unfortunately) he is a constant presence in my heart. There are so few people about whom I would say 'that person has a truly good soul' and Jhonnie has always been one of them.

So please send him my warmest love. My thoughts go out to you, and to him, and to your children; and I keep my fingers crossed for a speedy recovery. Could you please add me to your bulletins?

With much love always

K

So Jhonnie, one helluva way to change life midstream. Some of us are opting for hair dye and yoga. Do you remember Conel's madman days of frenzied cycling? Nope, bikes should only have three wheels and be one foot high and be kept in the playroom.

I'm in Wiltshire at the moment, staying in Danny's parents' spare cottage, supposedly to write another chunk of the novel-that-never-gets-finished. Do you remember Danny? He was in B3 with me – curly-haired blond cherubim? Not that he'd be flattered to be described like that, now that he's a serious diplomat with a receding hairline and a sculpted body. Anyway, his parents offered me the use of this tiny cottage. It has needless to say brought up all kinds of memories of school; and of being young. I almost drove into Marlborough yesterday: I had a strong urge to visit the Rose Garden, to stand under one of those stone arches, in an alcove, and light up a cigarette in memory of you, and in honour of those rollercoaster teenage years. Also my chest is not in such great shape these days – inside and out, force of gravity don't you know – so I've had to cut right back on the smoking. One of the reasons I find the habit so difficult to kick is because I associate it with pleasure, moments of pleasure spent with good people, drinking good wine (not that we did much of that in the Rose Garden) and

having good conversations. I miss not having your warm and wise
voice close by.

I don't know how much you can take of my chatter in one go.
I will visit the Rose Garden, damn it, and smoke one in your honour.

I love you, so bloody well get better soon. katri xxxxx

I quite liked sitting in the dark, just before dawn, with a cup of
tea, reading the incoming correspondence. I could quickly tap
out a few replies and then gather my thoughts before kids, dogs
and hospital schedules took over. The phone would ring at all
hours, and as each day passed fewer calls were surprising.

'Chris, I did warn you that it wasn't pretty.'

'Well you might have told me about the colostomy bag!'

'If he's got a colostomy bag this morning, he didn't last night.'

'He does. It terrified the children. I didn't know how to
explain it.'

I pictured the man monster she'd insisted Connar visit a
week before, and knew that the recognisable Jhonnie propped
up in 7B was a vast improvement.

'Do you mean the catheter? He can't walk. He can't move.
He's not putting up his hand for permission to be excused.'

'You should have warned me so I could prepare the
children.'

'Chris, I was peeing in a catheter when the kids visited
with Patrick in hospital. What were you expecting? He's just
coming out of a coma.'

'But he has no idea who he is, or where he is. You can't
expect me to put them through that.'

'What?'

'I won't take them back in there. They're over it. They've
done a drawing and made a tape.'

'They don't get to be "over" it. How will he ever know
who he is if he doesn't see his family? This is one of the hard
but important things they'll have to do in life. He is their

father. You don't have to go again. We'll pick them up and drop them off. Pete's offered.'

'Your lawyer says you've cut off Jhonnie's payments.'

'I've done nothing, and he's Jhonnie's lawyer. I don't have access to any of Jhonnie's money.'

'The school fees have come in. I don't have that kind of money. I've never seen the school fees before. What do you suggest I do?'

She was crying, and anybody who tried to cry on me just now was getting very little in the way of sympathy.

'Jhonnie's not writing any cheques for the foreseeable future. If you want to talk about money again, take it up with Jhonnie's lawyer. And Chris, stop fucking crying.'

Then Hugh turned up with fresh lattes. Hugh was very keen to see Jhonnie Unplugged. He was desperate for everything to be okay. I probably didn't inspire confidence because everything was so new on 7B. I didn't know the staff or the routine, the taps or the cracks in the floor. That would only be a matter of time. It would be morbid to miss 6C.

The big difference in the neuro ward was that nobody was about to die, but very few patients were compos, so there wasn't the urgency or service we'd experienced to date. We were finally enjoying the same appalling understaffed, underfunded, overstretched resources that patients in every average ward of every average hospital suffer every day. It was important to strike the right tone to get the best attention. Not too bossy, not too compliant. Try to listen to their problems, understand their position and then lobby like mad to get what you need for your man. Patients without advocates would have to wait. My appearance as the thoughtful, reasonable, vigilant wife and mother would get me to the front of any queue, as long as I didn't push it. We were back to square one. Nobody knew us, or our story, and nobody seemed to care, except for the social worker, Liz. She'd heard about the episode with Chris and the kids. We discussed reasonable strategies to get past the whole 'colostomy' stumbling block, and for the first time I felt I was being heard. She'd organised a meeting with the rehab doctor, who was assessing Jhonnie as we spoke.

Jhonnie slept for most of his assessment, and when he was conscious he recognised nobody. For Jhonnie, when he could answer, the year was 1980. He was in London, and when asked about his career, replied very politely that he was a courier. The nice young doctor wrote down every word.

'He's not a courier, you know.'

'No, I didn't. What did – does Jonathan do?'

'He runs great big advertising companies.'

'Does he?' Young Dr Davis looked nonplussed. 'Where are you, Jhonnie?'

'Airport.'

'Try again. Where are you?'

'At the stadium.'

'What time is it?'

'Miller time.' Jhonnie laughed to himself and dozed off. I interpreted.

'That's an advertising campaign, from America, for a beer.'

'Okay. Jhonnie. JHONNIE.' A really big shake and Jhonnie was awake, nearly alert.

'Explain these proverbs, what they mean to you . . . a stitch in time?'

'Some employment of software companies may be beneficial later on.'

'Look before you leap?'

'Some software companies may cause you trouble if you don't know what you're getting into.'

Dr Davis did not appear at all dismayed by Jhonnie's answers.

'I promise you he doesn't normally talk like a bad IBM brochure.'

He gave Jhonnie a pen and paper and asked him to copy some simple shapes on the page. Either his hand was too weak to manage any control or he simply hadn't understood the task. After he'd failed these rather arbitrary tests the doctor tied both his wrists to the bed.

'It's standard procedure, just while he's so disoriented.'

'And how long will that be?'

'No idea. Nobody can answer these questions. Until he can pass a series of tests, he'll stay here, which is the best place for him. Once he can walk, hold a pen, and is no longer confused as to time and place, he'll be ready for rehab.'

'Where does he go for that?'

'Ryde.'

'Oh fuck, does he have to –'

'The brain unit at Ryde is really the only place –'

'Can't he go to Vinnie's? It's just up the road from our house. Ryde is so far. It's so – I'm not even sure I know *where* it is.'

'You don't seem to understand, rehabilitation from brain injury is very specialised.'

'But he knows what a stitch in time is. He's not a courier. If he goes to Ryde how can I spend the days with him?'

'He'll be busy. You won't be able to spend the days with him. He won't be lying down.'

'What will you do with him at Ryde that you can't do here?'

'Teach him how to make cheese on toast, and buy a stamp. It's a very involved program. But that's a long way away. He'll be here for months.'

My nose was running. Hugh got some toilet paper from the en suite that Jhonnie would possibly never be able to use, and I wiped my eyes and my nose, but they just kept running.

'And when he goes to Ryde, how long?'

'I don't want to paint a grim picture. We don't know what kind of progress he'll make. With any luck three or four months –'

'In Ryde?'

Liz comforted me. Hugh and I were both crying as Dr Davis continued on his rounds. Down in the car we cried for a long time before Hugh felt strong enough to drive.

'I'm sorry you were there for that. I thought it would be a good day.'

'It's really good you make me come here. I mean – I don't know how to – this is the least I can do –'

'It's not supposed to be punishment. I thought if you came along you'd be part of his recovery – and you wouldn't feel so . . .'

'Oh Ruth, I'm so sorry. I'm so sorry.' And he pulled over and we cried a bit more before he faced the expressway.

EMAIL FROM RUTH TO JHONNIE'S LIST

Too deflated to write when I got home. Lousy day. Jhonnie was so exhausted from moving into the ward he remained mostly unconscious day and night. I spent the day hunting down the whole new team. His neurosurgeon checks out well and he seems happy enough with Jhonnie's recovery – all consistent with a very, very, very serious head injury. (I wish they'd grade these things like diamonds – Jhonnie appears to have a fine white head injury!) The meeting with the social worker went well. She'll be a help to the kids the next time they come in. But the rehab registrar had all the bad news. Nothing we didn't expect to hear, but he makes the future sound daunting. Months – too early to say how many, in Ryde rehab (not a bad place but quite a drive from home). As he talked about re-educating Jhonnie to make cheese on toast and operate simple machinery, my ears glazed over.

They want to know Jhonnie's level of ability before the accident. What was Jhonnie able to do? What wasn't Jhonnie able to do is the much shorter answer: get to a meeting on time, and ignore a fresh loaf of Infinity sourdough bread. Other than that, he was capable of pretty much anything. Paint and draw beautifully.

Run big companies and take care of little babies. Master any ball sport. Heli-ski, with a hip flask. He had boundless passion for his kids, for rugby, for good ideas, for me. He could make Yorkshire pudding, and model planes. Write and deliver wonderful speeches (guests at our wedding would remember the speech that had most of the female guests sobbing in the loo). He could ignore petty gossip, alarm clocks, SupaCentre crowds and my nagging. He couldn't resist laksa, gadgets, loud music, *Blackadder* accents, bloody bike riding. When Jhonnie focused, he really could do anything.

I have every reason to believe he can do this.

Just a really lousy day.

more later rr

Day 9

Wнат аn odd routine. Julia said it was like running a little
production office on a small independent film. I stared out the
big filthy window by Jhonnie's bed and wondered why anyone
would choose to make a small independent film if the schedule
was so gruelling and the outcome so questionable. I was determined that Jhonnie would turn out better than a cheap
Australian film.

Sitting by his bed now for hours at a time had a repetitive
yet unpredictable quality. The nurses would shake him so hard
I thought I could hear his ribs, and he wouldn't or couldn't
respond. They'd scribble more notes on his charts, leaving big
blank gaps where Jhonnie had performed no tricks.
Completely asleep he couldn't tell them the date, or his name,
or how many children he had. Ever impatient, I realised I could
tell them, but that probably wasn't the point. They didn't
actually care how old Jhonnie was, just that he knew. Another
half an hour passed, looking out at those light white clouds
drawn straight from a *Simpsons* sky, and looking at his swollen
blue fingers in the shabby plaster cast. Both arms were tied to
the rails of his still-too-short bed. Both arms in restraint. Was he
flailing uncontrollably and clocking himself on the head with
his plaster? I hadn't seen it from Jhonnie, but most of the men

around him, at least the ones that could move, threw their limbs about like robots that had run amok. Jhonnie wasn't going anywhere. He was still peeing into a catheter. He couldn't stand up, yet he was tied to his bed. Another nurse came and went, and smiles were exchanged and then his little corner of 7B was left in neuro-silence. Then, apropos of nothing, Jhonnie muttered quietly, but still articulately, at about the level that one whispers in the cinema during a foreign film.

'You can get the tickets at McDonald's in Marseilles.'

Jhonnie had been asleep for most of my visit, but appeared to be touring the south of France, on the cheap.

'Can you, babe, what tickets are they?'

'Rugby World Cup tickets.'

'Really, McDonald's will be pleased. Jhonnie, where are you?'

'With my honey-bunny?'

'Honey-bunny has brought you some beetroot carrot juice. We're going to rebuild your brain from brightly coloured vegetables.'

A little light reading had revealed a world of catering distraction. When Jhonnie gave up smoking we went to a health farm. I stayed five days, then returned to William. Jhonnie stayed on, to get the nicotine out of his system and clock up a new record for the most spa treatments enjoyed by one white man in any given fortnight. He'd become something of a health farm zealot, which accounted for the recent penchant for racing bikes and heart monitors. I'd come away from the experience convinced of the detoxifying properties of the 'super foods' they were flogging. We were already big fans of beetroot, pumpkin, capsicum, carrots and rocket. Health farm mumbo-jumbo was just another endorsement.

In terms of detoxification and getting Jhonnie's metabolism moving as he came out of a coma, I had grave doubts about what I'd seen of hospital food. If they were offering thin gruel through a straw, surely we could do better. If I couldn't, or wouldn't deal with the actual science of brain injury, I could certainly cook my way out of it. Until he could eat solids, the juice from brightly coloured fruits and vegetables would accelerate our date with a jaffle maker in Ryde.

EMAIL FROM RUTH TO JHONNIE'S LIST

Very much better day. Obviously my last email was a shocker, because most people reading this have stopped patting Jhonnie, and started patting me. Completely dropped my bundle, having got him out of Intensive Care, to be briefed on care and handling of vegetables, just ran out of foof.

Anyway, Jhonnie was much more alert today. Still polite, conservative and a delight for the nurses, ever the people pleaser. Jhonnie is making an enormous effort, as if he is in a new business pitch. When he's uncertain of an answer he'll refer to some research, or tell me his people will get back to me. I tell him that I am his people, and he is very patient.

He stood up today. It took five physios, but he stood up, for nearly two minutes. I apologised to the one who was about half the size of Kylie Minogue. (You can see them all drawing the short straw for this gig.)

The kids were coming this afternoon, and Jhonnie looked more like a bum outside a refuge for homeless men than a brain surgery patient. So I gave him a big scrub, and a shave, and briefed him on his children. Connar: 12? (close), Madi: 10? (not as close), William: six? (whatever), and Patrick. No Patrick. Well, Patrick would be 14, then. I told him that our baby was three months old, and after some consideration he agreed but added that 'Sure, but he's been in Corporate Affairs for much longer.' And given those over-achieving Blampied boys, that may well be the case.

We had our first kiss today, after which Jhonnie said 'Spicy.' Something Madi said as a toddler and now an ongoing family joke, so I felt that he was very much with us. When the doctors did their rounds, Jhonnie knew his name, was out but a decade on the date, and when asked who I was, said rather saucily that I was 'the Salad Girl'! No wonder Jhonnie never took drugs. God knows what's going on in there.

I haven't spoken to Chris Blampied since, but I thought the visit with the kids went well. Jhonnie did very few tricks of lucidity, but both Connar and Madi told him basketball and play-date minutiae that I'm certain will help to resettle his dust. When we woke him and he saw the whole gang at the foot of the bed, his entire body jangled with excitement. Not a lot of that going down in that neuro ward. I'm sure when he looks at those two kids he sees normal – about the only normal in his fucked-up CT-scan-head-injury world. I know the kids don't really see their dad yet, but they are most certainly bringing him back. Don't want to put too much pressure on them, it's all very confronting. Chris and I didn't even spat in front of Jhonnie, so this must be serious.

The main thing: I read Jhonnie all your emails: Vivvy's evocative recollection of Robot Land that Jhonnie created for her when she was a kid – he smiled in recognition. Sally's description of the Wallabies going through their paces with the Easts' sprogs (sorry foreigners – World Cup, only 29 more sleeps). Maggie's updates from London – 'Is she my best friend?' Yes darling, always. And a great long letter from his school-time best pal, Katri, revisiting rose-bushes where they smoked at Marlborough. (Well, if you're going to name a posh school after a cigarette, what can you expect?)

So emails are flooding in, and I read them, and he says, 'What a fuss.' You don't know the half of it, you Jhonnie, sleeping bugger, scary . . . When he comes good, I may kill him.

William asked me this morning, 'Do you remember before Dad was in hospital?'

Yes, but not very well.

more later xrr

Day 10

THE PACE HAD TO CHANGE. We couldn't keep up that Intensive Care sprint, with all the love and adrenalin in the world. I couldn't push Jhonnie into consciousness and wellness any faster, and I couldn't undo the accident. But now we were out of Intensive Care, another learning curve, another set of challenges, lay ahead. The new ward, 7B, was a whole new world, with more worn linoleum and more scuffed corners. The other patients were more awake and consequently more troublesome.

When men wake up with head injuries they are often wild. They've usually done something completely stupid to land themselves in hospital, and when they come to, the cocktail of anger and embarrassment can be explosive. When I saw how Jhonnie's roomies behaved I could see why he was such a favourite with the nurses. It was only when I sneaked a look at his charts that I discovered he was screaming in the night and disturbing the others. They were wheeling him out into the corridor, where he apparently shouted into the drafty darkness and annoyed only the nurses. It reminded me of the Bad Boy corner in the nursery at Royal Women's. All the newborn screamers would keep each other awake at one end of the room while the good babies and good mummies slept. Of course, that reference was only pertinent because Patrick and I had so recently made our escape from Royal Women's. Neither of us had been screamers, although I always come close. Not good at hospitals. Never been good at hospitals, and now I had no choice.

Did Jhonnie know that he screamed his nights away in an empty shiny corridor? He would not have been reminded of a maternity ward. To watch him was to see a kid in an imaginary game. We see an empty playground. The kid sees dragons and castles. And Jhonnie was walking through vivid scenes, mysterious to any onlooker.

It was only with the recent correspondence from some family and friends that the gaping vacant block of his past had become so apparent. I knew only a handful of well-worn anecdotes about life before he turned 30. The bad family stories were very bad. The lovely summer holidays were very lovely. The adolescent high jinks were standard, and a lot like my own, but without the beaches and bongs. But nobody in Sydney, perhaps nobody anywhere, knew the truth of the world that was opening up in his head as he made his way back from a coma.

Jhonnie was unfolding the messy map of his childhood and youth. While I was navigating ward 7B, Jhonnie was buying burgers in Marseilles. And when he cried out in the night, where was he then? When had he cried out like that and nobody came? While I wondered if there was any way I could be with him during the night, the nurses assured me he'd never remember any of this – that is, if he ever remembered anything again. Perhaps he would stay in Marseilles, forever.

After my tirade to Jhonnie's family, letters had started to dribble in. Julian had been the first to reply, as to how utterly hopeless the entire family are when it comes to taking action, but still sent nothing I could read to Jhonnie. Vivvy was very quick and colourful in her response. It was obviously difficult for Justin to write. Every family member knows another by a pet name. Confusing at first, like a clubhouse code designed to alienate outsiders. Jhonnie was 'Pog' to Vivvy and her mother. Justin was Eric Von Stromm, but only to Jhonnie, whom he flagged by many names from Biggie to . . . well, far too many nicknames to adopt or keep track of. As Jhonnie slept I read the new mail.

EMAIL FROM JUSTIN TO RUTH AND JHONNIE

Dear Ruth,

Your letters are an inspiration, I'm amazed at your bravery and the humour in your writing through all of this, Ruth. Thank you for the daily updates and for explaining things in ways that even I can understand. I know it doesn't feel like it but I am with you through every second of every day – as you wrote yourself, Jhonnie is amazing and accomplished at everything he does, and even though I'm not there with you to see him or help you, I know this is going to be no different. All my love,

Justinxx

Dearest Big Guy,

It's your little brother Eric here. I am practising being very lazy on a daily basis and cannot wait to show you how good I'm getting at it. Unfortunately the rest of LA is not, but I'm trying to convince them that it is the way forward. I am also trying to keep up the drinking, something that both you and Ruthie taught me when I was still an innocent wee lad in Falls Creek – we spent most of the time playing cards, drinking and being outrageously silly and I have the pictures here with me to prove it.

Ruth sends me daily updates of your recovery and tells me how well you're doing. I can't wait to see you, Big Guy – we are going to have some blissfully silly and lazy times together.

All my love
Eric Von Stromm

A combined note from Jhonnie's parents was hard to follow, and probably didn't make much sense when read to a comatose man by an exhausted wife. But it was something new to read, and something from the family.

EMAIL FROM JHONNIE'S PARENTS TO JHONNIE

Darling Jhonnie, While we are all hanging around waiting for Ruth's update, flashes from the past keep coming to my mind. ALL our summer holidays, Ischia Sardinia San Sicario. Lots of memories are coming back. I remember that summer in Ischia – we had rented a beautiful villa with a private mooring (Note from Michael – I think it was Elba) and you and Julian were taking Justin out to swim. He was just about one year old and couldn't even walk and you were putting him in a rubber dinghy and swimming with him – floating alongside miles and miles away – I must have trusted you both. Imagine how you would feel. I wonder if you would let little Patrick go off in a rubber dinghy. Get better soon and we will come to be with you. Meanwhile you are in our thoughts every minute of the day. Your Mum and your Dad.

He didn't stir for my entire visit. I sat stonily silent once I'd finished the emails, drank his beetroot juice and rubbed his feet. The juice was beginning to de-emulsify and Jhonnie didn't look like waking up, ever. I had to get William into the allergy specialist, because his allergic reactions to products that 'may contain traces of nuts' was bordering on the anaphylactic. He couldn't start school without us knowing if a few sesame seeds were going to kill him. And Pat had missed his three-month check-up at the baby clinic. (We'd had a bit on last week.) And as I reached down and discovered that I'd put on odd socks after my shower at 5.15 am, after Pat's first feed, I realised that my back was dangerously close to immobile.

Not a peep out of Jhonnie or the guy with the frightening halo of wires and bolts around his head. I dialled Meera's

number to get some appointments rolling. That very moment a
new stiff bossy nurse frowned into the room, glaring at my
phone, my hide, my behaviour in her ward. Usually I walked
out of the ward to use the phone, but I had almost forgotten
that I was not alone. She glared.

'Hey, this is me, maverick, living on the edge. Get over it.'
She laughed.

'Any movement from himself?' I detected a faint but sweet
Irish accent.

'Nothing.'

'He was up all night again. He doesn't appear to be in
pain. He's having, well, bad dreams. Open windows, flapping
shutters, and a room full of birds. Ring any bells?'

'Not unless he's got a Hitchcock DVD in there. Is anyone
going to shave him today?'

A hint of the bossy frown returned, with some Irish cheek.
'You, maybe.'

Shaving an unconscious man is something, I'm guessing,
only nurses ever do. I'd never shaved anyone else. I hadn't
shaved my own legs since discovering hot wax, decades ago.
When a nurse in Intensive Care had handed me a razor and a
can of foam, only a few days ago, I had been too embarrassed to
do anything other than just roll up my sleeves and get on with
it. Most of the nicks I'd inflicted that day had well and truly
healed, and in the greater scheme of things, with a shaved head
full of staples and a bulging black eye, there was really nothing
to mention.

It must be said that without the co-operation of the
shavee, pulling skin over the chin tight or dragging that top lip
long and taut, the shaver faces some definite challenges. More
so when the shavee is horizontal. But now Jhonnie was more
upright, which made the world of difference, and I felt quite
confident and creative. (How much worse could things get,
with a safety razor, and anyway, he was in hospital if things got

wildly out of hand, right?) I took care of the bits the other nurses had missed, around the neck, the ears. He cleaned up really well with his own razor and shaving cream. Only much later, maybe a year later, when I raised with friends for the first time the difficulty of shaving an inert husband, did anyone suggest an electric alternative. Funny that. You think you're fine. You think you're functioning well enough to give your brain-injured husband a passable, if still rather dangerous, shave. And you completely overlook the existence of the electric razor.

I left and visited my mother to pick up some chicken soup. Clichés have foundation in truth, and our family conviction that chicken soup can improve any situation has been proved so many times that I will not even begin to defend its potency in print. An organic chicken had not died in vain to save her son-in-law's life. She'd left out the parsnips, the carrot, the celery and the matzo balls. This was the clear broth that, in conjunction with the prayers of powerfully devout nuns, would have Jhonnie back on his feet in no time.

Normally some time with my mum provides a steadying counterpoint to anything that's going wrong elsewhere. So as we sat in our positions at the kitchen table, hers by the sink, mine by the condiments cupboard, my state must have been a disappointment to both of us. I wasn't all there. I couldn't concentrate. My head was stuck somewhere in the hospital car park or that appointment book at home, and Mum kept chatting in tiny, tiny detail about little things I'd missed, and a few things she'd clipped from the paper that she thought I'd like and obviously wouldn't have time to read. Did I want to take them now, or should she keep a little folder for me? Did I need a chicken sandwich? All that beautiful chicken breast from Jhonnie's soup would be perfect with some mayo and celery. That rye bread I liked so much wasn't fresh, but it was very good defrosted, or even toasted. I have the feeling she may have been babbling. But I couldn't eat the most excellent chicken sandwich in Sydney, even if it would have made my mother feel momentarily better.

I sat in my car outside Mum's house, my childhood home, on a perfect September day. Just like the day of the accident. Just like September 11. Sun on my hands on the steering wheel. Happy suburban tracksuit mummies walked by with strollers, and I had real trouble turning the key in the ignition. What a dreamy day to take a baby for a walk by the sea in the stroller.

On returning to 7B I encountered a vision. Lurching, leaning, immodestly covered with a surgical smock that was far to small for his six-foot-six frame, a giant man made a small step. Surrounded by a team of physios, and purple in the face with effort and excitement, Jhonnie Blampied picked up one foot and put it in front of the other.

'Whoo-hooo!' he cheered himself loudly, and half the floor in the hospital that day heard and cheered with him.

One step, then steady, then back in the chair. He was very, very happy, and then he was asleep.

EMAIL FROM RUTH TO JHONNIE'S LIST

Jhonnie walked. Not very far, but they were impressed. It completely wiped him out, and I had to shake him from a deep sleep to drink two bowls of my mother's chicken soup for lunch. Instant improvement – Jhonnie checking out tomorrow. Kidding.

All the cooks are kicking in. Eleni spent the night at our house and catered extra-ordinarily. Farfalle tossed in a fresh sauce of marinated cherry tomatoes, flat parsley and baby bocconcini. My mother has made her famous sour fish, and Helen is coming 'round with minestrone and fresh bleeding meat from our favourite butchers. If bad hospital coffee serves to make our situation only seem more depressing, great Parmalat lattes may be saving our lives. Every day the team at Parmalat (it's been Latteria for years, but we just ignore that name-change nonsense) have made up rosetta rolls and large prefect coffees for the crew at home before we set off to schools, hospitals and physio appointments. This is as much about ritual as caffeine. Parmalat was the last stop I made on the way to delivering both my children (decaf – but good decaf) and the first stop on the way back home with a newborn in the back. Parmalat is about as close as I get to a lucky rabbit's foot. As soon as Jhonnie can meet the challenge of a chewy rosetta roll, I will speed from Darlinghurst to RNS, to make sure it doesn't go cold. Worth risking the speeding ticket.

More conversations with the rehab people. Yesterday he told them he was a courier. Presume they were planning to retrain him to throw packages into bushes or leave them at the wrong address. No, I told them, he wasn't a courier.

Jhonnie asked me today how to get out of here, how to get to 'Jhonnie's room'. I told him all the doctors and nurses were going to remind him how to take care of himself, and eventually he'd walk back to Jhonnie's room. I told him they were going to teach him how to make cheese on toast. He looked appalled. 'Why would I want to do that?'

When the nurse took her observations this morning she asked Jhonnie if he knew where he was. 'The Mater,' he replied (a *very* much nicer hospital quite nearby). We told the nurse that he had recently been at the Mater with my mum for a charity function, and maybe he was remembering that. Jhonnie became fully alert – looked around at his tired plain public hospital surroundings and said, 'This is definitely not the Mater.' We all laughed.

Letters from all over the world are pouring in. Not sure, but these updates may be going to hundreds each day. What a popular boy. I'm piecing together an intricate puzzle of the missing Jhonnie – as useful for me as for him just now. I miss him so much, and gathering childhood chunks – before he was a raging Wallaby – feels like a practical way to put Jhonnie back together. His sister

Vivvy's letters, which refer to details as tiny as furniture and corner shops, seem to hold his attention. Remind him he's no courier.

We are coping well enough here, I think. Veal for dinner. Polenta or potatoes? Esther has just arrived with a bottle of gin. Imagine that goes with either.

I will start taking up offers to walk Devlin dog. He's taking all this pretty badly. More later.

Day 11

ANOTHER EARLY START. BREAKFAST, a bottle for Pat, and get us all dressed for the park. Just another weekend. William had stopped asking when his father was coming home, now. I don't know what was really going on in that serious little blond head, but for the time being, he'd stopped asking. He just seemed to roll with the passing parade of kind-hearted friends who'd scoop him up for weekend activities. It was the time of year when families spend entire weekends at sporting fields, with take-away coffees on tartan rugs. William loved all that. So a day spent with the English family that began with a walk in Rushcutters Park and a coffee probably seemed about right. Fiona and Peter English were tactful in their inquiries about Jhonnie. We all chose our words carefully, in a park full of kids downing hot chocolates. Nobody said, 'How fucked is he?' and I never said that I was terrified of growing old with a sleepy amnesiac. We had coffee.

'Don't eat any nuts, and keep your jacket on. Just because you're excited doesn't mean you're not cold. You know what I mean. Kiss and a both arms?' We hugged. Then I waved my brave little boy goodbye and pumped back up the hill with the stroller, to begin another day in 7B.

Yahoo and Lulu drove down from the beach to pick me up and visit Jhonnie. I could tell they were nervous but pleased to be helping. I knew that if Jhonnie had been in any kind of shape he would've loved to see them both.

Jo came to watch Pat, and we all talked at once, happy to see each other for a few minutes before we set off. For a moment it seemed as if Lulu, Jo and I might have just gotten together for a little shopping excursion, perhaps some new shoes, in Paddington. But we hadn't.

In the ward on weekends there were far fewer staff (many of the offices were locked and darkened) but many more visitors. This imbalance created a somehow less medical, less serious atmosphere. Patients recovering from brain injury and brain surgery don't exactly attract casual passing traffic, but still, when the predominant uniform is more Mambo than scrubs, it is possible to forget that a lot of these guys are just coming back from the dead.

The man in the bed opposite Jhonnie was dressed in pants, a shirt and an elaborate neck brace. His wife was bringing him shoes. He was leaving. When Jhonnie had first entered the ward, he'd been a silent sleeping fellow, and his silent wife, when she visited, sat bedside with her *Who* magazine. I don't recall that we ever spoke. Today, he was preparing to leave, and when I walked in with Yahoo and Lulu, the man in the neck brace stood up and shook Yahoo's hand. Apparently he'd been an extra in one of Yahoo's movies. Appropriately, he'd landed himself in Royal North Shore by falling out of a tree onto his head.

All the patients who were alert enough to recognise Yahoo seemed pleased by the appearance of the king of sight gags and pratfalls. When Jhonnie finally woke up he was so delighted to see them both, he became quite the jovial performing seal. Two weeks of nothing but me by day and Pete by night might have been wearing thin, even though he forgot we'd been there the minute we stepped outside. Bored. I think Jhonnie might have been bored, and visits from the Serious family, my mum and

Anna Ritchie brought out his best. The effect he had on each of his visitors was interesting. His progress has been so gradual that I had no way of knowing if this Jhonnie, this recovering Jhonnie, was a welcome surprise or a shocking disappointment. I wasn't worried about the impact of his behaviour and appearance on the visitors, but more how their response would affect his recovery. How much more did Jhonnie need to improve before we could take our chances with other visitors?

A large chunk of my thinking was stuck in Intensive Care. But those acute and frightening days were behind us. This was a hospital ward, and Jhonnie might be bored. Discussions with Pete reinforced my gut feeling that Jhonnie needed protecting from the uncensored visit for a while longer. If he had a bad experience he would never remember it, but the visitor might have broadcasted it to the world. Nobody needed to know how bad he'd been, until he was a lot better. Some of the more undignified aspects of brain injury aren't for general consumption.

Yahoo and Lulu seemed to think he was amazing. Perhaps they were being nice, but they were all moved by his sweet good manners. My mother and I agreed we'd be unbearable in his position. Yahoo wanted to get out a camera. He'd never seen anyone quite so relaxed and funny without the aid of drugs and alcohol. And that really was something.

Jhonnie was very happy to be visited by his family and friends on a beautiful sunny day. Another, younger man in 7B shouted and howled at nobody, and then at a nurse. Maybe Jhonnie's happiness, his ability to enjoy this moment when really, the big picture, the big clock, looked lousy – maybe that would get him back home faster than the doctors had planned.

EMAIL FROM RUTH TO JHONNIE'S LIST

Our best day yet. Perfect spring morning. William, Devlin and I went to the park early; met friends, there abandoned small boy and headed for hospital. With each passing day I face the trip with less trepidation. Yahoo and Lulu picked me up and drove, and I tried to prepare them. Jhonnie actually looks pretty good now. Most of the extreme head swelling is gone, and nearly all the tubes, and other than a broken hand, completely black shut eye and a variety of dropped-in-a-ditch abrasions, Jhonnie looks really good. He's either completely asleep or sleepy. He is often Romanian, constantly dealing with computer people, and occasionally in extreme pain.

On arrival he was unwakeable. The nurses told us he'd had a bad night. I shook him into consciousness (Yahoo and Lulu had driven all the way from Palm Beach, after all). When he came to, he was very happy to see them. Jaunty, chirpy, visiting the 'swing doctors', he told us. He wanted to leave and I explained what it would take to get him up and around. He was very happy with the explanation 'Up, up and around!' He knew that I was his wife . . . Cathy (oh well, close enough).

And how many children today? 'Too many!'

Hilarious.

Mum arrived with the sour fish, complete with tiny hidden bone, and for a minute it looked as if Jhonnie would survive a life-threatening head injury only to choke at the hands of his mother-in-law. After days spent at home minding Patrick (some of the worst), Anna Ritchie nearly collapsed with relief at this, her first visit with the recovering Jhonnie.

He stayed awake and really engaged for an hour and a half. We didn't read him the Fitz Files or any of the wonderful new letters from friends and his family in the northern hemisphere. We didn't read because he was talking to us.

He's back. He thinks that they put cocaine on his toast for breakfast, but he is most definitely back. Yahoo, Lulu and I nearly sang show tunes driving home.

Every night Pete visits, reads and holds his hand. Pete tells me that last night they were speaking French. Pity the patient waking up next to that conversation for the first time: fall out of a tree in Sydney and wake up in an English boarding school French class. Creepy.

I put the last of his clothes in the wash at the end of the week: jeans, his bath towel and robe. Chris, our cleaner, folded them up and put them back on our bed. Somehow Jhonnie goes through 42 pairs of socks a week. Last week I remember thinking I couldn't imagine doing our laundry and not pairing up all those black socks. A week later the laundry doesn't seem poignant. It's just laundry. I really think the worst is behind us. Bugger, the last time I said that my husband fell off his bike.

Day 12

I'M GLAD I LEFT THE martinis to Esther. There were more phone calls from the Blampieds in Italy and the UK, and it had already become apparent that these conversations shouldn't be fuelled by alcohol.

That White Rocks veal is magnificent. Can't believe I wasted it on a vegetarian. Even so, Esther and I made busy conversation about rugby tickets and their potential buyers, and plans to perhaps take Connar and Madi to a few games. William really didn't care about the World Cup and he was growing tired of the flimsy lies about Dad having a rest in hospital. William was only just five, but the world as he knew it had come to an end, and nobody was telling him what to expect in its place.

A tidy morning of banking and baby clinics was in order. I parked the car early down in Double Bay. Meera grabbed pole position with Patrick, waiting for the clinic to open, and I dashed to grab a mountain of cash from the hole in the wall. The machine ate my card. Inside the bank five customers stood by a sign on a pole and a velvet rope. No time to apologise, or make eye contact with the appropriate manager. I announced to nobody in particular, 'The machine has eaten my card. I need the card, and the money, now.'

Every face in the bank made the same expression. How awkward. This madwoman is right on the verge of making a scene. In a loud polite whisper, such a contrast to my booming broadcast, a staff member assured me that the machine would be opened tomorrow. If I could just come back before close of business –

She never finished that sentence. I'm not certain, but my arms may have waved about my head as I shouted. 'Listen here, I have a husband with a life-threatening brain injury and a three-month-old baby. Give me my money and my card NOW.'

How suddenly and certainly I now knew what my husband's injuries involved. Hysterical displays in banks. In the film *Traffic*, there's a scene where a desperate and pregnant Catherine Zeta-Jones shouts at her hit man through the phone 'Get out of the car, and shoot him in the head!' It is that defining, deliberate moment when a middle-class lady-like woman with really nice shoes becomes an animal. That morning at St George Bank, Double Bay, I had my Catherine Zeta-Jones moment.

Back in 7B, Liz the very helpful social worker greeted me out by the lift. This is a place devoid of atmosphere. It's shadowy; in some corners 7B barely exists. One end of the ward was completely shut down, probably a budgetary consideration. When they say they don't have enough beds, they don't mean the hotel is full; they mean they can't service another patient, and sometimes whole wards and corridors gather dust and clunky wheelchairs, taking on an attic-like quality so highly favoured in those not particularly scary movies Nicole Kidman is so keen on making. There were no ghosts in 7B, or if there were, they were talking to somebody else. The only thing that lightened the awkward haunted atmosphere was a smiling face. Not a face on auto-smile, but a real, look you in the eye, open face. And Liz had one – a clear eye and an honest response to good and bad news. And there she was, as the lift doors opened.

'Just the girl I was looking for. Quick, come see. I hope he's still doing it.'

She turned on her heel and marched me quickly to Jhonnie's room. All the other curtains were drawn. Patients were all asleep, or enduring disgusting procedures best performed behind pulled curtains. But not Jhonnie's. Most mornings began with a peek at his charts, just to see if he'd taken up inexplicable Gregorian chanting in the night. Every morning, the opening lines of his charts were the same: 'Mostly drowsy. Occasionally alert but confused as to time and place.' But not today.

Propped up in bed, with a lot of pillows, neatly tucked smooth sheets, and a cup of tea on his tray table sat one quietly alert Jhonnie Blampied, wrists untied, smile on face.

'Hello, you. How's the hotel treating you this morning?'

I planted a kiss on his cheek, and Jhonnie turned his head to kiss me back. He was actually there, sitting up, kissing.

'Do you think it's safe here?'

'As long as you don't come down with golden staph, I think it's as safe as anywhere. Are you frightened?'

'Oh, no. I'm not frightened, but you can't be sure on the Gaza Strip. You . . . hear things.'

The Gaza Strip?

'Jhonnie, just for the record, are you Israeli or Palestinian? Not that there's anything wrong with that, but this is kind of late for a nice Jewish Catholic girl to discover she's married to an Arab.'

'Ridiculous! I'm English!'

That voice, so plummy, so young. I appeared to be married to one of the little boys from *Goodbye, Mr Chips*.

'The bombs went off for most of the night. I can't believe they're not evacuating.' Conspiratorially Jhonnie pointed to the mystery men, his roommates, behind drawn curtains. 'When we do, they'll be fucked. Pack of vegetables, the lot of them.'

'How many guys are in here, Jhonnie, with you, in the Gaza Strip?'

'Too many to get out in daylight. My best bet is a motorbike, don't you think?'

'I think we might have had enough of bikes for a while.'

Confused as to time and place, constantly, all of us. No idea where we are or what's going on. Liz had wanted me to witness the civilised Englishman enjoying his cup of tea. Tarzan in a drawing room. I had wanted to kiss my husband, sitting up in bed, as though nothing had ever happened. What accident?

Perhaps Jhonnie was the only one with enough sense to steal a motorbike and get out of the Gaza Strip under cloak of darkness. Perhaps it was time to bring William in, after all. Boy's Own adventure in the Royal North Shore might amuse them both. For my own journey into the unknown, today I helped Jhonnie shower in a chair in a cubicle that could fit into the economy-class loo of a small plane. We both got very wet, but it was certainly the place to clean his teeth and shave him, then just go mad with the hand shower. The taste of Colgate my guerilla declared delicious. Swaying dripping wet and cold wrapped in tiny towels while two male nurses held him upright was apparently not so delicious.

Maybe this was the time to take up smoking again. Cigarettes are usually brilliant company in a disaster. There hadn't seemed any point at first, or at least very little opportunity. It's not as if you can smoke in hospital, or near a baby, or in a restaurant, or an office or a nice bar. But I had started to remember nicotine appeal as I had those many bizarre phone conversations at ungodly hours, out by the garbage bins so that William, and anybody else in the house, wouldn't know that things outside the world of 7B were even more strange, and more Gaza Strip, than the world inside.

I had mostly reasonable conversations with Julian, Jhonnie's brother in London. He was a born organiser, the eldest. This accident gave him some kind of pivotal role which apparently he didn't enjoy elsewhere in daily life. It was becoming clear that while his heart was breaking for his brother, and our family, his job was to protect his parents. He had everything under control at his end.

'But Julian, your dad rang and he's furious because he says he's tried ringing the hospital and they won't put him through. He thinks Jhonnie's in some Third World antipodean hellhole, and he's insisting I get a phone put next to Jhonnie's bed. So I can't tell him that Jhonnie is surrounded by nude guys with bolts holding their skulls together. There are no phones on the whole floor. Now that Jhonnie is actually improving, it might be okay to tell him the truth.'

'It'll kill him.'

'It's not my business, but do you have the right to decide what your father knows? I wouldn't ever want to be protected from the truth by my children. Would you?'

'Trust me on this, Ruth. It wouldn't be better if Dad knew the truth.'

There was a shudder in his voice, the voice of Blampied experience. Perhaps he was right, and it wasn't my place to impose some overbearing Ritchie frankness on this family.

'Hey, did you two ever have birds in your bedroom, a room with shutters that banged, maybe?'

'Why?'

'Jhonnie is very restless at night, and the nurses say he's cold and there are birds flapping, and I wondered if it was something from home.'

'Not home, no. We were left at school once during the holidays. Christmas, no, it can't have been Christmas, but we were the only kids left at school. The school was shut down except for this dormitory, and there were pigeons or starlings in the rafters. And it was cold, but, no it can't have been Christmas. And Jhonnie cried a lot, but nobody came. You know, I think the housemaster may have actually left for the night. He probably thought nothing would happen, and nothing did.'

'So this is after your mum died. Why didn't your dad come for you?'

'He did, at some stage, probably the next day. He must have been caught up with work, or with Gabriella, in London.'

'But you were in Oxford.'

'No. We were still in Jersey. We didn't go back to England for years and when Dad finally took us back, to Summerfields in Oxford, it wasn't much better. We were still at St George's in Jersey. We were day boys, but when Mum died we started boarding.'

'What about the aunt and uncle who lived across the road from St George's?'

'They weren't close.'

Not a hint of irony in that delivery. Poor Julian, I found myself thinking. And not for the last time.

'How old were you?'

'Maybe six.'

'So, Jhonnie was . . . five and a half. William's five.'

I don't know how strange or foreign the experience of head injury or brain damage was for those other corpses in Intensive Care or the shouting angry men in 7B, but Jhonnie Blampied had seen it all before. It seemed that in a cruel yet provident twist of fate, life had uniquely prepared Jhonnie to cope with a coma. All alone in the dark, not knowing what will happen next, or who will come.

Every day the charts read the same: confused as to time and place. I hoped he continued to tour the French Riviera and fill his days with sunny nostalgia, until he felt considerably better. Every time I walked into that ward, when he was awake, his eyes brimmed with delight and surprise. He must have forgotten that I was there every day, and had hours in the night of not knowing if anyone would come. Then, every morning, armed with beetroot juice and some of my mother's chicken soup, I practically jumped out of a cake.

EMAIL FROM RUTH TO JHONNIE'S LIST

For most of today Jhonnie was in the south of France, driving a Renault which had been specially built for his needs. (A Renault?) When the nurse inquired of his whereabouts, he told her 'Monaco.' She corrected him, 'Royal North Shore.' 'Well then, that's quite close.' I must say that this recovering Jhonnie is adorable, and as one friend put it, 'He's come back as a surrealist.'

I left him to his French touring and started reading your emails to him. For the first time Jhonnie, seemingly asleep, laughed in the appropriate places, and sighed. Letters from his mum and dad, a brilliant collection of anecdotes from Julian about their granddad's stories of the trenches in WWI.

Jhonnie was completely there.

He remembers you all. Some of the details of long since rusted motorbikes, rosebushes, ice-cream parlours, ski trips, beers and sports seemed clear and present to him. He recognised local pals as if spotting faces at his own surprise party. At the end of each one, 'Good man.' 'She's lovely.'

We agreed these letters are just amazing, but Jhonnie observed, 'They seem a bit freaked out. Why are they all writing to me?'

'Because they love you.'

'Yeah, but they wouldn't write like that unless I was nearly dead.'

It was only in my silence that Jhonnie knew for the first time that he had nearly died. It was as if he'd arrived, white-knuckled, at the bottom of a terrifyingly steep ski run, looked back up the mountain and shaken his fist in exhilaration and defiance.

So I hope none of you are surprised to find that Jhonnie Blampied thinks defying death is a bit of a hoot.

I started to explain about the emails, and how we had been reading to him for days. And when he was completely gone, supported by machines in Intensive Care, how I read rugby columns, and letters and talked about food – salt and pepper crab featured regularly. So I explained that we just talked and talked until eventually he woke up. He looked at me, bemused.

'Well, that was a complete waste of time. I didn't hear any of it!'

On the home front, Connar and Madi have visited again and Madi delighted in asking her dad if he was still Romanian. I'm taking William and Patrick in tomorrow afternoon, if the morning goes well. William has been largely distracted by our good and generous friends. A footy match yesterday. Cranbrook Fair today. It is a fantastic time of year. Football finals on every playing field at every hour of both days of every weekend, and only 27 (26?) sleeps until the World Cup.

Helen's minestrone for Jhonnie's dinner tonight and Susan and I are roasting a chicken.

I'm starting to line up local visits, paving a clear way for the kids to have time on their own with Dad.

Played music in the car today for the first time. Sang really loudly and out of tune. Things can only get better.

Day 13

I'D NEVER SPENT SO MUCH time with Jhonnie in the entire time we'd known each other. We didn't even have a honeymoon. Jhonnie was always in meetings, on call-waiting, on the way home. But now I knew exactly where he was, every minute of the day. The layers of irony around the fact that he'd never remember this time together, or that he wasn't exactly all there or – well, the irony of the romantic nature of this whole episode lurked nearby somewhere.

Now I spent every day with Jhonnie. Sometimes I'd go back and forth three times (that parking pass was a winner). Sometimes I'd go for a meeting with doctors that didn't eventuate, then I'd go to a hardware store and buy another laundry rack for drying Pat's little white things, then I'd go back and just sit outside a doctor's darkened door in those miserable shiny hospital corridors. And sometimes I'd go with a friend and we'd spend an hour with Jhonnie and another hour driving around, looking for a park, just to buy some milk.

I love my friends. How had they all managed to move heaven and earth to help us? All this time just hanging around, keeping me company, sitting with a mostly sleeping giant. We passed so many emotional hours together on those trips. I had decided to stop being frightened of our future and as a result

I wasn't feeling as sorry for myself. No more howling through the hospital car park to nobody in particular, 'He can't stay here forever – he has four children. He has three sons!' Having given the fear and self-pity a little break I was constantly overwhelmed by other emotions, even with humility at our situation. Who had time for this?

Suddenly everybody's parents were dying. People we'd known our whole lives. It's the age: after the fortieth birthday parties come the funerals of the dear parents. That's where we were at – oncology wards – not Intensive Care. My friend Andrew's mother was in a nearby hospital dying of cancer, as was the father of my old school friend, Jane. All of Mary McKillop's bony-kneed nuns had very full dance cards, just with our immediate circle of friends. We'd happily testify, if they all got up from their deathbeds and drove back home in one piece, so Mary could finally nail that sainthood.

Andrew would leave one bedside and go to another. He and Jhonnie made each other laugh with a series of absurd exchanges. Afterwards we walked to the cheerful resort café and commiserated over some lukewarm grey frothy milk. My old friend and I talked about our kids (nine between us), our parents and our past. We'd met in a cafeteria on the first day of university, 25 years earlier. We had rated the sexual possibilities of our fellow students to pass the time, and the cigarette machine had scored rather well.

Andrew smoked at hospital, and I felt like joining him. While we appeared to be drowning in responsibility we agreed that we weren't so different from the teenagers who drank and smoked our way through 'big school'. I could never have known then that Hugh and Andrew would be there for me, a hundred years and all those children later. Remarkable, even though, as Andrew pointed out, Hugh had to be there – because he'd nearly killed my husband. Andrew still smoked Camel filterless, bless him.

waterlemon

EMAIL FROM RUTH TO JHONNIE'S LIST

I think siege mentality is finally subsiding. The adrenalin-pumped first two weeks of this crisis have passed, and all involved are just plain pooped. I went 'banking for Jhonnie' the other day, and realised nobody else in the queue was about to explain a 'life-threatening-head-injury' to the bank manager. Even the project manager, my amazing sister, Julia, has stopped diarising with me, because I must have shut down a bit. (She was up with Patrick on and off until four, when I came back on deck. God bless Julia Ritchie.)

So the siege has passed (of course, more American soldiers die every day in Iraq, since the war finished, than in the actual – well anyway, now that he is breathing and talking on his own, I feel more likely to crash the car, lose my phone, drive away without the baby.)

Hugh came with me today – important for him to see Jhonnie at every stage of improvement, because he was the man who put Jhonnie in a helicopter two weeks ago. We'd brought in a great lunch, but spent most of the visit in the bowels of the hospital in X-ray and replaster rooms.

Hugh brought his camera (he's a wonderful professional photographer, and all those black-and-white pictures of our children looking wistful and gifted are his doing). Anyway, Hugh's camera passed a day in the neuro ward. Jhonnie's bed, lined up for X-ray like a jumbo taxiing at Heathrow, takes up no more room than any other patient's. But people line up there, no say in the matter. Jhonnie, awake for the first time for this routine, read some very bad medical puns off hospital posters, and identified them as such. He was grateful to Hugh and me. 'This would be boring without you. Thanks.' He has no idea how many lost hours we've squandered in these corridors since his accident.

We fed him the very fine lunch, completely avoiding the catering horror of RNS. After lunch Jhonnie, ever the excellent host, offered, 'Chocolate cake, Mr Bond?' (an ancient ski holiday reference). Hugh replied, 'You're a hard man to kill, Blofeld.' Jhonnie smiled.

I asked Jhonnie today if he remembered what I do for work. He told me I was a writer. I asked him what I was writing about now (usually TV, restaurants, sex, garbage). He said, 'I hope you're writing about me.' And I told him I was.

The big medical review tomorrow, where we get more appallingly frank recitals of 'what can be expected of a head injury of this severity'. But I'm bracing myself, because they don't know Jhonnie, and they don't know our family. They just know head injuries.

Took William to karate this afternoon, instead of going back to hospital. Sarah drove us, because I am so tired I can barely remember to zip up my jeans. Watching a bunch of little boys kick the air with purpose and discipline is just plain wonderful.

Susan and I have just had a candlelit dinner with William, complete with disco ball, and as I write, I can hear them giggling upstairs with Patrick.

Scarlet-Fucking-O'Hara. Tomorrow is another day.

more later

xrr

EMAIL FROM PETE TO RUTH

Ruth

A visit of two halves last night . . .

First half: silence apart from his snoring. Just held his hand. Very peaceful (apart from the snoring).

Second half: after the nurses stirred him to turn him over, we were chatting about his investment strategies in a Russian–French drinking game. It resulted in the cancellation of a rugby tour. Go figure.

New investment strategy was Mandarin Centres because they were community-based. We were, after all, in Chinatown (the only hospital that would have us). I asked if he remembered how to make a cup of tea, he thought so but would be glad if I would help him. Ditto a sandwich. My pleasure.

I am taking in (if it's okay with you) a small cassette tape machine so he can record his thoughts. It may end up meaning nada, but knowing Jhonnie it may be the answer to life, the universe and everything.

Tearful Justin on the phone yesterday; it's sunk in I think.

Jules very pleased (he says) that someone has told The Family (i.e. Michael) to quit bickering and get their act together. (I had written to Jules, and said to Michael, that if they turned Jhonnie's injury into another source of feud/grievance I would wash my hands of them.)

Esther and self hoping to be at your house Monday night to sort rugby tickets, if that's okay.

Is Saturday still good, and if so, what time? Nicole will bring veggie-filth.

I will bring wine . . . would you prefer red or white?

Twenty years ago, as a very junior copywriter, I was sent to Disneyland and Hawaii with a TV film crew to pull in some stock footage for holiday package ads – non-specific cliché stuff: windsurfers gliding on the horizon at sunset, a small child running with clouds of balloons in front of the Disney castle. It was a two-week shoot spent evacuating various hotel mini-bars and standing thigh-deep in warm tropical water, holding large sheets of polystyrene above my head. At the end, as there was no edit or air date, I stayed behind in Maui and scuba dived for two weeks with a young producer friend. I was 21 years old. (It was exactly this sort of gruelling work that prepared me for the various challenges of life as home-typist, mother, step-mother and vigilant wife to the brain injured.)

While shooting in Disneyland, in 40-degree heat, and capturing all the magic that old papier-mâché mountains and giant rats have to offer, we would slip behind the bright clean façades to swap magazines in the camera, change lenses, douse ourselves in iced water. Nobody in Disneyland proper is ever thirsty or sweaty. It is the happiest kingdom of them all, and legions of wildly obese 10 year olds walked around with four-gallon tubs of hot buttered popcorn as living proof that it doesn't get any better than this. But Disney staff have to disappear into the wings to sneeze.

Behind the scenes, among the ladders, mops, buckets and stools that apparently hold the whole operation up, the Disney characters would take their breaks. There's no green room for Goofy. He just pulls off his own head, in his personal furry sauna, and leans on a ladder, his real face almost comically purple with heat exhaustion, drinks warm Coke and smokes cigarettes. We had been given strict instructions not to shoot any of the characters behind the scenes, especially in such disarray. It was probably too dark, but one morning our cameraman shot a few minutes of the dwarves on smoko – every single one of them Grumpy. I never saw the footage, but it must have looked like an outtake from a David Lynch film.

The bowels of a large hospital such as Royal North Shore are like the buckets-and-mops side of the Disney set, with one major difference. There is no bright shiny papier-mâché façade. It's just that the machinery below ground appears even more run down than the highly polished broken linoleum above ground. We descended in an elevator as big as a Darlinghurst one-bedroom apartment, below the ground, to what might have been a world of medical hobbits. Catering. Garbage disposal. Laundry. And the plastering rooms. Hugh took pictures. I figured we weren't supposed to. And we waited in corridors with the wildly disoriented and unconscious for hours, until a young Irish intern took another look at the snapshots of Jhonnie's various broken bones, and had another crack at replastering – at first – the wrong arm.

Under different circumstances the nosey photographer and copywriter would have had a really good poke around. Everybody who was conscious wore a uniform except for Hugh and I. We seemed to be the only hand-holders in the entire maze, and this area was vast. Long shiny fluorescently lit tunnels connected rooms large and small that were often obscured by low-hanging, large ropey air-conditioning ducts.

'Is that black and white?' I asked Hugh, with only vague curiosity about his process.

'Yes. I'm thinking of doing some in pin-hole. I think the effect would be surreal.'

'Oh, and this isn't surreal enough for you without special effects?'

Hugh and I both laughed.

'Thanks for coming, guys. It's so sweet of you to take me out.'

We both looked at Jhonnie in wonder.

'Just don't ever complain that we never take you anywhere nice.'

'When's he getting out of here?'

'What, down here, the last remaining Nazi prison camp that the Americans forgot to liberate, or the whole wonderful hospital?'

Hugh just set off his shutter. The despairing wife will eventually offer up a decent picture.

'Oh Hugh. Enough. I haven't washed my hair since – what day is it?'

'January 12, 1978.'

'Thank you, Jhonnie. In that case I haven't washed my hair since New Year's Eve 1978.'

'A good year.' Hugh cast his mind back to our first year together at university.

'Wasn't it? Were you driving the Mini Moke then?'

'Guess so. You?'

'Just had my driver's licence. Was driving anything I could get my hands on.' I recalled my brother's old Fiat. My sister's old Alfa. Old cars, first cars are like favourite dresses. They stick with you forever.

'Kawasaki,' Jhonnie chimed in, dreaming of a long-lost motorbikes.

'Enough with the bikes, you. When will we get out of here? Before we can go to "Wonderful Wonderful Copenhagen" (my new code song for Ryde Rehab), Jhonnie has to know not just who he is, but where and when.'

'Where are we, Jhonnie?' Hugh aimed his lens at Jhonnie and made ready to let loose on 'Cheese!'

'Denver Airport.'

'The rehab doctors ask you to explain proverbs, and you're not giving them much help. Like, when he said: "A stitch in time," you told him that "Some employment of software companies may be beneficial later on." Nup. We're not goin' anywhere fast.'

'I don't know why they're asking me. Stupid. I've got a plane to catch.'

Snap. Hugh took a few more pictures of the remaining dwarves with our papier-mâché heads in our hands.

Day 14

There are many good things to report. Last night our friend Susan used a cheese knife and a bread knife to carve the chicken while I was on the phone – after this, the whole world will know its way around my kitchen, and my baby. All my great girlfriends, including Simon, are spending unprecedented long chunks of time with Patrick, and declaring him the best baby ever.

Oh, Jhonnie, that's right.

Doing better, but looking exhausted. Told me today that he was off to Beer & Ciggie school. He's forgotten he's a non-smoker. Must say this episode is testing my resolve.

It was a very long day at the hospital, but when my sister, Julia, and I took William in for the first time after school, Jhonnie's face lit up, and he asked for a camera. William climbed up next to his dad and fed him strawberries. After a lengthy karate perform-ance, and some tediously charming detail about the Cranbrook Fair, we came home in time for Patrick and a bath and more lamb chops. Jhonnie and William played I Spy With Jhonnie's Good Eye.

Jhonnie continues to thank all the nurses for his injections. I feel like I spend the whole day thanking everybody, and haven't come close to gratitude yet. Tomorrow he will have been out of Intensive Care for a week. He still can't walk and hold his head up

at the same time, without the assistance of three small women.
Such a lot to learn, for all of us.

more later

xrr

William honestly seemed unfazed by his father's appearance. I
tried to look at Jhonnie through William's five-year-old eyes.
I would have found him slightly frightening and confusing.

They had a lovely relationship before the accident. Jhonnie
worked hard and wasn't around much, but he was a nappy-
changing, teach-you-to-swim, put-you-on-your-bike-for-the
-first-time father. William adored him because nothing they
did together was as tedious as toilet training or teeth brushing.

Jhonnie certainly enjoyed parenting more than I did. But
it was a bit like playing bridge – something he loved, was good
at, and really wished he could do more often. Jhonnie was a
very involved, absent parent. 'Where's Dad?', 'When's Dad
coming back?' were questions William had been asking since
he could talk. So for him, the change in routine had started
with that damned new baby, the arrival of Meera, and then the
disappearance of his mother to hospital every day.

I'd worked from home since William was born. We'd
probably had too many hours of 'Watch another episode of
Thomas the Tank Engine. Mummy's working.' Once, when he
was two, and a tape came to an untimely end, William stood
up, held his arms out to the screen and demanded, 'Be more!' It
could have been an advertising slogan for Nike. It could have
been pilfered for my weekly column. I wasn't destroying a
child. I was building a critic.

Basically William and I were a team of two, and he knew
the family, his crew, could expand to include Daddy, Madi,
Connar, Gogo (my mother), Doody (Julia), Anna, Tracey, Eleni
and so on. But his place on his 'cooking chair', in the kitchen,
by my side, was a certainty.

No matter how much I'd continued to take William to karate and horse riding, nothing had really been the same since the arrival of Patrick, and now this.

William had seemed nervous in the groaning elevator, and the shiny darkened corridors of 7B. The kind smiles of nurses who knew it was his first visit didn't help. I couldn't predict how he'd fare, but I felt certain he wouldn't faint on seeing his father in a hospital bed.

'Hi, Dad. Want to see my two-knuckle punch?'

'Sure.'

William's karate demonstration was full of focus and purpose. His posture and facial expressions reminded me of little Nadia Comaneci, just before she scored a perfect 10 on the balance beam apparatus at the 1976 Olympics. Serious William with his thoughtful old man face. He looked like my dad, aged five, doing karate, in a neurological recovery ward. Jhonnie was enchanted.

After he finished, William climbed up beside Jhonnie on the bed, remarkably careful of broken limbs and plaster. They shared a punnet of strawberries. William had to remind his father not to eat 'the green bits – they're not the *actual* strawberry!'

We knew it was time to go when it was time to go. William was never one for small talk. He told his father all his news, looked at me and finally offered his 'Now what?' shrug. Now we go home. William didn't hesitate to kiss his father goodbye.

In the car on the way home William had no questions about Jhonnie's condition. He seemed to have absorbed enough in the afternoon, and preferred to move on to topics of dinner and sleeping bags and rock climbing.

Except for the few unfortunate occasions where he caught the tail end of his parents' fights, William had almost never seen me break down and lose it. When my cousin Tracey was diagnosed with breast cancer I went outside, sat on the grass and sobbed like an animal. When I returned to cook dinner, red-faced but recovered, William remarked, 'Tracey has made you very sad.'

Only months later, after a miscarriage, I came home from hospital, went to bed flattened by nausea from the general anesthetic, a theatrically timed flu and a grief that shocked me with its enormity. I was so overwhelmed by that unmistakable pain that only comes with a major death in the family. (I'd only known it twice: my grandmother and my father. But that was the feeling.) I'd hid in bed all weekend and read Ian McEwan's *Atonement* in 36 hours. It was like disappearing to another country. And when I'd put the book down, and come back, I couldn't shake my sadness. After two days William came in and sat by me in bed for a long time, saying nothing. He finally patted my arm and said, 'I'm sorry that baby went away. I wish that baby would come back.' Then I broke down and howled. He was four.

William has a nice simple take on things. But I was worried that too much howling and not enough karate would make him a very dour kid. I was so busy saving Jhonnie's life. What on earth was I doing to his children?

EMAIL FROM RUTH TO JHONNIE'S LIST

The rehabilitation doctors and the neurosurgeons all gave Jhonnie glowing reports today. This is the first time in two weeks that any medical practitioner has said that they feel Jhonnie will recover (they never say 'fully' – but I think they came as close as we are going to get). Eleni noted this enormous shift. She was with me on Day 2 in the Intensive Care family conference. I had thought, as he'd survived, I could assume he would recover. That's when he explained that only 50 per cent of these brain injuries recover well enough to go home, in care. The other half (surely not our half) stay in institutions for the rest of their lives. They never go home.

But that was Day 2. And now, when I explained to Jhonnie for the 9000th time how he came to be in this predicament, he apologised again. I told him he would have to be grateful to me for the rest of his life. 'I'd have thought it is you who should be grateful to me.' Really, and why would that be? 'For giving you all this lovely time on your own.'

Funny bugger.

Well that might be enough for a while. Tonight I'm having Hugh's leftover prawn gumbo. Jhonnie had the rest for lunch. William is staying over at Eleni's and Patrick is asleep upstairs. So I might take Jhonnie's advice and, for the first time in two weeks, enjoy some lovely time on my own.

Xrr

Day 15

JHONNIE AND I HAD BEEN friends for years before I learnt his mother had died when he was four. He always referred to his stepmother, Gabriella, as 'Mum'. A wonderful mimic, he often amused dinner parties with Gabriella monologues. A six foot six Pommy bloke made a rather convincing tiny Roman coquette.

He didn't say anything negative about his large, almost eccentric family. All warm, loving and whacky, it never seemed strange that no two Blampieds ever resided in the same country, or continent for that matter. I'd met them all in various combinations, first when they visited Jhonnie and Chris in Australia, and later when we holidayed with them in London or Umbria. They were great fun around a table, breaking bread, drinking wine. Gabriella and I shopped and cooked together with surprising compatibility, in just about any location. I could see that she was rather hard on daughters-in-law, but we'd really had no problems, and anyway, I didn't scare easily.

There was nothing dark or sinister about the 28-year-old Jhonnie Blampied who migrated to Australia in 1989 with his new bride, Chris.

Eleni had been creative director then, and hired Jhonnie after interviewing him while on a trip to London. She was importing strategy planners because she'd run out of good locals, and, one spring day, in walked Jhonnie. He caught the last gasp of '80s advertising excess. Eleni and I, both our boyfriends and nearly everyone we knew worked there – or at least turned up to drink weak Mexican beer from bottles with a lemon stuck in the neck. That agency was like a forerunner to *Big Brother*, but with clients, and drugs, and a much bigger budget.

Jhonnie had fitted in straightaway. In his first week we worked on a piece of business together, which we managed to lose by Friday. Our war stories in the bar that night were hilarious. Jhonnie's imitations of the slimy client who found our presentation too obscure captivated the crowd. This guy was great. He played cards, and pool. He skied, he ate and drank like an ad-man, and as he stood head and shoulders above any crowd, he was very easy to spot at the football.

Jhonnie and Chris spent their first Christmas in Australia with my family. I left the agency a few months later, and moved to Melbourne. After I left advertising, the Mexican beer-drinking multitude, with their red Reebok high-tops and their unnecessarily large four-wheel drives, disappeared. Yet we remained friends. The '80s finally came to an end. I went back to university in Sydney. Jhonnie and Chris had a baby. My boyfriends came and went. I lived in Kings Cross, kept my own hours, and as Jhonnie and Chris surrounded themselves with all the brightly coloured plastic that becomes attached to every young family, I remained delightfully, perversely single.

Chris threw Jhonnie out for the first time when Connar was a toddler. She just 'thought there'd be more'. At the time I wondered how much more she was expecting. More stuff? They had plenty. More height? Not possible . . . Jhonnie was the most generous man in the world. How could there not be enough of him to go around? But perhaps he really wasn't there. Perhaps he'd withdrawn into that busy distraction I'd experienced after both our boys were born. Where did Jhonnie go?

At the time he moved in temporarily with me. I'd just broken up with my boyfriend, so our mutual puddles of self-pity formed a lake on the roof of my Kings Cross apartment. It was a strange month, spent in tears of commiseration all around. After we'd had a cry, we'd have another beer, and another cigarette, and stay up 'til all hours playing Risk on the computer. All the friends were relieved for Jhonnie and Connar when Chris eventually took him back. We knew he would go back. We just never understood why he wanted to.

My house was always full. Esther was around, and Matt, my bestie at the time who had stepped in to fill the gap left by the sudden departure of the beloved boyfriend. Matt worked for Jhonnie, who was, all these years later, the chairman and CEO of the agency for which Eleni had hired him. Matt and a loose gang of Darlinghurst floaters would come and go, and eat and drink, and after they left, Jhonnie and I would sit up for one more ciggy and a short post-mortem.

It was on one of those nights, after a laksa and plenty of cards, that Jhonnie told me his mother had driven him to school one day where they lived in Jersey, flown to London, to the mews flat that she'd kept from before her marriage to Jhonnie's father, taken an overdose of pills and drank herself to death.

Nobody came to pick up Jhonnie and Julian that day, or any other, for months. They were day boys, and even though there were no boarders under the age of seven, Jhonnie and Julian precociously began a life of boarding. No two versions of the events of their mother's death concur. Forty years later, each family member simply retells the story they've been telling forever, whether it's true or not.

Jhonnie recalls that he was called to the principal's office and told, 'Blampied, your mother's dead.' And then sent back to class. Julian says they were told together, and the nurse stayed with them for the rest of the day. Jhonnie's father tells a version where if he hadn't married Gabriella the courts would never have given him custody of his own kids. And the boys agree that for their entire childhood they were encouraged to express boundless gratitude towards their stepmother, who didn't have to put up with them at all, by rights. There was to be no mention of the boys' dead mother in the Blampied house, ever. Jhonnie wasn't told until he was 27 that his mother had committed suicide, and then the news came from a stranger.

There are also many conflicting stories about their childhood. Dickensian abuse at posh schools. Wild summer holiday escapes in Ischia and Elba. With each trip we made back to Umbria it became apparent that Jhonnie's memories of his childhood bore very little resemblance to those of his parents, or his siblings. In fact none of them matched. Their own versions were kept in splendid isolation from any other Blampied, in different countries, on different continents.

But Jhonnie and Julian always agreed that their maternal grandparents provided their childhood oasis. (Had they never discussed their daughter's tragic death? How did they ever recover from it, other than by loving her two little boys?) Now Jhonnie's friends poured in page after page of letters that we read at his bedside, yet family communication was a struggle. After some nasty emails and phone calls from me, Julian's letter arrived on Day 15. Not surprisingly their beloved grandfather, John Young, took centre stage.

I took Jhonnie a beetroot juice, and a latte. (There's no point in rehabilitating him into a health freak.) He was groggy when I sat down. I opened the folder and started reading new emails. Hilarious Wallaby material from one friend. Another wrote explaining that it wasn't a Renault but a Peugeot cabriolet that Jhonnie had driven at university, and the two of them had holidayed in France, with the big guy behind its wheel. It appeared Jhonnie was actually flicking through the sketches of his past: each incident like a single frame of animation that moved his story along at high speed. Jhonnie seemed only mildly interested in these stories. I started Julian's, with a long introduction that sent him drifting. At the mention of the old man, he rallied considerably, an old man himself, roused for Christmas dinner. He listened, transported.

EMAIL FROM JULIAN TO JHONNIE

Remember when we used to drive down to Grandpa's in Kent? We were always late and so drove far too fast in order to make up time. He once asked how you coped with my driving and you replied that you didn't mind as you just shut your eyes. Other times, on our way down to the 'chippy' by the power station, Grandpa would turn to you and say 'Jhonnie, do you think we'll get there?' I also remember one of those journeys from London when you had really pissed me off about something, I wanted to get it off my chest and then you turned to me and said very calmly, 'You know, Jules, if I was you I would have stopped the car and got out and walked by now!'

You were so right. It made me laugh and actually taught me a bit of a lesson.

And old Grandpa. He would be 108 now. His England football cap, 'John Young playing on the left wing for England in Mesopotamia scored the only goal in an otherwise boring match' – eat your heart out David Beckham! His tomatoes until eventually the wind blew his last greenhouse down, and his stories of going over the trenches in the 1st World War dressed in women's night-dresses as camouflage against the snow and it all getting ripped off on the barbed wire so that only the cuffs came back. When he was stationed in Malta and one of the chaps in his mess was having an affair and used fishing as a cover. The fishmonger would put some-thing in his bag to take home to his wife and then one day Grandpa persuaded the fishmonger to put a few mackerel fillets in instead and when he got home the game was up!

How about when we were in Sauze d'Oulx with Dad and his architect friend had just separated from his wife, and Dad said, 'Look, all you have to do is remember that women are just a bit of skirt' and quick as a flash you replied, 'Watch out Dad, here comes Mum' and he got very flustered. Ah, Mum & Dad! The day in Ladbroke Grove when we had the lecture about treating the place like a hotel and they stormed out, slamming the door for dramatic effect and you turned to me and said, 'Huh, the service isn't good enough, I'm checking out . . .' Vivvy heard, burst into tears and ran off to tell them that Jhonnie's leaving home.

Ladbroke Grove, remember decorating? The day you were at the top of a ladder painting the living room and Dad had moaned about our work rate and you looked at me and said 'Sure could do with a hand up here . . . to pick my nose!' I still laugh about that. I remember your decorating career. In your year off you trained with some idiot and it was going to pay for your trip round the States but at the time you obviously didn't realise that the States is bigger than just New York! Ladbroke Grove, a Sunday afternoon film on TV. Dad and Suzy were asleep and the door bell in the film went. Suzy barked and scuttled round to see who was there. It woke Dad with a start and he went 'Ooh! Bloody dog' and went to open the door to find no one.

And the decorating takes us back to Grandpa. You went down to decorate his living room and he couldn't get over the fact that you could paint the ceiling without a ladder. Then in his last days when he could remember everything. You called him from Aus and he wrote on the top of newspaper, 'Spoke to Jhonnie. He's doing well.' It kept him going for days.

Anyway, that is enough from me. I don't know if you received my last email. You always were crap at replying. Lots of Love, Jules x

When I looked up from the letter Jhonnie's face was wet with tears. Completely alert, but apparently confused as to time and place. He bit onto his bottom lip, a failed attempt to stop his chin from wobbling, like a brave little boy. I wrapped my arms around him, mindful of the ribs, and the hand and the eye.

'Darling, what is it? What's wrong?'

'Grandpa's dead.'

How much bad news could I deliver to a man who was lost somewhere between Monaco and the Royal North Shore Hospital? More than a decade had passed since he'd first learnt of his grandfather's death, and the discovery may well have hurt more this time around.

I made it home just in time to feed Pat a bottle. We sat on the couch together quietly. My friend Susan had christened Patrick 'the velvet worm' because of his soft fluffy head and rather stupendous collection of velvet pyjamas. I often joked that the only reason I had children was so that I could pat them, and stroking Patrick's little velvet head now proved very soothing.

If Jhonnie had to rediscover all the bad in his past he could also find new joy in the treasures of the present. That would be a good day, when he could hold Patrick again. It would be like giving birth, but without the doctors' bills or the caesarian. And that's as far as I got when the doorbell rang, and Hugh arrived with coffees and some cameras. We were off to 7B for lunch, and after our last visit, Hugh obviously wasn't prepared to brave the ward without some digital wide-angle wiz-bang armour.

Day 16

EMAIL FROM RUTH TO JHONNIE'S LIST

There was no Day 15 update. Sorry. It was a good day all round. In the evening the laksa boys took Jhonnie piping-hot noodles from the Malaya, and they were all very impressed with his efforts. (Jhonnie is yet to drop bundle, sulk or grump. He remains tirelessly positive.)

But today was particularly interesting. Andrew took me to the hospital with more of Eleni's excellent moussaka, apple pies and chocolates, and Sam came to join us. (Sam hadn't seen Jhonnie since ICU and was gobsmacked by his progress.)

The doctors say Jhonnie's ability to articulate his sense of what has happened to him is extraordinary. He understands that he's been away, is coming back, and is in the middle of processing a lifetime of information.

He knows now, most of the time, that he has fallen off his bike, and is already philosophising on the subject. 'You see, I fell over, and lost my balance. I was heading that way anyway. So it was inevitable. Losing your balance – these are things you have to take responsibility for yourself.'

We all nodded, stunned. He's also had a dream that Hugh is freaked out because he has a gift to change people's lives and he can't cope with that. I told Jhonnie Hugh had indeed been freaked out because he thought he might have killed him and was unsure how he would ever face me if he had.

'No, it's not that. Hugh has a gift.' Hmmm, with a camera certainly, and a vat of prawn gumbo most definitely. But if any of you would like Hugh to take you bike riding and help change your life (head injury optional) I'm sure that can be arranged for a small fee.

Andrew and Sam were still marvelling at the youthful British accent. Jhonnie said he'd been wondering how God would sound if he fell over and got up, so perhaps Jhonnie had come back with a 'God-fell-over' accent. Well, yes . . . why not.

He talks very calmly about feeling lost and alone in the night. No matter how often we tell him I have been with him every day, amnesia sets him adrift in the dark. He talks about being lost and alone with Julian when they were little boys, and all the feelings are very familiar. Very matter-of-fact relaying these spooks. The nurses have told me that when he has very bad nights they move him out into the corridor. That can't inspire too much comfort or confidence. And every morning he is completely delighted to see me, as if we were meeting with the dog in the park. Amazing.

So, now well into our third week, and the emergence of Guru Jhonnie. I'm thinking of getting him a TV deal. Feel sure that his God-fell-over accent has ratings-winner written all over it.

Connar and Madi are seeing him again this afternoon. He talks about them every day. William has gone away with his best friend from school to the beach for the weekend. Haven't taken the baby in yet. My hours at the hospital are probably too long to juggle for his schedule. But he continues to be world's most congenial baby.

I keep showing and reading Jhonnie your new letters (well, they're all new to him). He loves them, and all of you. So many truly extraordinary things have happened in the last 16 days. Thanks to all of you for everything.

Tonight, fish!

more later

xrr

Jhonnie's friend Jem took the kids to see their dad and forwarded an email to the Jhonnie list. So every visit sounded comprehensively better than the last . . .

EMAIL FROM JEM TO JHONNIE'S LIST

Well, I took Jhonnie's kids Connar and Madi in to see their dad today and it brought a lump to my throat. Obviously they were pleased to see each other, but didn't the kids' faces light up when Jhonnie said he remembered them coming in before!

'And Dad, the right hand side of your mouth is now smiling too.' 'And Dad, your black eye isn't as bad as it was, it's actually going yellow, which is the last colour after it's gone black, blue, purple and green and then gets better. And it is getting better coz the whole middle bit is now yellow.' 'And Dad do you remember me being born?' (yes) 'And Dad you've got your old laugh back.' 'And Dad you're nowhere near as weird as that bloke in the bed next to you.' 'Do you want to share some sushi with me?'

Now the bloke in the bed next to him may be wearing a nappy (which he's very keen to show the whole ward), have his head in something that looks like armour and keep asking someone, anyone, to please help him escape from the castle before those bastards with the guns come to shoot him, but I think the point is, even relative to that Jhonnie is getting better.

Perhaps more importantly he enjoyed the sushi, he remembered having the laksa last night (and it didn't have any bad side effects).

His short-term memory is still a bit suss. I had to tell him again that I was going to Fiji tomorrow (second time in 24 hours), but maybe that's just clever mental blocking coz who wants to think of Fiji when some bloke keeps showing you his nappy.

Anyway, look after him while I'm away. Talk/email Ruth if you want to visit and tell Jhonnie if he doesn't keep on improving we'll put him in a nappy . . . now that should motivate him!

Day 17

I HAD THE STRANGEST CONVERSATION with Jhonnie's ex-wife. Chris and I spoke on the phone about how well the kids' visits were going. How lovely for Jem and the other guys to take turns. They're all so busy. Haven't they been good friends.

'One of the boys at school told Connar his father was going to die. He was absolutely destroyed by it. Went to the school counsellor. Apparently he's been in a state of shock for two and a half weeks. Total shock.'

'Well of course. How dreadful. How has the school been handling it?'

'Well that's the funny thing. He hadn't told anyone, not a teacher or a boy, about Jhonnie's accident.'

'But didn't you tell them? I mean, of course he's in shock.'

'Well apparently.'

'Kids can be so brutal. How is he now?'

'I gave him a bath and put lavender oil on his temples.'

'Right. I'm sure the social worker could suggest somebody good for him to talk to – perhaps a child psychologist. Liz – she seems to be really, I don't know, intuitive.'

'No. I'm giving him Rescue Remedy every day now, and he's fine. I meant to say, you should be giving Jhonnie Rescue Remedy.'

'O-kay . . . Thanks, for that.'

I bit my lip and thought, 'We gave him Rescue Remedy, in the form of a helicopter pilot, a brain surgeon and a nice long spell on life support machines.'

The retelling of this conversation at dinner took on a sketch comedy quality that made some of the lines difficult to deliver with a straight face. Pete and Nicole, Julia and Anna Ritchie, William and I pulled together all the normal preparations for a big Saturday night roast dinner. William wanted to light all the candles in the house. Julia produced a bottle of Taittinger from nowhere. Pete had brought a few sensational reds. Big fat salty black olives went into the little crystal ashtray that had done the same pre-dinner job at our home in Northbridge when I was a child. Olives and ice buckets, and Scotch and busy hands and tinkling crystal. Mustard in pots. Corkscrews in bottles and serviettes – white, ironed, nice. The very sharp steak knives. A baking dish of pan juices for gravy. Aprons and oven mitts. I felt strangely elated. The news at the hospital that day had been all good. This dinner became an artificial punctuation mark. Without consulting each other we'd all decided that as of today, the worst was behind us.

'Does anyone want hot English mustard, or are we just having French?'

'I'll just stick with Rescue Remedy, thanks.' Pete couldn't help himself.

I nearly choked on my olive for laughing. It was a happy, happy gathering. We were celebrating, really celebrating. William laughed for the first time in weeks.

We toasted Jhonnie first, but continued to toast each other throughout the night. What about the good old days in Intensive Care, huh? Wasn't that a hoot? How about that mad social worker? How about that doctor on the helicopter – the lifesaving angel from central casting? We'd come so far (literally only one floor, but tonight we weren't counting). It was a celebration of the fact that things were getting better not worse, and we were so lucky to have each other to handle this difficult test. The mad parents. The crazy siblings. The . . . Rescue Remedy. What next?

Julia was unusually buoyant. 'I've produced American disaster movies that had more credible twists and turns than *Blampied – The Head Injury*. Remember the giant octopus movie with the largest glass tank ever built in the southern hemisphere? Technically, less challenging than some phone conversations with various Blampieds.'

I drank Pete's red wine and smoked Julia's cigarettes. We had a party. It was only on the stairs on the way up to bed that the first inevitable whiff of an anticlimax reached me. We had to do it all again tomorrow. It wasn't over. We were all just three weeks more tired than we were at the start. And in just three hours, Patrick would sing out for a bottle.

I lay awake thinking about Connar and the mean kid at school. Rescue Remedy aside, there was nothing good about this situation for any of the kids, and fixing it was completely beyond my control.

Jhonnie had told me once that when he was left at school, at the age of four, to become the youngest orphaned boarder since Charles Dickens put down his pen, a much bigger boy made fun of him in the playground one day. He had apparently teased this undersized blond moppet about his mother running away and never coming back. With a strength that surprised the entire playground, Jhonnie had picked up a rock, smacked it into the bigger boy's head, knocked him to the ground and kept smacking until his head split and blood ran from his ears.

I've heard Jhonnie tell the story so often, using exactly the same phrases and pauses for emphasis, that it is impossible to know if he just nicked the boy or damn near killed him. But the fury of his frustration is palpable, nearly 40 years later. Jhonnie expressed nothing more than mild indifference to his dead mother, but recalls clearly his anger at the kid who'd dobbed on her. Rescue Remedy wasn't going to fix that, and I doubted very much that it would help a 10-year-old boy who had been too frightened to tell anyone at school that his father had nearly died.

Day 18

EMAIL FROM RUTH TO JHONNIE'S LIST

Yesterday Jhonnie's neurosurgeon told us that he was officially out of the 'acute phase' of the injury, and Jhonnie's biggest concern now, after rehabilitation, is his eye. This is the first time Jhonnie has met the man who cut his head open nearly three weeks ago. I introduced them. Our filmmaker friend, Susan, caught the moment on tape. (Jhonnie may want to see this when he is much better. His thoughts on his accident and recovery are very interesting just now.)

After the doctor left, Jhonnie remarked that he couldn't be his patient. He's never spoken to him. How would that doctor know what was wrong? Hmmm. Good point, Jhonnie, but he seemed to have managed okay. After all, it wasn't exactly brain surgery. Well, now that you mention it, it was!

So, the eye! Weeks ago I was happily trading body parts (his, not mine) to save Jhonnie's life. 'I'd give his right eye to have him back.' Now I'm getting greedy. I'd like the eye back. The doctors aren't ruling out surgery, or some natural recovery of the third nerve (controls eyelid, eyeball movement and focus).

Last night the Swans lost to Brisbane. Esther, Hugh, Simon and assorted others all watched their demise at the ground, while the rest of Team Jhonnie had roast lamb here, and a bottle of

Taittinger. Pete, Nicole, Anna, Julia and I sat around cooing at Patrick and congratulating ourselves, and Jhonnie, on making it this far.

Don't know if I will keep writing every day now. We'll be organising more regular visits for Jhonnie, so all those offers of help will be taken up in weeks and months to come. Taking Patrick in for the first time today, with a leftover roast lamb dinner, complete with my breaded mint dressing. That should fix him right up.

Acute phase over.

more later

xrr

Day 19

JHONNIE AND I SAT QUIETLY by his bed, in two of the ugliest
chairs in Australia. It takes three people to get Jhonnie into these
chairs, and once he's there, they pad him with pillows and run
away rather quickly (perhaps I just imagined that part). I'd stopped
bringing large quantities of rather diuretic fruit juice, now that he
was no longer catheterised. A dash from his bed or chair to that
less than glamorous en suite had no chance, even if the nurses did
respond to the bell. We had little coffees and little rolls. Jhonnie's
went cold as he dozed through the early hours of this morning.
I patted his hand and gazed out that tedious window, relieved, not
for the first time, that he would never remember any of this. Now
I too would need a head injury to forget it.

Jhonnie woke with a start.

'Where is she? Where is she?'

'Who, darling? I'm here.'

'The baby. I can't find the baby.'

'Patrick is at home with Meera and William.'

'No. Not Patrick. Oh no. We've lost the baby.'

A wave of bitter disappointment darkened his face. He
seemed to be experiencing genuine fresh grief. His hands and
ribs and countless other tiny annoying injuries all pained him
as he doubled over.

'Where's that baby we lost? Where is she?'

I'd had a miscarriage before Patrick. Jhonnie had been certain that baby was a girl. Was it that or was it Patrick? Had he just realised that he was missing out on Patrick's entire life, stuck in this shiny creaking hellhole? Maybe 'she' was his mother, and he was confusing himself with a lost baby. I could make up theories about the true meaning of these vague rants all day long, but Jhonnie would never be able to tell us what was really going on.

I thought about getting the nurse, but just then a giant walked into the room. Very few men have Jhonnie's physical presence, though certain hospital orderlies, Tongan furniture removalists and rugby players fill a doorway like Jhonnie Blampied – or Peter FitzSimons.

I didn't know Peter well. We worked for the same paper but our paths rarely crossed. So his appearance at Royal North Shore Hospital at the bedside of a rugby-mad total stranger on a busy morning was a generous surprise. He nodded to me, but went straight to the patient.

'Hello, mate. How are you doing?'

Men. Can anyone make sense of the way they speak to each other?

'Hey, Peter. Do you know who this is, darling? It's Peter FitzSimons, come to visit . . . you. How about that!'

'Yeah. That's nice. Hello, Peter.'

Jhonnie was unmoved, not in an indifferent way. He was very happy to have Peter Fitz sitting on the end of his bed. But his appearance seemed anything but a surprise. Perhaps in Jhonnie's head, all sorts of oddballs were popping in regularly – John Lennon, Marilyn Monroe, his dead mother, and his favourite sports columnist. A real live Peter FitzSimons was probably a waste of time.

They talked about football, and hospitals and wives. Peter told him he was very lucky to have me. They spoke as if they knew each other. They didn't. And Peter's voice broke a few times and I wondered if he was going to cry. He didn't. He stayed for about half an hour. When I walked him out he looked pleased but relieved.

'He's amazing, Ruth. He's better than I thought. I don't know what I was expecting, but he's amazing. You're amazing. Bless you, Ruth Ritchie.'

'Peter?' I was very serious.

'Yes.' I could have asked him anything.

'You know he thinks you're Ian Thorpe?'

We laughed in that horrible corridor. I thanked him all the way to the elevator and raced back to witness the transforming effect of this celebrity visit. Jhonnie had fallen asleep and dropped his half-eaten cold frittata roll to the ground. Damn. I had been counting on that roll for lunch.

EMAIL FROM RUTH TO JHONNIE'S LIST

Well, after thousands of words from me, here are the first pictures. As Jhonnie would say, 'Up, up and around.' Yet to find a hospital gown that covers his bum. Jhonnie enjoyed (really enjoyed) a visit from Peter FitzSimons (for northern hemisphere folk – Jhonnie's favourite columnist and an ex-Wallaby) today. He must have wondered how Fitz happened to just stroll in to his neurological ward. Unfortunately the visit was wasted on Jhonnie's three other roomies – completely out to it. Jhonnie has remarked, rather unkindly, that he's 'woken up in a vegetable patch', and I constantly remind him he was no better than a very big choko only a week ago. We need to get him into rehab.

more later

xrr

Chris was ringing more, helping more. Not helping, co-operating. Not co-operating, just not hindering. I hadn't heeded her Rescue Remedy advice, and yet he was on his way to rehab.

'Ruth, that's really great news that he's going to Ryde. Will that be much nicer?'

'I'll find out tomorrow. I don't think it's Betty Ford rehab. I'm expecting gruesome head injury rehab. But he'll have his own kitchen, or share it with a bunch of . . . I can't imagine that it will be a Gold Coast time share, no.'

'Have they told you when he'll drive? Because I'm trying to work out if Connar should do rugby this term, and I won't if Jhonnie can't drive him.'

'I don't know, Chris. I reckon after they pop him up in a chair and remind him how to clean his teeth without sticking the brush in his eye, they'll move straight on to the operation of luxury German performance cars.'

Silence. Or was that huffing?

'There's no need for that tone.'

'He may never drive again. He can barely walk. He still doesn't know how many children he has. Does this information affect the choice of Connar's extracurricular activities?'

'I can't see why you have to be so unpleasant.'

'I know. You have a special unique blindness. Chrisocentric vision. Do you have any idea how preposterous, how insensitive it is to ring me about . . . after-school rugby plans? Wake up, honey. You've got much bigger problems than just getting the taxi back on the road.'

'I will not be spoken to like this.'

Before I came out with my best 'But ya are, Blanche. Ya arrrre,' she'd hung up. I could picture her tripping to the bathroom for the Rescue Remedy.

For years I had test-driven strategies for the care and handling of Chris with my cousin Tracey. How could the wicked stepmother and the nightmare first wife ever break from their almost comically evil stereotypes? We'd made no progress. If anything our relationship grew worse.

Employing tricks of the psychologist trade, Tracey

reminded me to never engage. Keep communication short and clear. Sentences without adjectival clauses. Nothing beyond clear-cut instructions. Drop off. Pick up. No chat. It will always go badly. And she was right. Tracey was right . . . But driving Connar to rugby? I rang Tracey, fuming.

'What a shock? Chris can't see beyond Chris's problems, and that has happened, in the last six or seven years, how many times? I can't hear you . . .'

Tracey relished this one. I was nearly laughing already.

'That has happened on more than 8000 occasions.'

'And so, the best indicator of future behaviour, is? All together now . . .'

'*Past behaviour.*'

'And the lesson we learn here is?'

'Don't engage.'

Day 20

EMAIL FROM RUTH TO JHONNIE'S LIST

He goes to rehab on Monday.

Three weeks ago today, Jhonnie waved goodbye on a beautiful spring morning, and he hasn't been home since. For those who don't know, here's what happened . . .

Jhonnie, Hugh and Philip took their racing bikes to West Head for a 20-kilometre bike ride, in preparation for the Sydney to Wollongong road race. Jhonnie's bike was new (a farewell present from the agency; in retrospect a watch might have been less dangerous). Although he had been riding a lot, he'd done bugger-all since Patrick's arrival, exactly three months earlier. And to make matters worse, he'd put on 15 kilos.

Hugh and Philip didn't see the accident. They heard it. They were going downhill very fast (40–50 km/h). Jhonnie rounded a bend and flew over the handle bars, landing, unconscious, 30 feet from the bike. He was having trouble breathing, had a fixed dilated pupil, and never regained consciousness. Hugh rang 000 and a helicopter arrived presently and delivered him to Emergency at Royal North Shore. We were lucky in many respects. Jhonnie wasn't alone. Hugh's phone had a signal (remote bush area, no passing cars) – or they could be waiting there still. The helicopter could have gone to Gosford (bad – country, 1½ hours from town) or RNS, with the best neuro Intensive Care Unit in the state. So, we were lucky all round.

When Hugh called me, I was hanging out with the baby and watching tapes of *Six Feet Under* for my September 11 column. I'd thought that *Six Feet* was a completely post-9/11 drama because every week it reflects on the abrupt absurdity of life – that it might change, end at any moment, when you least expect it. That preoccupation separates it dramatically from other TV drama. So that's what I was thinking when the phone rang and, on hearing Hugh's voice, I said, 'What have you done with my husband?'

And after that, absurdly, abruptly, nothing has ever been the same. But three weeks later, three weeks after that helicopter doctor gave Jhonnie a 50–50 chance of survival, and gave me his phone number so that I might tell him if those odds had worked in Jhonnie's favour – three weeks after brain surgery and kind introductions from every chaplain and social worker in the hospital – Jhonnie is wearing underpants, eating sushi and complaining that he's sharing a room with three complete head cases. Good thing he missed the first two weeks of this ordeal. Trust Jhonnie to sleep through the really ugly bits.

So rehab will be a whole new chapter. Any local who wants to visit Jhonnie before he goes (if you haven't seen him yet, please check with me – only two visitors at a time), do not take wives, kids, strangers in there. This is not like visiting a friend with a broken leg, and while Jhonnie looks very much better, he is still very fragile, and shares a small space with some pretty scary people.

I will update locals on the visiting situation in Ryde after he gets settled. We've all come such a long way in just three weeks. Thanks again for all your kindness. Our house is full of loving cards – welcoming Patrick to the world and wishing Jhonnie speedy recovery. Spooky. Don't take this the wrong way, but I look forward to some dreary time when all that arrives in the post is bills.

more later

xrr

Day 21

PHIL, HUGH AND I WHEELED Jhonnie out into an extremely ugly corner of scrub that we laughingly referred to as 'the garden' to share a thermos of great take-away coffee and crispy baguettes.

Hugh was nearly au fait with the whole hospital experience by now. (Even so, he didn't push the wheelchair.) I had forced him into his discomfort zone, and he had coped, if not exactly thrived. Philip could barely speak for the whole visit. He had taken all the bikes home that day. He had left the scene of the accident under the uncomfortably cloudy assumption that a man he barely knew, a man he'd only been riding with for a few hours, was probably about to die. Sitting in the ugly garden three weeks later was really the only way to scratch that image for good. So Philip, also a photographer, didn't have much to say.

Seeing Jhonnie in sunshine, in real daylight, breathing fresh air, was novel. I couldn't imagine him moving through the real world anymore, not even in a wheelchair. I couldn't picture him in the car. I couldn't picture him in a Westfield shopping centre with Rebel Sport and Myer bags hanging off his chair. I couldn't imagine anything but our life in Royal North Shore. Now I was so good at it, it was almost over. My parking ticket, that precious money-saving slip that had been tucked in my bra every day for three weeks, would soon be meaningless. I could forget all the names and the phone numbers, and the fastest elevators and the best intersections at peak hour, because we were on our way to Ryde. We didn't say much about that over lunch. We talked about Philip's impending wedding. When the rolls were all eaten I made Hugh push the chair, and we went back up to good old 7B, tucked Jhonnie back in bed and I got my instructions for Ryde Rehabilitation Centre.

Julia was meeting me there. She'd backed off in recent days. Plenty of her own work, life, laundry to catch up on after installing herself at our house. But she decided to meet me at Ryde. We were casing the joint. Trying to get the lie of the land, the dirt on the staff, the good oil on how to play rehab and win. Tracey knew some of the staff there, and had the most realistic expectations for what was to come. We hadn't talked about it much, but I could tell she was preparing me for a tired Pacific resort without cocktails full of umbrellas.

Julia must have sensed that it would be bad. Not bad per se, but bad for me. She arrived with notebooks and pencils and rubbers, and a variety of pens in different colours. It wasn't orientation week at Sydney University, but she'd come prepared for any eventuation. Lucky. I was prepared for nothing.

EMAIL FROM RUTH TO JHONNIE'S LIST

Well, I've seen rehab, and while Jhonnie is desperate to get out of his acute ward at RNS, the future looks like a cross between *Cuckoo's Nest* and a barely acceptable retirement village where one might deposit a distant elderly relative and then drive away at guilty high speeds. It's not that bad. It's another institution, full of really broken people who are trying to piece their lives back together.

Once he's there, and we do an episode of *Changing Rooms* in his immediate environment, I may not notice the depressing rec room with the 10-year-old television and the not quite clean personalised mugs. Yes, what Ryde Rehab needs is Jamie Durie and a Balinese water feature. I took the grand tour and looked nonplussed at the training steps – three steps up and three steps down – where patients learn how to climb, well, steps. Three steps. That's brilliant preparation for our three-storey house.

The room where he lands on Monday is fairly awful – undeniably hospital – and shared with three other newcomers. Still no room in the brain unit, where he will eventually land and have his own room. And I can bring in towels from home. (How anybody, let alone a six-foot-six man, is supposed to remember how to dry themselves with a frayed tea towel is beyond me.)

The whole experience was strangely deflating. Ryde itself is Nowheresville, and a decent hike from our place. The petrol is five cents cheaper per litre. Normally that'd be a good thing, but today I just found it disconcerting. I drove away from Ryde, through that shocking way-out-west traffic, to visit Jhonnie back at RNS. I've left Jhonnie's CDs in his stacker (and his voice on the home answering machine), but those CDs have become a strange soundtrack to this whole ordeal. Today, playing Ben Folds Five, and thinking of Madi and William loudly singing 'Kiss My Ass Goodbye' only weeks ago, seems like another planet.

Jhonnie had a pretty good day. Phil and Hugh (partners in bike crime) visited today. The last time Phil saw Jhonnie he was unconscious in a helicopter. So today was pretty important for him. Connar and William are visiting this afternoon with Julia. Jhonnie is entirely focused on family/kids, getting back home to us. He is angry at missing what seems to be Patrick's entire life, and frustrated with life in an institution.

The irony of this is not lost on Jhonnie. As he put it, he's spent his entire life in one shithole institution after another. He even stayed in the same job at the agency for 14 years. The first time in his life he actually embraces freedom and breaks out on his own, he goes for a simple bike ride and winds up . . . back in an institution.

So, no visitors until his brain injury bed or team assessment (next Thursday). Visiting hours are tricky, because of all his appoint- ments with physios, OTs, psychs, etc (basically 3.30–8.00 pm) but the weekends are completely free. Devlin Dog will finally put in an appearance. I'll update locals with address and times for visits when we know the routine.

Thanks again for all your support. I know marathons are only interesting at the beginning and the end. This is neither.

more later

xrr

The euphoria of the day's conference proved to be exhausting. We had overcome another hurdle, and in the cliché-ridden world of near-death catastrophes this had been a day of triumphant milestones, turned corners, personal victories and red letters. Lucky old us.

Julia sensibly remembered everybody's name, and asked really practical questions about Jhonnie's schedule, and clothing he might need. (He'd been nude for the entire month of September.) Julia Ritchie, film producer, stepped up to the plate while Ruth Ritchie, dreamy dopey writer, just checked out. This would be so much better than hospital. We'd be able to sit on grass, outside, and have picnics, with the dog. Devlin could come to rehab. But there is something about the miserable manicured nature of the gardens in such institutions that is frightening. Nothing random or spontaneous in the planting. No love. Just a government contract of weeding, pruning, fertilisation and maintenance. Why would Devlin even want to pee there?

Tiny details like the gardens and the coffee stains on the walls distracted me from the job at hand. Perhaps, because I knew my big sister, my competent, capable sister was very, very present, I just had to disappear. I cried on the way home, and then pulled it together for cheerful cups of tea for the assem- bled welcoming party.

I could feel an explosive Catherine Zeta-Jones lurking just under the surface. So many total strangers had metaphorically patted my back all afternoon. I typed out the good news in a hurry on my return. But Julia went home, and Eleni waved goodbye, and finally Meera left me home alone with William and Patrick and all the uncertain optimism about Jhonnie's recovery.

I encouraged William into the bath and was already nearly an hour late with Patrick's bottle. We lay on my bed, the late-September sun setting rather suddenly, leaving us in darkness. Pat was nearly asleep in my arms. Only the bulb in William's bathroom provided a pilot light at dusk.

Two weeks of walking at high speed up and down the hospital car park had murdered my slowly achieved patience with babies. Come on. I needed Pat to pass out so that I could illuminate our gloomy home, and start our dinner. 6.30. William was starving and whining in the next room. Sleep, Patrick, I command you. Pat gurgled back and rolled around. In the last two weeks he'd gained so much more control of his movement. I could have watched him explore the doona by the tiny green light of the phone all night, but William and I were planning to share a romantic spaghetti. We need to move this bottle/cuddle/roll-about routine along. And then the phone rang. I answered quickly so as not to break Patrick's milky spell. It was Jhonnie's father.

'Ruth, is that you?'

'Yes, Michael. I've got so much to tell you. Listen, can I just get the kids a bit organised and I'll –'

'Tell me, what news of Jhonnie?'

'Thing is, I'm here alone in total darkness, with the boys, and I just need to –'

'Listen here – I'm very busy. We're trying to organise our tickets to St Petersburg.'

And then Catherine Zeta-Jones snatched the phone from my hand.

'You're busy! You're busy? You can go to hell!'

And I hung up. I didn't really spend any 'lovely time on my own'. I hurled William into pyjamas, and parked him with a bowl of pasta in front of the television while I made the grave mistake of engaging with the rest of Jhonnie's family about how much I had hurt Michael's feeling by hanging up on him.

EMAIL FROM RUTH TO VIVVY

Vivs – just slammed the phone down on your dad. He rang while I was feeding Patrick, with William moaning that he was hungry. Me here alone. In my attempt to explain this situation to Michael, that I needed to call him back, he cut in, 'We're very busy here. We have to organise tickets to St Petersburg!' To which I replied, 'You're busy! You're busy? You can go to hell!' and hung up.

Sounds bad, but in terms of Ritchie restraint, think I did well. Didn't call him names or pass on any uncensored Jhonnie. Today: 'Your parents want to come for Christmas. What shall I tell them?'

'They've left me in one shithole after another my entire life, and they want to come get me now?'

Don't pass this on to your folks. I know they have their own problems and frustrations – none of which mesh very well with mine at the moment.

Anyway, our boy is getting better. Sure rehab will be a whole new challenge. Don't know what to do about your parents. Actually, don't have your current phone number. Email me, or give me a call before 9.00 pm Aust time and we'll catch up. Hope you are holding it together. (Whatever that might mean?) I know this is very scary. Something none of us ever thought we'd have to go through. You make so much sense in your emails – not just because you love Pog so much, but perhaps because a personal crisis – where you suddenly jump the tracks from everyday society to something very strange – has been such a big part of your journey.

I know you've often found me a pain in the arse, but I have never underestimated your bravery in dealing with such a tough hand. Very glad that your big brother is made of much the same stuff.

We will all sit around a table and eat and drink too much again. Not soon, but one day.

Love

rr

Vivvy's reply was a complex cocktail of justification and self-pity. Their frail father couldn't possibly be held accountable; he'd been through so much and I'd misunderstood. He worried that I would hate him now. After all he'd done for Jhonnie and Julian, jeopardising his own marriage to Gabriella by caring for them, protecting them from the awful truth about their dead mother. A 40-year-old saga suddenly came into play as an explanation of current telephone etiquette. She described the valiant hero of a Danielle Steele novel, not the pompous old bugger who had bailed me up on the phone. She explained that Michael looked mortally wounded and that she was in floods of tears. Quite an achievement, I thought, from all the way down here on the other side of the planet.

EMAIL FROM RUTH TO VIVVY

Dear Vivvy – sorry things are such a mess there, and genuinely sorry about your dad's sadness and vulnerability, BUT guess there's not a damn thing I can do about it here and now. Hate him? How is it your parents manage to make other people's tragedies all about themselves? The only times they have spoken to me in the last three weeks, they've cried. They ring me to cry, to perhaps impress me with how much they love Jhonnie, or how difficult this is for them. If they want to cry they should bother somebody else. Does he think that I have a spare second in a day that begins at 3.30 am and doesn't stop until 10 at night – a free moment to think about hating *him*?

Can we just focus on Jhonnie!

I'm heading off to hospital now. Will call you this evening if I get a break between infants. Chin up. (What appalling advice – chin anywhere you like!)

Xrr

EMAIL FROM VIVVY TO RUTH

Dear Ruth – sorry if this last email was a bit emotional – I was trying to give some background info to explain some of the family things that happen. There is nothing I'd like more than to see this family fully functioning and sometimes I try to make that happen and create a worse mess! Their main concern is Jhonnie and I was wrong to go into anything else . . . as a dad he wants to be there and can't be and as a dad he is very worried about him. I think that when something like this happens it can affect extended family in a strange way, especially when the family has issues – it somehow brings them to the surface – but I absolutely promise that everyone's concern is Jhonnie right now but there's nothing we can actually do, which is a bit frustrating.

Yesterday was just a bad day so guess I was a lot more emotional than usual – want to see Jhonnie and Dad okay with each other but I can't make it happen and shouldn't try. I have been coping well – it's just rare days like yesterday where I feel overburdened with Mum and Dad's feelings as well as my own stuff and cope badly.

All present and correct at this end today!

love Vivvy

EMAIL FROM RUTH TO MICHAEL

Michael – I am not writing to apologise for hanging up on you. You got off lightly. Unlike you and your family I have not felt the need to burden you with the difficulties of my domestic situation here, so perhaps you have no grasp. So, when I say that I have two hungry babies here, one crying, and I am alone – don't ever interrupt me with 'St Petersburg'. Because I will tell you to go to hell. Got it?

Don't ring me anymore with your nonsense. And don't tell lies to Pete, who spends every night with Jhonnie followed by hours of self-absorbed crap on the phone with you. These tickets to St Petersburg, have you had them for months, when you were too fragile to breathe, or did you buy them last week – as in last week when Jhonnie was in a coma, or last week when we simply didn't know if he was going to be a vegetable?

For the last three weeks we have been told to lie to you – you're too fragile, to lie to Vivvy – she's not well. Justin's going to Corfu, but Mum and Dad don't know. Don't care. WE JUST DON'T CARE.

I don't care if you hate me. I don't care if you hate each other. I don't care if you feel guilty as hell for things that happened 30 and 40 years ago. I care about Jhonnie and our children.

Frankly I don't think you are strong enough to watch Jhonnie learn how to clean his teeth again, but Jhonnie is, so don't come here and give him the added burden of worrying how his accident is affecting you.

Now go to St Petersburg or get on the phone and have a big boo-hoo to anyone who'll listen, but stay away from us.

I have copied all your children and Pete on this letter. It will take a very big bump on my head for me to forget how you have made a freakishly nightmarish situation worse with your unfathomable selfishness. Have a think about that in St Petersburg.

Ruth Ritchie

If only I'd sent it. If only I'd actually broken the tangled knots of nonsense and sent it. But I didn't. Instead, Pete and Julia endured hours, long shouting hours, over days and then weeks in telephone calls with various Blampieds, debating what a meanie pants I was, and how difficult this was for *ALL OF THEM*. The three of us decided it just wasn't a good idea for me to speak to them any more. There is a place, especially in the stressful landscape of an ongoing medical disaster, for the hotheaded outburst. There's an instant sense of relief, in much the same way that a headache can pass with a purging flood of tears. Those heavy stones on the chest, that feeling of bending, cracking ribs under the weight of pain, pass momentarily with an outburst from the Incredible Hulk. Unfortunately the Hulk can be frightening to anyone who isn't amused by green body paint.

My broadsides at Chris and my frustration with Jhonnie's family should have been completely understandable under the circumstances, but I couldn't help wondering how I might have frightened people unintentionally. I just had to keep an eye on the length of that list of people Julia and Pete were protecting me from. Or was it the other way around?

Back in Royal North Shore, Jhonnie's last days ground on slowly. Physio routines became relaxed, or non-existent. Jhonnie only needed one nurse to assist him to the bathroom. I cleaned his teeth and helped him shave every day. It's wrong to say that the overworked staff at 7B had dropped the ball, but I liked to arrive just outside visiting hours to see what level of care he was enjoying. So many patients sat propped up in bed, meals untouched a few feet away on trays they couldn't reach, only to be reprimanded sweetly by another patronising attendant hours later: 'We've been naughty. We haven't touched our jelly, and our tea's gone cold!'

Not their fault. Nobody's fault that the acute cases must be treated first. As the acutes get better, as they become more self-sufficient, with the best intentions in the world, quite frankly, if the situation isn't life threatening, they can wait.

One afternoon Jhonnie attempted to take himself to the bathroom. Only three metres from his bed, but medically he needed a stamp in his passport and a fancy visa to make the journey. He used the curtain rails that provide a modicum of privacy around each bed to guide him. He was the only patient in the ward who could reach and even think about using the flimsy, dusty fixture as a handrail. Crash. The whole thing hit the ground, the beds, the machines. Luckily the bed next to Jhonnie's was empty. Although every family on this floor would appreciate the irony of having survived brain surgery, Intensive Care and unspeakable mashed potato only to die in a freak curtain rail accident, we were lucky the bed was empty. The nurses were at a loss to know how to restrain him. Now that Jhonnie could stand up, and would be aware if he was, say, tied to a bed day and night, they had to watch him like a hawk. And I know none of them was in the position to do that effectively.

I arrived half an hour early one morning to find Jhonnie sitting calmly in a bed full of his own shit. He had less awareness of his condition than Patrick. No cry. No sign. Jhonnie sat calmly in the centre of a large mess. I grabbed a towel, kissed him hello and sprinted.

'I'll be right back with a nurse, Jhonnie.'

'Don't go. You just got here.'

They moved quickly. I don't know how long he'd been sitting like that, or how often it happened. Any day now, a team of professionals would be teaching him how to make cheese on toast.

Pete still visited every night. They spoke French (or talked pretentious shit, as I preferred to put it) and talked about the rugby, edging ever closer – Jhonnie now knew most of the time that the World Cup was about to start. Esther and Pete ran an elaborate email scalping scheme that didn't make anybody any money. They had takers for 'that brain-injured guy's tickets' all over the country. Brothers of friends, and clients with cousins and apparent total strangers ended up knowing about the accident, or had once played pool with Jhonnie in

Morocco. The six degrees of Jhonnie's ticket separation was almost a serendipitous story of its own. As Pete and Esther filled Jhonnie in about the happy recipients of his tickets in Melbourne, Brisbane, Gosford, Canberra and Adelaide he appeared to be delighted, as if hearing the news they'd won the lottery. So many of them had. Jhonnie appeared to have bought more rugby tickets than I had taken hot dinners to Royal North Shore.

Jhonnie's neuropsych reports improved gradually. His PTA (post-traumatic amnesia) scores increased from a daily average of zero out of 12 to about six out of 12. Rehabilitation at eventual freedom would require 12 out of 12. He was beginning to be bored by the constant questions about who and where and when he was. He still got many of the answers wrong but his pleasant exasperation with the process led us to believe that he could recall being asked the same tedious questions only hours before. He very occasionally understood that the results reflected the speed of his recovery. He seemed more often to be baffled by how few of the staff had any idea where they were, and it was slightly unprofessional for them to keep asking him.

EMAIL FROM HUGH TO RUTH

I'm free anytime next week to help you with Ryde if you want.

I have to tell you that the most touching thing about Friday was Jhonnie saying, 'What's brought me back and what keeps me is going has been Rufus, even when I had no idea what had happened I was clinging to the thought that I had to get back for her . . .'

I'm sure he's told you that personally but it wouldn't hurt to hear it from me too.

It's been a miracle and you've been amazing.

Hugh

EMAIL FROM RUTH TO HUGH

Dear Hugh

Don't make me cry. You have been very amazing, too.

    xrr

So confused by receiving a compliment from you, I may have to go for a brisk walk. I will take you up on Ryde offer. Maybe Wednesday afternoon, and we'll take the kids?

EMAIL FROM HUGH TO RUTH

Ruth

You know I'm far too much of an egomaniac to throw compliments around . . . and if I don't spray them around towards you it's just because I expect a lot from you . . . I always thought you were just so bloody talented at life and it's taken me years to realise that what you have achieved in your life is mostly the result of sheer bloody hard work and if I've never said it before then I'm saying it now, unfortunately at this most difficult of times . . . but I don't know anyone who could have held up under the events of the last few weeks as you have, and turned it into the miracle that it's become, of teamwork, of family and of love. It's not over yet, but I hope for you and for Jhonnie and for all of us that the hard yards have been fought and won.

    hh

Day 25

For no reason anyone explained, Jhonnie had to move out of 7B and upstairs to an ordinary hospital ward for his last night before shuffling off to Buffalo. It was a move we could have lived without. I'd already started shipping home some of the kids' art, and odd boxes of long-life juice that Pete had brought in. There were dictaphones, and unopened books, and presents from well-wishers that made each trip back to a distantly parked car just that little bit more tedious. Now I had to take Jhonnie a large overnight bag of clothes (I packed for a health farm, but without the trashy novels). We pulled his art and photos down from the windows to reveal yellowed tape stains and the ugly industrial wasteland that surrounded the hospital. It was like moving out of a particularly skanky share house at university. I kept checking his two drawers, knowing we wouldn't find that missing bag of dope, or one lone earring. And it was a Saturday. Weekends were hopelessly understaffed and half-mast around here. I had the kids with me, and Therese. Juggling little eskies and strollers and baby bags was easier with two adults.

Jhonnie met Patrick as if for the first time. He couldn't hold this baby, this velvety nodule in a little yellow jumpsuit. We lay Patrick on Jhonnie's chest, on the unpunctured lung, unbroken rib side. He stroked him with his good hand. William explained the various features, the care and operation of this little baby. Jhonnie didn't recognise Pat at all, but appeared to fall in love with him instantly. Therese and I would look at each other and look away. Teary heartwarming little vignettes at every turn.

We'd brought in a poached chicken salad full of wild rocket, fennel and dazzling red ox-heart tomatoes. I cut crusty rolls on the tray-trolley for the last time, and didn't worry about the crumbs. We were just about to eat when a young family wandered in. I assumed that they were lost. Backlit, I couldn't see their faces, but when I heard those unmistakable voices, I could barely hide my surprise.

She had one of the few Irish accents, with an inbuilt lilt of disappointment, that's actually annoying. His voice was classic East London, the standard issue dialect of ad-men everywhere since the early '80s. They were a couple that had been friends of the Jhonnie and Chris Blampieds. Not the Jhonnie and Ruth Blampieds. (Their marriage had temporarily broken up at the same time as Chris and Jhonnie's. Ever since, after a few drinks, she would moan to me, with a long wistful look, 'You had better take care of my boy, mind!') After a while, as is the natural law of attrition with the division of friends, we never saw them again. We hadn't seen them in five years. But they turned up today, with flowers, and biscuits, and *their kids*. And Jhonnie had no idea who they were.

''Allo, mate. Look at you then. Sitting up in bed. Looking a million pounds.' Her eyes began to water melodramatically, and she grabbed fast for Jhonnie's good hand. I could barely speak. I removed Patrick from the action. I passed him to Therese. She walked out to the hall and came back, hovering.

'Hello. What on earth? What are you . . . ?'

I genuinely struggled to remember their names and couldn't introduce them to Therese. I think the inappropriateness of this gathering struck me in the moment. There I was with my kids and my oldest friend from school. Therese and I had met in kindergarten, taken our first Holy Communion together, gone to Loreto together, studied communications at university together. *She* had sensitivity to privacy, to the privilege of being involved with Jhonnie's recovery, and yet these blow-ins were oblivious. As for their great lumpish children, who stood, jaws dropped in astonishment at the appearance of the brain-injured man, I had never known their names and had no interest to learn them now.

'You'll have to excuse us. We're about to have lunch.'

He pulled up a chair. She lurched onto the bed.

'Have you got a kiss for your Uncle Jhonnie?' she whined to the daughter. The kid didn't. She was frightened, and hid behind her father's chair, not wanting to touch this total stranger with the bulging eye and swollen shaved head. What can they have been thinking?

He acknowledged me.

'He's doing great then. Yeah. Chris told me he'd be leaving on Monday, so I thought we'd better nip in. Give him our love. Cheer him up. When are you going to be up and around, big fella?'

Jhonnie smiled benignly, confused as to time and place and gathering.

I could feel my face reddening with anger. She leaned over and whispered into Jhonnie's ear.

He kept his bouncy tone afloat.

'And this little man must be . . . Billy?'

'William.' William looked less benign than his father.

I finally took her aside. Did I drag her off Jhonnie's bed? I might have.

'I'm going to have to ask you to leave. And if you are speaking to *anybody* else Jhonnie used to work with, *a decade ago*, tell 'em this is not the time or place. I'm afraid Chris gave you the wrong impression.'

She looked affronted, then gathered herself together for the patient. 'Well you enjoy your lunch then, darlin'. We'll be moving on then. Some little presents in there for you. You open them later maybe, when you're alone.' She spoke as if to the deaf or elderly.

He dawdled, inconceivably.

'And what are you doing for work now, Ruth? You're not in advertising anymore, are you? What are you doing then?'

'Taking care of Jhonnie,' I replied stiffly, and turned away. They couldn't still be standing there, surely?

After they left, I served the chicken salad and rolls, and cracked open a bottle of mineral water. (Where was that Scotch bottle when you needed it?) What a surreal invasion. Even around here, the encounter had been unusually odd. Jhonnie seemed unfussed and finally decided, 'This chicken is delicious. A lot of the nurses are Irish now. A lot of them are fat.'

It could have come straight from the mouth of William.

Jhonnie and his bed piled high with belongings went to 8C. Therese went ahead with the boys. I stopped to look back, the way they do in the finale of every long-running sit-com, at the set that has been the scene of so many high jinks. There was really nothing to see, with the bed gone, and Jhonnie's messy, kid-like niceties evacuated. This was just another empty corner, by a window, in a dull, broken-down hospital ward. At the door two ambulance men stopped. They were out of breath and looking for me.

'Are you Mrs Blampied?' (Wrong pronunciation, again. It came out 'Blamp-eyed'. Mostly people went for Blom-peed. I'd insisted that our boys have names anyone could spell and pronounce. Blampied was burden enough without adding the complication of Sacytcha! Mental note: before next medical catastrophe, change name by deed poll to Smith.) 'The nurses said you might still be here.'

'I am.'

When they introduced themselves, I noticed one was holding the heart rate monitor Jhonnie had been wearing on the day of the accident. They hadn't brought him in. They just started to work on him when the helicopter arrived. Somehow the bit of gismo had been rolling back and forth on the dash for a month. They hadn't thought to bring it in before because they assumed that Jhonnie would be, well . . . anyway, a nurse in Emergency had just told them he was alive.

They were bowled over. Alive.

'He's great. You just missed him. We're going upstairs and then to Ryde Rehab.'

They beamed. They were amazed. They were so happy they'd just caught me.

'Thank you. Thank you for everything you did there. Thanks for saving him. Damn. I wish you'd seen him. Damn.'

I burst into tears, and one of the ambos put his arm around my shoulders, easily, automatically. What bizarre jobs they have.

'You must have had a bit of a shock.' He laughed a little. Okay to laugh, now. Who knew that I was so close to tears. They wandered down the hall marvelling to each other. I could tell from the tone of their voices and their gestures they had mentally buried that big guy on the racing bike a month ago.

Upstairs, Jhonnie was confused and panicking. He had to get to a meeting. His suit bag was still on the baggage carousel. The clients were expecting him. He calmed down when I found him, but none of the nurses knew us, and he couldn't convince them he was supposed to be going home in the car with me.

A different ward. Different light. Different trolley. I couldn't operate the bed. Perhaps Jhonnie only functioned in the tiny world of 7B. I hoped he was ready for rehab. This place was fine, actually, just a normal hospital ward. Nobody here was going to die, yet. An unscheduled visit from Father Kelly seemed to bookend our stay here. Jhonnie didn't recognise him. When I explained that Kelly had prayed by his bed in Intensive Care (how close were we to last rites?) and now Jhonnie was a Catholic, we all laughed, and they talked about rugby. Father Kelly couldn't hide his amazement at the recovery.

We looked at each other in the hall.

'Miracle?'

'Miracle,' he concurred.

And then a young man who had worked as a junior suit for Jhonnie briefly, in 1990, walked down the corridor with a bottle of red wine. I headed him off at the pass, and told him Jhonnie couldn't see another soul, or him, for that matter.

'Well, he might like the wine.'

'He's brain injured,' I hissed, as if that would mean anything to this near total stranger who must have thought there was professional mileage in visiting the great man in hospital. I know I was rude. He apologised, limply, and turned on his heel. He turned back, and offered me the wine.

'Well, maybe later.'

I took it. Maybe, in the car park, I thought. Now we couldn't get to Ryde fast enough.

Day 26

EMAIL FROM RUTH TO JHONNIE'S LIST

How can I put this politely? No, why should I put this politely? Prepare to be offended: people who Jhonnie doesn't know or even like are 'visiting'. People not on this list. People we don't socialise with. People Jhonnie would never visit in hospital are turning up to have a look.

I'm not going to swallow an argument for misplaced good intentions. You all ask what you can do to help. Nothing. Absolutely nothing until instructed otherwise.

Jhonnie finds these visits unwelcome, confusing and a complete imposition. I find them an invasion of our family's privacy and genuinely destructive. I am really angry.

This is not a peep show.

Tell anyone who asks you that Jhonnie is not receiving callers until further notice. The handful of regulars is all scheduled and knows the routine. The rest of you can take your curiosity elsewhere. I am off to move Jhonnie into rehab. To everybody else who has offered nothing but love, support, brilliant emails, lasagnas, dog walking, child minding and wonderful constructive suggestions, thanks for your friendship and sensitivity.

I'm not one bit sorry for the tone of this email. I'm only sorry that I had to write it at all.

more later

xrr

That was the end of Royal North Shore Hospital. Part of me missed it already. The new address was inconvenient, uglier (hard to imagine, but true), and much harder to juggle with a small baby. And although I knew this was the only way to get Jhonnie well enough to come home, I felt somehow usurped. Jhonnie would have a full dance card: speech therapy, physiotherapy, occupational therapy, hydrotherapy, neuropsychological testing, counselling, cheese-on-toast making and stamp buying.

Would there be nothing for me to do? I would be on the road at peak hour, twice most days, like real people, in offices. I'd escaped the tyranny of peak hour traffic in the clogged arteries that pump the pergola-building masses from their renovated homes to their very promising jobs. I'd managed to successfully avoid these realities for . . . well, forever. It was payback time. I had happily knocked suburbia in feature articles for decades; now suburbia was fighting back, placing gourmet kitchen showroom-shaped hurdles in my path.

Behind the wheel I became a Monaro-driving hoon, again. I turned the music up to 11, sang wildly out of tune, and buzzed slow drivers at the lights. If Jhonnie had stayed in rehab for a year, I would have taken up drag racing.

I arrived at Ryde before visiting hours, but a long time after Jhonnie's ambulance, to find him sedated, tucked neatly into a cot in a four-bed ward, quite close to the front door.

It's a funny old rambling place. New wings butt up to old. Chipped paint, maybe 20 layers deep, on high-arched door-jambs meet broken-down 1980s particle-wood joinery – the kind that can never be properly cleaned, or fixed, or loved. The kind of stuff that nobody steals when it's left on the footpath on council pick-up day.

The whole place – the buildings, the furniture, the crockery, the gym mats, the staff, the patients – looked as if nobody would rescue them from a footpath. At least Jhonnie was asleep.

His cubicle was bare but for his overnight bag (hopefully no point in unpacking *here*) and a huge free-standing floral arrangement in a bucket sent by my cousin Tracey. She knew this hospital, and from her more recent experiences as a patient, she knew that some lurid natural colour might just improve a very dank beginning. She was right. As Jhonnie slept I got lost in the outrageous tropical cocktail of lilies. Tracey and I always sent each other peonies at the beginning of November. It was a month early, so crazy loud lilies, sunflowers and artichokes would have to do. Tracey's flu had finally passed, but she still didn't sound great. I couldn't tell if there was something else up with her health, or if she knew darker truths about Jhonnie's case that she'd decided not to share.

A nurse glided in to check his charts. More charts. More new faces. More tired nurses. I didn't bother to introduce myself.

'He gave us a bit of trouble. In the navy, is he? An officer? He put up quite a fight.'

'No. He's in advertising.'

She laughed out loud. 'Well he's very concerned about the Nazis taking his wife and kids prisoner.'

'Well, he would be. We're Jewish. Jewish enough to be taken by the Nazis.'

Why was I even having this conversation?

'So, he's not in the secret service.'

'If he is, all those McDonald's conferences have provided an ingenious cover.'

I sat for hours and Jhonnie finally woke up just before I had to return to the kids. He was still groggy and stressed about my safety. The paddy-wagon (ambulance) had taken him to the border. He couldn't convince the guards (nurses) that it was time to head for the hills, and join the resistance, but not without his family. I would be waiting for him at a previously agreed secret meeting spot, and if he wasn't there, I would know he had been captured, or killed.

After a month at Royal North Shore, I would have thought that a little road trip down the M2 would have been diverting enough, without the introduction of Nazis. When I was a child my father had warned me that if it happened again, if Holocaust II ever made it to Australia, he and Julia and I would be the first to go. Good to have a getaway plan, and some portable assets, and cash, in a safe. Some kids just learn how to ride a bike with their dad. Not us.

Jhonnie finally came good, and was impressed with the novelty of his new surroundings, and while he could appreciate that he was no longer active in the secret service, he was still very concerned about our losing contact when I walked out that door. The guy in the other bed looked amused. I didn't care about our lack of privacy, about his obvious eavesdropping. He was held together by springs and wires and haloes of taut steel. I didn't ask how he had come to be in this nearly comical predicament, but he looked like the Coyote immediately after he's sucked in to another of the Roadrunner's ploys.

We roamed the hideous gardens, Jhonnie walking as slowly as a woman two days after a caesarian (me, four months and a lifetime ago). We decided to explore the facilities and have lunch in the 'rec' room. Right name, wrong spelling. An oddly configured space filled with ill-matching couches and chairs, draughts – abandoned mid-game – and a kitchenette corner, where patients made instant coffee with hot water from the tap. We ate lunch with blinkers on, facing a stained wall. It was a late lunch, as a result of Jhonnie's exhausting escape through Europe. We held hands and didn't say much. His roommate seemed to have followed us in and sat quite close by, 'not wanting to intrude', listening to every word. What, nothing on television?

'I can't believe I get to do all this with you,' Jhonnie said rather romantically, to break a silence. Finally it was time for me to go. The 20-metre walk took 10 minutes.

I'd brought Jhonnie Thai take-away for dinner. Not homemade, but spicy, foreign, not hospital food. A reminder of the outside world, a life ahead, a thing that any couple might pick up when one is too tired to cook, a normal choice: that's what a take-away container of red duck curry, pad thai and boiled rice had come to represent. We found a crusty microwave oven and a nurse who might, or might not, heat it up for him later on, because they serve dinner at five. But he'd just had lunch. Couldn't someone help him heat it later? We'll see. All beyond my control.

I left through the wrong door, misguided by the wrong exit sign, and wandered around the grounds for precious minutes looking for my car, trying to get my bearings, swearing under my breath. The adrenalin kicked in as I sped down Victoria Road. Just try to book me, I thought. That would make a nice switch for the police officer. Mad woman shouting from her speeding vehicle, 'Catch me if you can! Car chase? I dare ya!'

I drove down inside lanes, jumping parked cars, a wild-eyed Catherine Zeta-Jones behind the wheel. I was speeding *away* from Ryde, not towards my kids and my next shift. I would have liked a cigarette, and a shot of tequila. I felt a shivering, rollercoaster thrill that seemed impossible as I passed the car yards and Hungry Jack's and bathroom showrooms of Victoria Road at dusk. Life went on, ordinary, repetitive, blissfully dull life went on, but not for me. I was speeding away from . . . from what?

There is something peculiar about going through one of those bone-breakingly frightening life versus death experiences. Like bungy jumping or taking drugs, or breaking the law – you really know you're alive when your husband tickles death. You can actually feel your heart pumping your blood and propelling you forwards in something quite like exhilaration. Now *there's* a guilty pleasure I would never have factored in to life's rich tapestry.

waterlemon

EMAIL FROM RUTH TO JHONNIE'S LIST

I think Jhonnie put it well when he said, 'I'm so happy to be here. I'm so happy you're here. Have you come to get me out of here?'

The road to rehabilitation appears to be as long and ugly as Victoria Road – the main artery from our house to Ryde. Nearly an hour door to door, and the street is lined with kitchen showrooms. It seems that everybody west of Taylor Square is enjoying cheap and brazenly hideous kitchens from the looks of these flourishing showrooms. So the kitchens get uglier and the petrol gets cheaper (81 cents! Really!) the closer I get to Jhonnie.

And so, nearly a month into this trip, we are the new chums all over again. Whole new cast of characters, shiny floors, broken drawers and endless forms to chew through. Really should have scalped my two-month parking card at RNS. (Worth a fortune.) After weeks of sliding that thing into the left cup of my bra for safekeeping, it can hit the bin.

Jhonnie was very disoriented by the move, in spite of his excitement at progress. He thought perhaps war had broken out and he was being taken prisoner, until he saw faces on Lane Cove Road, and they looked normal, and he started to relax. (Glad the ambo didn't go down Victoria Road!)

But we got him settled in, walked around and got our bearings. Jhonnie and I are such hotel pigs. When I think of all the glamorous bar fridges, gyms, pools and foyers we've dived into with enthusiasm: Venice, London, Bangkok, New York, running wild like naughty kids. We've been so lucky. Now I'm obliged to consider us lucky yet again, as we sit in a hideous rec room, Jhonnie eating my goulash polenta and broccolini, while a man three feet away, held together by more pins than William's Meccano set, watches TV and eavesdrops. We're really lucky to be sitting together, having a conversation, having lunch. We had to remind ourselves over and over. We also had quite a time deciding if the dribbling stains on the wall were Coke, urine or coffee. If this was a hotel . . . yeah well that's all ahead of us.

The visiting hours are shocking. The place is butt ugly (Brain Injury Unit will be better). The road trip is a shocker, and everybody involved is so tired that an injection of Rugby World Cup adrenalin can't come around soon enough.

No Foxtel at Ryde, not yet, and we're working on it.

Jhonnie said today that he really can't see the meaning in this yet. He'd already taken all the steps towards changing our lives by leaving that job. He thinks maybe that the meaning will be for somebody else – clearly not the uninvited morons who plagued him on the weekend. Then he said with what seemed like hilarious insight, 'Perhaps it was just an accident.'

More later

Xrr

I wasn't getting accustomed to having a husband who spent a good deal of his time in a Steve McQueen film, but I certainly found these episodes less alarming than one might imagine. I was assured that the delusional aspects of Jhonnie's amnesia would decrease as he recovered, and also that any sudden change in routine or undue stress could rock his world. Nobody was shocked that Jhonnie had gone on something of a brain-damaged trip, simply because he'd left home – the only home he'd known since the accident, the Royal North Shore. I didn't miss it, but at least I knew it. We would both get to know Ryde soon enough.

EMAIL FROM TRACEY TO RUTH

From someone with a tolerably tasteful kitchen west of Victoria Road . . . I NEVER GET ON VIC RD – it's invariably shitful. I would think about going towards the M2 (Channel 10) and veering left. Given that I can usually get to you off peak in 30 mins – it's worth a try. This is the beginning of the last bit of this horrible journey. Give JB our love.

Trace

w a t e r l e m o n

Jo's husband James came back from a trip. In all her cheerful, bouncy support, Jo hadn't mentioned that she'd been coping with two kids on her own. I must have known, because James had sent funny emails from hotel rooms across America. A keen cyclist himself, James had been looking forward to the big road race with Jhonnie. Since Jhonnie's stunt our legions of lazy friends felt vindicated for their commitment to couch/beer/ TV; and all the others, the running/riding/swimming minority, were just a little bit jumpy about leaving the house in trainers.

EMAIL FROM JAMES TO JHONNIE

Dear Jhonnie,

I met a Tohby last night. Must have had the same spelling teacher. I'm sorry, big boy, I haven't got out to see you yet. Unfortunately, I've been away. Well, fortunately for me as I was in LA, NY and London, but unfortunately for you as you were deprived of my company. Still, I must say the communications room is working very well. Regular emails, photo shoots – are the film rights still available? I know some people now, and if we can't get this up on HBO or at least *Australian Story* – with a lovely inspirational song by Delta Goodrem – then we are not even trying.

Can I just say, that if you didn't want to do the Sydney–Wollongong ride, then all you had to do was say so? Actually, the real piss off for me in this whole affair is that you have just ruined any chance of me getting back on a bike. I know that's a little bit selfish, but you should see Joanne when I suggest I might just ride to work. Insists on an ambulance following me all the way. I have to get off and walk across intersections, and wear a very daggy orange reflector vest. Hardly the Lance Armstrong image I was hoping for.

Anyway, the other good news of course is that you are now part of my listening demographic. The aged, the home office worker, the sales reps in cars and those in institutions – that's my

195

gang in the afternoons, so welcome! Find the AM dial, turn to 702 and it's just merry japes all afternoon.

I'm hoping to get out to see you in the next week or so.

We'll try not to turn up when World Cup games are on – which might be a challenge in the next month. Fantastic to see the last bunch of photos, and you looking so strong and handsome. Or was that Patrick?

Thinking of you often,

Love James

Letters were flying in every direction. So many new emails came in from all over the world. And angry phone calls flew between the Blampieds and Pete and Julia. Pete was still visiting every night, but now making the much longer inconvenient pilgrimage to Ryde. Then, in the car on the way home, he would phone-a-Blampied, and often listen to their complaints and fears for the whole trip home before getting around to an update on Jhonnie. I don't know how he did it, but my decision to speak to them no more had certainly created breathing room.

Jhonnie's laksa mates who were keen to buy into the visiting schedule had been away on school holidays, but came back, for the Cup, and spent evenings with Jhonnie as well.

I walked in one afternoon to find Jhonnie telling Sam how this accident had been the most romantic episode of his life, because even in coma, he could hear my voice, and he knew he'd be okay. He remembered being shown his life, like a very long montage in a B-grade movie and he felt he would just be prepared to let it all go. He'd seen it, after all, until it got to me. Then he'd hear my voice and follow it out, until he got here. And that's the only way he'd know if something was real or not. Like the Germans trying to take him prisoner on the way from Royal North Shore. He worked out that that was probably a fantasy because I wasn't in it. That's how he got confused. He was looking for me and the kids, but I wasn't actually *in* it. So even though, at first, he didn't know who or what he was, or who or where I was, he just followed me. And fell in love all over again, as if for the first time. Wouldn't everybody want that chance if they could take it? The chance to meet your wife and fall in love again, without the distractions of work and traffic and phones and deadlines, wouldn't everybody grab at that?

Jhonnie couldn't recommend the restorative, romantic value of a good head injury highly enough. In marriage counselling terms, he appeared to have tripped over the new dirty weekend in Noosa.

Sam sat slack-jawed. Jhonnie happily skipped onto the topic of his new annoying trainers and how they're already falling apart in the pool. Sam looked at me. I must have been blushing.

'He's amazing. That's amazing!'

That he is.

Meanwhile my mother had been busy stirring up help and prayers, and sour beef and beans, in every direction. She went to the Nut Shop (one of our family's regular sweet-tooth pilgrimages) and bought up kilos of toffee-coated brazil nuts, boxes of smoked almonds, assortments of pistachios, choc-coated prunes, Vienna almonds, hazelnut clusters dipped in dark chocolate, and milk chocolate ginger in quantity. She packaged up hampers of these nutty assortments, and then asked for the addresses of various friends and some lovely mums from William's preschool who had taken up the slack since the accident. That afternoon they all arrived home to nut heaven and a sweet card from my mother. There's a good chance that no one is as fond of nuts or milk chocolate ginger as my mother, or the rest of the family for that matter. But they all found the gesture adorable. They're lucky Dad wasn't still alive or it might have been mud crabs, a sack of broad beans or a case of cherries.

Mum came to visit at Ryde, and talked to Jhonnie about his family. She couldn't help thinking that they just didn't understand the Herculean effort involved in getting him back on his feet. They must just be frightened, and frustrated at being unable to help. She decided to write a letter – from one parent to another – to break the unpleasant impasse.

Dear Michael and Gabriella,

How awful for you to be so far away from your son at this harrowing time, and (like me) to realise how little you could do if you were near.

On the day of the accident Ruth had to race to the hospital, where I joined her to sit out some of most horrendous hours of our lives. We had the comfort of knowing he had been flown with least possible delay to the Royal North Shore Hospital, one of the very best in our entire country for such emergencies. We sat in an adjoining room as hour by hour they reported to us every procedure. You might picture Ruth's feelings, still not up to par from the caesarean surgery, and the usual ensuing sleeplessness from three-hourly feeds. Not knowing if her dearly loved husband and father of her children would survive, become a paraplegic or lose his mental faculties.

All I could do was phone my dear friends the Sisters of St Joseph nuns to pray in force to their founder, the blessed Mary McKillop, who is beatified and in line to become Australia's first saint. I still feel Jhonnie's incredible progress to date is the miracle they need. Such a huge wave of intercession and positive thoughts surely works, no matter what religious belief.

In the time Jhonnie has been here he has established himself in the real affections of many, many genuine friends and the lasting love of both my daughters. You probably don't know Ruth well but she is a steadfast character and has real strength — Jhonnie couldn't have a better partner. Julia regards Jhonnie as a dear brother and in the last weeks has given every waking minute (and her formidable skills as an organiser) to rallying all possible help and liaising with the incredibly generous Pete. Ruth visits the hospital daily, to shave him, shower him, take him palatable food, drawings and recordings from all his children.

In all of this I am a comparative bystander. My impaired vision makes my practical value limited; I can say I am incredibly proud of my generous seemingly indefatigable daughters. I miss seeing them; I miss talking to them (I deal on the telephone with Julia — hesitant to even phone Ruth when I know she is averaging about three hours' sleep a night.

Now Jhonnie is finally being admitted to the top rehabilitation hospital. We think his mind, with a few lapses, is being coaxed back to complete memory. Ruth and correspondence from overseas organised by Julian really help.

As parents there is not much practical help we can offer but to stand by, stay healthy (they don't need anxiety over us as well) and try to radiate our love and concern. Remember, your son is a real candidate for complete recovery — he has a patient and accepting nature, which is a real bonus. Ruth has the backing of long-time loyal women friends, some from kindergarten days. She will need energy and resolve for the restoration ahead. Jhonnie is lucky. I can't honestly and dispassionately think of anyone with all Ruth's attributes to weather the storm.

So though you are not here, and it is not quite the

same, consider us as surrogates until there is the best possible
outcome, and you can be reunited with your son again.
   Regards
   Patricia Ritchie

I hadn't heard from Julian since the St Petersburg incident. He had been furious at my treatment of his father, then furious at Julia and Pete by proxy, so I hadn't missed our lugubrious conversations. Maybe Mum's letter, accompanied by another reassuring note from Julia, would smooth the waters.

And then the phone rang.

'Are you Ritchie women trying to kill my father?'

'What? Julian, did you read Mum's letter? She thought if they had a better understanding of what we're —'

'Oh we understand, all right. You don't think we love Jhonnie, and you don't think we have any rights to come and take care of him.'

'What? Can you hear yourself? When has there even been a question of any of you "caring for him" with or without a head injury? If I was on the other side of the world in a coma my family would hire a Learjet to get to me —'

'And your family can afford to.'

'Boo-hoo. Yours can only afford Fantasy Island weddings in Corfu and little excursions to St Petersburg. Nobody here can believe that there is not a Blampied alive willing to come here and help Jhonnie. And now, I'm so relieved you didn't come, because I'd be expected to make you endless cups of tea and pick your wet towels off the floor, while you ran around like headless chickens.'

'How dare you? Jhonnie's accident has devastated this entire family!'

'I dare. We can hear your theatrical grieving on the other side of the planet. It just doesn't do us any practical good.'

Who hung up? I can't remember. But I believe that's the last conversation I ever had with Julian Blampied.

EMAIL FROM PETE TO JULIA

Jules,

Julian has been on the phone to me too, incandescent with rage . . . which has prompted me to write to him as below, today.

I thought it prudent to copy you in case this stuff does another lap of Europe before coming back garbled.

I haven't copied Ruth, just to save her the trouble, but feel free to discuss/show/copy as you see fit.

Brace yourself, Pete xx

I am struck that twice in the last two days you have called to shout at me about what others have said and done, and while I don't mind, I am not sure this is helpful to you.

I suspect it's unhelpful to you because on neither occasion did we talk about Jhonnie, and on one occasion I was sitting next to Jhonnie and your fury directed at others prevented you speaking to him.

Tit-for-tat? Let me give you just one recent example of (what I see as) a futile, even destructive, point-scoring mentality that seems to pervade the family history (judging by the list of items you mentioned on Monday). You may construe the letters recently received from Pat/Julia as a selfish irrelevance, and wonder at their purpose. Is it not then trivially easy to see that early messages from Europe about burglaries, bad-luck/ incompetence with emails (including forgetting fax facilities) and trips to St Petersburg might also be construed as similarly selfish irrelevances, especially to people who have just spent six-plus hours by their loved one's bed in Intensive Care and are now juggling the needs of two small children, and fearing the worst outcomes?

I applaud your motives for taking on the liaison role but is it still needed? Michael and Vivvy (the ones believed by you to require shielding initially) have had frequent direct contact with all of us and know the whole story.

I'd prefer to be able to share with you the good news of your brother's progress than discuss third parties.

In closing, I would be happy to talk further for as long as you like, especially if it can be in a civilised and constructive manner.

Jhonnie has come to see this injury as an opportunity to review his life and its priorities. I am sure you can guess better than I can how he will feel about the past.

I am, however, confident he will make up his own mind. I already know I am going with his judgment of these recent events whatever it is, rebuke or praise or indifference.

He's my mate . . .

Day 29

EMAIL FROM RUTH TO JHONNIE'S LIST

Sorry for the gap in emails – hours of driving in inexplicable traffic, and very long hours at Ryde getting Jhonnie settled have taken their toll. We are all exhausted. Yesterday, a full month after the accident, we packed up the car: Julia, Hugh, William, Patrick and a rather good lamb beetroot leek eggplant salad. What a workout. Jhonnie was overjoyed. Hugh brought in his new jazzy camera and took some very happy pictures. You've seen a few by now. Jhonnie fed Patrick and read to William. I lay on Jhonnie's bed and wondered about checking in myself.

Today he is moving into the Brain Injury Unit, with his own room. They are very, very impressed with his progress. The occupational therapist – a nice uncomplicated girl (what's she going to do? Remind him how to acquire small companies and asset strip them?) – anyway, she says that after Jhonnie has demonstrated he knows how to buy a stamp (tricky. Usually that's 'Ruth, where are the stamps?') he might be ready for day leave. Maybe next weekend.

Next weekend.

Next weekend, as in the opening game of the Rugby World Cup?

Well, yes. He could do that, if he can remember how to make

a cup of tea and buy a stamp. Right. Amazing. I tell Jhonnie that there is a very real possibility he could attend the World Cup, to which he replies, if he can have day leave he'd rather come home.

Now, some of you may be thinking, how romantic. Greater love hath no man than to give up his Wallabies for his wife. But to those who know better, this is, if any more was ever required, proof of the severity of Jhonnie's head injury.

So, day passes and rugby matches are all within our grasp. In the meantime his schedule is busy, and for Jhonnie's sense of continuity we're keeping visits to Pete, Hugh and the family.

Jhonnie's brother Justin rang my mobile phone while I was sitting by Jhonnie's bed, and I passed him the phone. They had a great chat. Talking to Justin straight afterward, I could tell he was nearly passing out with delight. There is something very reassuring about hearing Jhonnie Blampied's sunny voice on the other end of the phone, even if he is still occasionally hiding from the Germans. So, one month later, and we are all holding it together. Patrick is now four months old and, as of this morning, off the charts for his age at four-month baby check-up. How like a Blampied. William is having sleep-overs with all his friends and a fabulous time at tennis, karate and horse riding (what head injury!). All over, our amazing family and friends continue to prop me up and every day we get closer to reclaiming our lives. Actually, that's probably crap, but every day I get more used to this bizarre situation, and can really only cope because I know Jhonnie *will* come home.

Thanks for all your ongoing support. Jhonnie knows how much he's loved, although still doesn't quite know the sensation he's created.

More later

xrr

EMAIL FROM JUSTIN TO RUTH AND JHONNIE
Bugger!

Well if that wasn't better than a million birthday presents wrapped up in a pizza, floating in a bathtub of beer – then I didn't just speak to my big brother!

Fuck me!

I can't stop smiling! I'm sitting at my computer speed-drinking a beer and I can't bloody call bloody anyone to tell them cause of the bloody stupid time difference in bloody LA!

Thank you so much Ruth – I am utterly totally and completely beside myself.

When you have a spare minute (and I know you don't) I'd love to talk about how he's getting on in more detail. Keep being wonderful . . .

All my love to you and the munchkins

Eric Von Stromm

Normally a new shopping centre is a treat. I can get excited about food markets in Adelaide, so really, a trip to a confusing little precinct known as Top Ryde would have been a welcome diversion under any other circumstances.

Jhonnie's trainers had fallen apart. I took his shoe size (enormous) and directions to this new mall. I don't want to insult the locals, but there is nothing 'top' about Top Ryde. Maybe I was tired, and certainly I was confused. I went up a down ramp. I searched in vain for pram parking (I need a disabled sticker NOW!) and I couldn't have gotten more lost or derailed if I was parking in Prague, in a blizzard, drunk. Sadly, that analogy does have a guilty ring of truth about it.

I seemed to have stumbled upon a unique shopping mall that should have come with a warning: *Beware: all the wrong shops, assembled for your convenience under one roof.*

I must have been close to tears by the time I found Tragic Feet – an unusual shop with precisely seven pairs of runners and a large staff of uninformed, uniformed 12 year olds. There were very few real shops in this mall. The real shops must have been somewhere else, because Tragic Feet could be found, logically enough, by the outrageously cheap hair-product outlet store ('You *won't* pay retail for your mousse!'), and the shop full of artificial flowers and hostess gifts made from broken mirrors and shells. Where was Athlete's Fucking Foot?

Back to the car, back down an up ramp and back to the hospital just in time for Jhonnie's next swimming lesson. It simply didn't matter that I'd bought the ugliest trainers in Christendom. They didn't fit. The physiotherapist and the occupational therapist both patted my back as I melted onto Jhonnie's bed and sobbed. Then Jhonnie pulled himself up out of his chair, out of the ill-fitting glass slipper, and scooped me up in his arms.

'There, there, little girl. Sorry my feet's too big.' And there it was. A month into this debacle, Jhonnie was actually comforting me about his accident for the first time. 'She's been through a lot, this girl . . .' he told the assembled therapists, who nodded politely while the brain-injured patient explained our plight, complete with new baby. And I cried.

The idea of leaning on my husband had become so remote, it never occurred to me that I would be able to rely on anyone ever again. Jhonnie was actually walking back into this picture a player, not just a near-deadweight to be nursed. Calling me by old pet names and trying to help. Jhonnie was coming back. I dried my eyes, and pretty soon our little group was laughing.

'I really fucking frightened the good people of Top Ryde. I think I stood in the middle of the mall, waving my arms announcing, "This can't be it! This can't be all there is?" I promise you I don't behave this way at Bondi Junction!'

Driving back to revisit Tragic Feet for the exchange, I marvelled at Jhonnie's patience. I couldn't do it. Just being unfamiliar with the shops, just not being able to coolly slip into my favourite parking spots, had totally undone me. I'd fallen apart trying to buy a pair of trainers because I was lost in Top Ryde. Since the accident, the entire world was Top Ryde to Jhonnie, and he seemed completely prepared to go up and down all the ramps to find his way home. Better him than me.

Day 31

EMAIL FROM RUTH TO JHONNIE'S LIST

Excuse my silence. The glorious goal of rehab has proved more challenging than Intensive Care. I had been warned, and really it's not that bad (or is it worse?).

The long weekend was a shocker. Unlimited visiting hours, how wonderful. Of course, nobody had told us that the entire place would shut down for three days. No rehab, no staff, no lights in the halls (thank you, Mr Howard, thank you, Mr Carr). Gyms, pool, everything locked tight as a drum. You could shoot a cannon off in the place – and if you hit anybody you'd have to go back to RNS – not a doctor, and barely a nurse in sight.

So. Jhonnie just sat on his bed, waiting for us every day. We took the kids and nice picnic lunches. William played soccer with his dad, and collected sticks in the grounds. We took Jhonnie for long walks and pushed him with a bit of painful yoga and Pilates. But schlepping and driving and timing Pat's feeds (he continues to be the most congenial baby, but a baby, none the less) is fraying every nerve.

Madi and Connar came back from holidays and Pete and Nicole took them to visit their dad on Monday. That all went really well. By Tuesday I was tired and really angry – went in and gave anyone who'd listen a serve – not blaming them, mind you, but if

208

nothing is going to happen here, then I'm going to bring in a trainer, and acupuncture and a massage, because Jhonnie is going mad in this prison!

See, none of this is Intensive Care – it's not life support. It is excruciating care, and although everybody here continues unabated support, the traffic and the shoes and the outrageous phone calls with hopelessly selfish interested parties are all taking their toll.

Jhonnie improves every day, but his frustration with the lack of rehabilitation that actually takes place in rehab is growing. Again thanks to everybody for the emails and all the good stuff.

more later

x rr

Day 34

I'D MISSED EVERYBODY'S BIRTHDAYS. Simon, Jo and Esther all celebrate birthdays within a four day period. This traditionally hectic, drunken, expensive little festival always coincides with the October long weekend. My friends must have celebrated more quietly or separately this year.

Meanwhile, we'd spent the long weekend buoying up the loneliest little boy in rehab. The anticlimax of the deserted wards was steeper because of our excitement at finally getting Jhonnie into the actual Brain Injury Unit. This was a new building, a separate wing from the original wards. The hospital had been set up as a home for destitute invalids, incurables with nowhere else to go. But that was at the turn of the twentieth century, before we'd built any recreational machines capable of carrying a man fast enough to inflict a serious head injury. The sparkling 'new' Brain Injury Unit was a place for angry young men who'd driven too fast, or too drunk, or walked off a cliff, or ridden wildly out of control on their shiny racing bikes. Perhaps they represented some new form of destitution.

They each had their own room, their own mugs, and their own unpredictable anger about their injuries. In a movie, this is where Jhonnie would make great friends with some seamy character played by Willem Dafoe who, while looking like a rat

caught in barbed wire, would turn out to be the most enlight-
ened man alive. If that was going to happen, he hadn't been
admitted yet.

There were three other patients in the unit. One of them,
a teenage boy, was very close to checking out. There was a 30-
something car accident and a 40-something stroke. And they
had no more insight into their conditions than Jhonnie had
about his part in the downfall of the Nazis. Not one of these
men had anything in common with the others, except brain
injury.

We made-over the room straightaway. We took in bedside
lamps, a portable TV, vases and flowers from our garden, and his
pictures went up on the walls. His window looked out on sad
men smoking on the verandah, so we kept the curtains at half-
mast. And none of it really mattered, because Jhonnie would be
dressed and out of bed all day, getting rehabilitated.

But first he had to ablute. Jhonnie had never been quick in
the bathroom. Now, on rediscovering the razor and the mirror,
he had become glacial. We took in big bathsheet towels from
his own bathroom. The standard-issue tea towel variety didn't
wrap around Jhonnie's waist for him to shave. The bathroom
was communal. But Jhonnie's shaving kit and toiletries seemed
to roll out and dominate the shelves over the other men's more
basic razors and deodorant.

'Shower, shit and a shave!' one of the men declared each
morning as he emerged from the bathroom like a shiny new,
somewhat bent, pin. If Jhonnie hadn't been six foot six, they
might have beaten him up for his 'extra rich emollient night
cream', electric toothbrush, dental floss, Q-tips and aftershave
moisturiser. We had been warned that brain injuries can leave
victims with a hygiene bypass. Not so Jhonnie. He spent an
hour each morning getting presentable.

Sprucing made him late for hydrotherapy or physio. They
reorganised his schedule, and finally the pieces began to fit

together. The speech therapist was gorgeous, and Jhonnie loved her. The physio reminded me of a curiously ageless nun, and she and Jhonnie seemed to talk more than work, but she got him up and down those three steps every day. In occupational therapy, the men in Jhonnie's ward had to take turns in opening tins of spaghetti and heating them in the microwave. Surely cheese on toast couldn't be too far off.

The hydrotherapy pool attracted another strange group, not only the men from Jhonnie's ward. Fully clad adults stood in warm shallow water, trying to lift their arms above their heads, trying to pass a ball from one hand to another, trying to just lie back and float. Before long this would be Patrick at swimming class, and I would at first be in the pool, then by the pool, talking to other parents with pride about our charges. The hydrotherapy pool was no different. A potent cocktail of chlorine, urine and steam, we'd been warned that swimsuits would perish within weeks, so old was best. The ragged attire of these patients didn't help the tableau. The smell and the humidity made it difficult to cheer from the sidelines.

There were a few other soccer mums on the benches. One Chinese woman had been here, encouraging her 22-year-old daughter who was recovering from an aneurism, for six months. I could see the girl in the pool. She wasn't performing appreciably better than Jhonnie. She hated the water, so she was really very reluctant to hit the pool each day. Jhonnie was a very strong swimmer, and always fond of a hot bath though preferably not in shoes. He was an obedient, enthusiastic patient. What a pity. Her daughter had succumbed to depression over the long course of the recovery. I suggested she stop her daughter from eating the food. Institutional food makes you lose perspective and hope. Eat those carrots for long enough and you'd end up drinking this pool with a few olives tossed in. She hadn't thought about the food.

It's always mothers. Not brothers, not daughters. Right

now, mothers are holding old faded beach towels on benches beside hydrotherapy pools everywhere, comparing the progress of their loved ones with other mothers. How was I ever going to get back to being Jhonnie's wife now that I'd seen him through potty training and swimming lessons?

Day 35

THERESE RANG ME TO SAY that Jane's dad had died. Their family (nine children, 86,000 grandchildren) had been counting on Mother Mary McKillop for a cure from cancer, but they hadn't been as lucky as Jhonnie. Jane was one of my best friends from school. We'd been emailing each other about our various hospital experiences, and I was keen to make the funeral.

Several school choirs, an altar full of clergy and every prominent Catholic in Sydney filled St Mary's at North Sydney, a church we'd frequented all our lives. My grandparents had secretly married there. All the big funerals after all the untimely deaths at school – parents, even some children – were held at St Mary's. The nearly sainted Mary McKillop was buried around the corner. In our choir days we'd all been wheeled in to sing our hearts out upstairs in the suffocating loft, at funerals. And here we were for Jane.

Therese and I met outside. An enormous contingent from our school and university lives gathered, and somehow grouped together on the long dark benches. Some I hadn't seen in more than a decade. So much happy eye contact and recognition – there was a buoyant sense of occasion in the church. We could have all been meeting at the Newport Arms Hotel: sunburnt, in string bikinis, sitting around jugs of beer and baskets of hot chips. And afterwards, somebody would have fashioned a bong out of a Mr Juicy bottle, and we'd get stoned in our cars until the hour got late, and roam en masse to the Harbord Diggers to hear Mental as Anything or Hunters and Collectors sing the same songs every week. After waving and chanting 'Throw Your Arms Around Me', cooling off and sobering up enough to get back in our cars, we'd find our way back to our parents' houses, and our funny little single beds. That was my history with this motley crew. But this was Jane's dad's funeral.

I cried intermittently throughout, because it was a beautiful service, and because it made great sense to finally sit in church surrounded by a lot of very emotional people, and just cry.

All the eulogies were great. A famous old judge recalled their days as law students at Sydney University. They'd remained friends for life, an unlikely pair: one a Noel Coward—esque raconteur, the other an apparently serious Catholic husband and father of nine. Yet they were both very droll. He recalled Jane's mother asking her husband one morning, through his *Sydney Morning Herald*, what he would like for breakfast. Jane's father had replied: 'Two soft-boiled eggs and my misspent youth.'

So here was a life cut short, but still a whole long embellished amazing life, and we all laughed and cried to mark its passing. I looked around at my old friends, old boyfriends, old netball team-mates. I saw a church full of 40 year olds I'd known most of my life. A lot of them gave me kind, knowing looks. They all knew I'd only just managed to get out of hospital to come to a funeral. From now on we were just going to have to settle for soft-boiled eggs.

Day 36

EMAIL FROM RUTH TO JHONNIE'S LIST

Wonder of wonder! Miracle of miracles!

Who knew 36 days ago that we might be quoting *Fiddler on the Roof*? (With any luck I may close with a few choruses of 'Sunrise, Sunset'.)

Today, thanks to a last-minute cancellation, we had our first family conference. Normally scheduled once a month, we snuck in early. Jhonnie's entire rehab team assembled and reported on his progress. Also in attendance were Tracey (my cousin, but also very experienced nurse and psychologist), and moi, the nagging wife. The centrepiece, the man driving the biz, was, of course, Jhonnie.

Anyone who's ever pitched a piece of new business with Jhonnie, or had him as a partner in bridge (or life), or seen him effortlessly find his way out of a Westfield car park, would have appreciated today's performance. Tone and manner, perfect. Just the right level of humility, humour, confidence. A suitable demonstration of language, insight, caution.

Brilliant. Even with a serious head injury, Jhonnie can still bullshit a team of professionals. I couldn't have been more proud. The result of all this show-ponying: Jhonnie is coming home on Saturday for an overnight visit. Now they're talking weeks not months before Jhonnie becomes an outpatient.

One more sleep to the World Cup, and I have an enormous piece of expensive beef to buy. *So* – no phone calls, no visits. The rehab team has stipulated this. The home visit is about Jhonnie's recovery, not our necessity to get back to normal.

To those with visiting plans this weekend, we'll regroup and reassess by phone or email. Sorry to have so many of you on standby. Nature of the situation I guess. Well, back to babies, dog and dinner. For the first time, I have absolutely nothing planned.

more later

xrr

While I had managed to successfully avoid telephone conversation and consequent confrontation with Jhonnie's family, they had been receiving email updates. Pete would keep verbal contact going, but I thought including them in the more personal medical details, and Tracey's thorough report, would be helpful, not to mention diplomatic.

EMAIL FROM RUTH TO THE BLAMPIED FAMILY

Dear Blampieds,

All great news about Jhonnie. The rehab conference went brilliantly today, so I am forwarding you my cousin Tracey's notes from the meeting as an attachment. (Not for greater public viewing.) He reported well with every department. Some of these notes might raise more questions than supply answers. The whole 'brain injury' domain is obviously new to all of us, and the learning curve is steep.

Ignore the details that are just crib notes for us, but you'll get the gist. Sorry I haven't been able to man the phones. My hours on the road daily are wild, and when I get in I try to really make up for robbing the kids of one, well let's make that two, parents in the last weeks. (They continue to thrive, and with Jhonnie's recuperation going so well, I may turn a little less focus on Jhonnie, and a bit more on them.)

Jhonnie is far more able to enjoy visits from friends without me! A boon on many fronts.

To keep him safe, able, not confused, comfortable outside a hospital will obviously present a whole new set of challenges. *And* – Jhonnie is cheating and bullshitting like mad. He will often start a sentence, lose track, and finish it with some quite acceptable neutral jargon – fooling any but those who know him. You could halve his IQ, and he's still miles ahead of the rest of his crowd in rehab.

They have really emphasised that this home visit is about Jhonnie's recovery not ours – and that includes me as much as you. If he feels good enough to pick up the phone, I'll dial the numbers, but I don't want his own high expectations to be taxed by his seemingly genetic inclination to please.

So please be patient. He is. (I'm not. Nearly murdered a plumber today who had parked across our drive!)

Our boy is coming back, so much sooner than they had given us hope. There's time for everybody, and everything. Luckily, the rest of Jhonnie's life!

more later

xrr

EMAIL FROM RUTH TO JULIAN

Dear Julian,

Have you been receiving recent emails (mainly the detailed report written by Tracey from rehab conference)? All very encouraging news. Could you please reply, just to let me know they are getting through?

Ruth Ritchie

Day 37

Jhonnie gave a ticket to the opening game of the World Cup to Esther as a birthday present. And I took his one. This would be my first outing, at night, in nearly five months. Not wanting to seem ungrateful, but Australia versus Brazil at Homebush Stadium wouldn't normally have been my first choice. Jhonnie's passion for the sport was infectious with everybody but me. There's nothing wrong with rugby union that couldn't be fixed with a few fast horses. But the scale of the event was thrilling. The exuberance of Australian rugby fans after years of anticipation created an atmosphere not unlike a teenager's party where you just know people are having sex. Esther and I drank enormous cold beers, shouted the national anthem, and had an earplug each of Jhonnie's little radio, to hear the match call. We jumped up and down in the cold with 80,000 other fans and had a ball.

Jhonnie watched the action on the couch in the Brain Injury Unit at Ryde Rehabilitation Centre, and he was completely happy. The day before, we'd walked up the hill from the hospital to a high vantage point where it was possible to look back to Sydney, in another direction to Top Ryde (shudder), and in yet another, quite close by, to the stadium itself.

Almost ironically too near and yet too far, Jhonnie was reconciled to watching the match in hospital.

We phoned him from the train, before and after. He was very happy with his lovely, lovely Wallabies, and even more excited about Pete coming to pick him up, complete with raging hangover, to bring him home for his first visit.

Esther, Pete and a huge gang were partying on. I jumped out of the train, ran down some side stairs at Central and into the last available cab in Sydney. After my first big night out, I was tucked up in bed by 10.30 and mentally marinating the beef for the following night.

Day 39

WHEN I POPPED THE GATE to let Pete and Jhonnie in from the street, none of us could wait at the front door for them to slowly negotiate the path. We might still have been standing there, Devlin, William, Julia, Patrick, me (in an apron!) – like a Norman Rockwell tableau, as Jhonnie took those first slow, shuffling steps back into his own home. Devlin broke ranks first. I had to tear after him so that he didn't knock the brain-injured man over.

The rehab staff had given us very firm guidelines as to what Jhonnie could and couldn't do. (No carrying boiling kettles. No walking with baby. Stairs must be tackled hands-free, carrying nothing, holding rail. No lukewarm tinned spaghetti, please.) A body blow from an overeager Irish terrier fell outside the guidelines.

So we met them only a few feet from the gate, and it seemed for the longest time that we wouldn't ever actually go inside.

It is almost impossible for an event that has been highly anticipated to meet expectations. We all have some anticlimactic childhood birthdays that left a sour taste after the candles had been blown out. (Was 12 the absolute fizzer? I can no longer recall.) But Jhonnie's first hours, first cup of tea, first roast beef dinner, first sleep in his own home were not an anti-climax; instead, I had a sense of us all just observing him, back in situ, back where he belonged, and the wonder of it gave very mundane domestic moments a rather grand, surreal quality. Look. He's packing the dishwasher. Our dishwasher. He's drinking out of *our* blue glasses, not hospital plastic. It's a miracle. And while he slept, which he did about 14 hours a day, I couldn't work out what to do with the time. Suddenly I had nowhere to go. The person I had been rushing towards for all this time was here, needing nothing. Godot was snoring upstairs in his bed.

He and Patrick slept, and Anna, my sister-in-law, came over with cake, and we had more tea, and Jhonnie woke up, and used his very own bathroom, and Anna looked pretty close to tears, and we all watched Jhonnie eat cake, slowly.

'This cake isn't for the birds. It's too good, isn't it, William?'

'I don't really know, Dad. It's just that . . . I don't eat cake, Dad, don't you know that?'

Egg and nut allergies had given William the healthiest diet in the eastern suburbs. He most certainly had a best-selling kids' cookbook in him. 'Then this cake is for the birds. When did you stop eating cake?'

William looked at me, only slightly disturbed by his father's dietary amnesia. Anna jumped in, offering him chocolate strawberries.

'Then I might have to get a bird plate for my head.'

Very occasionally Jhonnie would make an offer or observation that he seemed to pluck straight from a Hieronymous Bosch painting, yet there was nothing in his demeanour, no dark transformation in his expression, that gave any clue to an interior world anything but sunny.

We lay in bed together that night, and didn't talk for long. Jhonnie's broken ribs and hip were giving him a lot of pain. He'd probably overdone it, he thought.

'I can't believe I get to do all this, with you,' he said, again. He said it often. Sometimes, every 20 minutes. And I lay next to him trying to mark the magnitude of the moment, our first night together, but I couldn't quite nail the emotion. Overwhelmed and exhausted came close.

Jhonnie awoke in the morning to find Patrick next to him in the sheets. He was confused as to time and place at first, and then, when he saw the little vanilla Paddle Pop kicking his legs in the air, Jhonnie's room came into focus. Home, with his family. His eyes filled with tears, and he touched Patrick's head tentatively, as if he'd just discovered him in a nest, and didn't want to frighten him away.

Eventually, Jhonnie stood up very slowly and it seemed to take minutes for him to reach his full height. He was very bent, the bad hip way out of whack, the entire left side of his body inches lower and slacker than the right. It took a long time for him to take his first step, and I decided not to help, because just then springing out of bed like a gazelle didn't seem tactful. He appeared to be slowly arriving at something.

'Do you know, little girl, that's the first time I've slept with straight legs in days? I feel completely different.'

'It's months, Jhonnie. You've been sleeping in a baby bear's bed, with your knees in the air, for months, not days. So I guess it's good to be home.'

Day 42

EMAIL FROM RUTH TO JHONNIE'S LIST

Can it really be six weeks? Sorry for the gap in communication. Exhaustion, not bad news. Everything continues to rocket ahead in terms of Jhonnie's rehab. The visit home was a total success. Jhonnie loved every second, and when he became tired (a lot) he lay down on his very own bed, with his legs straight, without his feet hitting a board, or a lunatic nearby shouting at him (unless you count me!).

The roast beef dinner on Saturday night was an unqualified success. Jhonnie made Yorkshire pudding. I didn't fight him about it. (How long will this utopian land of tolerance thrive?) Julia stayed all weekend and kid wrangled. This really will be a challenge when he's home full-time, but his improvement is astonishing, so there is hardly any point planning for Jhonnie's return as he may well be sharper than me by the time he's released.

Jhonnie brought home a mountain of homework, mostly neuro-psych exercises to test his powers of deduction and recollection. His rehab team were all impressed with the results. I've taken the brave step of a few days' break from Ryde. I'm finally seeing the dentist (broken teeth, go figure), buying some baby things, and just walking around trying to breathe normally. Jhonnie will be back home for another weekend visit, and I have a menu to plan!

Regarding local visits, Jhonnie's rehab days are now jam-packed. He says he really doesn't care too much about visitors, outside the kids, as the end is in sight. I think he doesn't want to feel that he's entertaining in such an awful place. Anyway, his call. So I'll try to contact those of you who were lined up for the next few days. He may feel differently next week. Chris is taking Connar and Madi this afternoon. Pete tomorrow and me for a big chunk on Thursday. Then another weekend of rugby and absolutely no beer. For all those who know Jhonnie so well and send wishes of beer-soaked World Cup joy – there is no drinking for 12 months after brain surgery. Glad we didn't know that from the start. He might not have found the will to go on.

Esther and I took Jhonnie's seats at the opening game on Friday night. I did so with mixed emotions. Reminded me of the Olympic Opening Ceremony, me turning to Jhonnie and saying, 'I hear hooves!' just before all those incredible horses cantered out from beneath our seats. I started crying and I didn't stop for hours.

So being at the rugby without Jhonnie, being at the rugby in Jhonnie's place – yeah, very bloody emotional. I sprinted like Cinderella before the last minutes of the game, and was home to feed Patrick by 11.05 pm. Jhonnie would have been horrified, passing up such a legitimate opportunity to carouse. Anyway, he can make Yorkshire pudding, and there's not a damn thing I can do about it. Six weeks, and they said he might have remained in a coma for that long.

more later

Day 43

I GOT THE FEELING THAT AFTER the weekend home visit phones rang hot, but I was left out of the loop. We'd had no mishaps, no dramas, but I could tell that the rest of my family were worried about Jhonnie coming home too soon, and my not being able to cope. I read between the lines in conversations with Mum and Tracey and Julia. They thought I'd crack, and Jhonnie would drop the baby, and I'd drive off a bridge, and William's teeth would decay. Something along those lines would be inevitable, if Jhonnie came home too soon.

No matter how old I get, I'll always be the youngest in my family, and the youngest of nine grandchildren, and probably the youngest wife of a brain-injured man with a five-month-old baby. My family believed me to be many wonderful things, but I was most certainly too young and stupid to identify the certain disaster of Jhonnie coming home too soon.

It's wonderful to have family and friends so close, so loving, so involved with every intimate detail of your life. Without them I couldn't possibly have managed, even as feebly as I had, with Jhonnie in hospital. Unfortunately one looks like a total bitch when the time comes to tell them to fuck off.

'Look, Rufus, I don't want to play devil's advocate, but –'

'Julia, you *do* want to play devil's advocate. You live for those moments when you can point out the errors of anyone's ways.'

'That's not it. I want him home as much as you do, so we can all get on with our lives. It's just that, objectively, you can't see the pitfalls.'

'They won't let him out before he's ready.'

'They're desperate for the bed. And you saw him in that assessment meeting. They might be brain injury professionals, but I don't think any of them could tell that Jhonnie's answers were complete bullshit. Rufus, it'll be like having another baby in the house.'

'And that will be fine, because I won't be driving to Ryde! The sooner he gets out of there, the sooner he'll stop acting like an invalid.'

'He's not acting! HE IS AN INVALID!'

She had a point. When Julia is self-righteously playing the devil's advocate role that she's so fond of, she speaks in exclamation marks. She doesn't raise her voice, she just punctuates wildly, and prefaces every sentence with 'I'm sorry, but . . .' then proceeds with a blast for which she is not one bit sorry.

'I'm sorry, but you're just not thinking this through. You want so much for this to be over that . . . just don't be in such a hurry.'

'I'm now married to a man who takes 20 minutes to clean his teeth. My long and cherished relationship with "hurry" is officially over. We're not going anywhere fast, ever again. But the sooner he gets out of an institution, the sooner I stop being Mrs Brain Injury.'

'All right. Well, as of today, he's officially out of the acute phase and into the very-much-fucking-better phase.'

'Why's that? Why today?'

'Because this is the first fight we've had in three months.'

I didn't go to Ryde for a few days. I took him back on

Monday morning, early, in time for school, and I stayed away until Thursday. Julia could well be right. With talk of Jhonnie coming home now in weeks, not months, this could be a calm before the storm. This could be that last month of pregnancy, when you can get your legs waxed and go to a movie, because after the baby comes home, you can forget about all that for the foreseeable future.

Even so, the prospect of Jhonnie's eviction from Ryde filled me with hope, and considerably less fear than my family believed appropriate. And in the meantime I had to work out if the mud crabs were any good in October, or if it was just more traditional to go with a big Saturday night platter of schnitzel and cauliflower cheese.

EMAIL FROM RUTH TO THERESE
Dear Therese,
Have you spoken to Jane? I rang her at Dee Why last night, but got the machine. Andrew McPhail's mum's funeral is tomorrow, same time and place and Michael Connors. What's going on?

Call me tonight if you want to rehash current status of . . . well, stuff. William and I are having candle-lit chops at about six. Free afterwards.

Xrr

Hugh and I met Andrew, his wife SJ and all the kids outside St Mary's for another wonderful big Catholic funeral. Mrs McPhail had also 'lost her battle with cancer'. As we milled and chased kids and hugged in the sandstone courtyard, we all tried to avoid the excruciating clichés of grief. Andrew, although he had been captain of the school, would have been voted the boy most likely to say 'fuck' at his own mother's funeral.

He made a beautiful speech. None of us knew how he managed to hold it together.

We'd all been making each other so proud in recent months, it was almost nauseating. I would have loved to go on to the wake, and drink beer, or even whiskey, slowly, anecdotally, purposefully, until Irishly drunk. Instead I went on to my equally Irish Catholic dentist, who'd managed to sneak me in to fix those cracked teeth. Hadn't we had enough rites of passage lately, enough brutal reminders of the random nature of existence, without dental icing on the cake of mortality?

I was beginning to feel like Hugh Grant, without the floppy hair. In my own dark version there were no weddings on the horizon, just profound moments with loved ones at funerals and hospitals. What was *Four Weddings and a Funeral* about, anyway? The fact that you can mark time your entire life turning up at other people's catered events and never leave yourself open enough to find love? Or was that whole premise just an opportunity for Andy McDowell to wear pretty hats?

We didn't have any weddings, but we did have light and shade. It wasn't all great funeral speeches. I had almost comical conversations with the curiously obtuse. Those early tolerant days of armistice between Chris Blampied and I were over.

In a very badly timed melodramatic escalation, Chris broke up with her boyfriend. Jhonnie's accident wouldn't have contributed to the split. But the split certainly contributed to Chris's emotional tailspin. We didn't know the details, but he sent me an email wishing Jhonnie well. He was curious as to Jhonnie's progress, as he and Chris no longer spoke. I felt as if the whole family couldn't stand one more upset. This latest romantic disappointment, along with the 'gravy train derailment', as Jhonnie referred to his accident, had rendered Chris a damsel in distress. I had neither the inclination nor the energy to untie her from the railway tracks. (Highly evocative transportation analogies really come into their own after a bike accident.) She had burst into tears on the phone to me, not because she feared for the life, for the future, of the father of some of her children. She cried, and I'm ashamed to say that I comforted her, about money.

While the Blampieds in Europe had managed to turn Jhonnie's accident into a catastrophe that threatened to wipe out their own personal wheat crops, Chris had managed to make it all about her bank balance. What was she to do? Where was she to turn? Who would pay for her personal trainers now?

When she wasn't railing against poverty she lapsed into total denial. This whole head injury thing was something I appeared to have made up, and as soon as Jhonnie got home, we'd be back to normal. Nothing to see here folks; move on. And often, straight after one of those conversations in fantasyland, I'd have a call or email from Jane or Andrew, who, while mourning the loss of a dear parent after an exhausting intense terminal illness, wanted to know how I was coping.

So we were officially up to two funerals and a head injury with some Blampied cameos for light relief.

Day 48

I WALKED DEVLIN IN THE PARK very early. A crisp spring morning, alone with my thoughts and an Irish terrier: there really is no better way to start the day. We ran down the Elizabeth Bay steps, across the waterfront then up the hill to Darling Point, past big mansions and even bigger trees. At 6.30 we had the roads to ourselves.

Even with Devlin's enthusiasm, and the filtered sun on my back, there was something I couldn't shake, an impediment to the morning. It was like a distant transistor radio, at a very low volume, set just off the station frequency. It was the sound of my own angry voice in my chest. My self-righteous, wounded, furious tirades. Thump, thump, thump. I couldn't get away from my inner fishwife.

So angry. So fucking furious. So frustrated. I really should have stuck with Catholicism, or bailed completely and investigated the Jewish thing, because about now, just being able to hand over and peacefully mutter 'God will provide' would have been better than my way.

Communication with the Euro-Blampieds had deteriorated so badly that Pete had written an all-Blampied email entitled 'Three Strikes and You're Out'. (He didn't send it, but the act of angry typing certainly made him feel better.)

Dealing with Chris on any level was proving disastrous. While not wanting to engage with her in a pissing competition for Woman in the Worst Position, I couldn't make any practical headway. And then Jhonnie's old agency had ceased his payout deposits. After 14 years and nearly two marriages of devotion to the place, some bean counter decided to save a few pennies by cheating the brain-injured father of four out of his entitlements. It seems he was obliged to turn up for one or two meetings each month, and since he was just lying around in hospital . . .

And we wonder why people have such low opinions of ad-men.

Somewhere in the last week I had crossed the line from Catherine Zeta-Jones to Jack Nicholson, and even as I walked my dog, a voice deep inside was spitting, 'You can't handle the truth!' to nobody in particular. While we should have been focusing on Jhonnie's impending homecoming, we were all distracted by vitally important war-room meetings. Goodness, chicken soup and love weren't buying us any leverage. Diplomacy hadn't got the Blampieds off our backs, Chris to sit up and behave, or the agency to honour its obligations. It seemed that we'd have to hire lawyers. It was too late to get down on my knees and pray. (If I had had to start with confession I'd still be in that little booth today, mentally rewinding the '90s.) For the time being I was stuck with deep breaths and the sound of my own relentless angry inner voice.

Day 49

EMAIL FROM RUTH TO JHONNIE'S LIST

Seven weeks after the accident Hugh calls me. Phil (who was riding with Jhonnie and Hugh on the day of the accident) has had a look at Jhonnie's bike, remembering the souped up little computer jobby on board. This thing apparently records, among other things, the top trip speed, which presumably Jhonnie had achieved in his steep descent just before collision. Hugh had clocked himself at somewhere between 40 and 50 km/h. But that was Hugh. Jhonnie's bike records 67.2 km/h.

Do dwarfs shot from cannons achieve that speed?

Tomorrow, when I go to Ryde for the family conference to rejoice at his progress, I may take a rolling pin, and give him a *real* head injury! 67.2 km/h. I know Jhonnie. I expect to have five-kilo children. I'm no longer shocked when he buys 40 rashers of bacon (just in case!) but this is excessive even for Jhonnie.

Speaking of high speeds. Jhonnie's recovery continues to hurtle. All the staff at Ryde luuuurve him. Never has a patient been so willing, so polite, so amusing, or responded so well to every treatment. What a surprise, Jhonnie is blitzing rehab.

His eviction is approaching, with longer weekend visits and a return home scheduled well in advance of our optimistic Christmas conjecture. Jhonnie's spirits remain, if not exactly high, well focused on his recovery, and his kids. He's still not really reading, and not much interested in visits other than the few regulars who've been on board from early days. With them and the family he is revelling in his progress without worrying about his 'performance'.

Jhonnie is speaking well. His amnesia is subsiding. He gets physically stronger every day (now swimming laps!) and the bung eye is his greatest concern. Even so, this is a head injury. He's been well warned about depression, confusion and the physical dangers of amnesia. Telling the same story five times is not a problem; forgetting that he *cannot* pick up Patrick could be.

Last weekend, a very successful home visit, I handed him the phone and offered to dial any number, and in spite of the hundreds of people so keen to hear his voice, he just thought the phone could wait. On this, I'm going to be guided by Jhonnie, so please be patient.

Everything on the home front is going well. Patrick, William and I have fallen into a nice quiet early bed routine, with the baby occasionally obliging by sleeping through that 3.00 am feed. Madi stayed over last Saturday night – a thrill for Jhonnie, both little boys, and a delight for me, as she is such a sunny gorgeous girl to have around the house. We watched rugby, and mucked around with Dad in bed on Sunday morning. Return to some kind of normality is in clear view now. Esther took Connar to Brisbane for the day to watch a great Wallaby win, and he came over on Sunday morning, with live reports of the game.

Seven weeks. Seven very unusual weeks. We are eating this elephant one mouthful at a time. I feel very confident, but bloody tired with it, that Jhonnie is coming back home and the worst is most certainly behind us. Again, thank you for the beautiful cards, flowers, prayers, thoughtful gestures – the . . . the everything that has helped our family get from September 3 to this point. We are just kiss-the-ground-lucky to have you all.

more later

xrr

Day 50

THERE WAS A LOT RIDING on this family conference. Jhonnie knew it. Every single day he said, as if for the first time, 'I'm really coming back into myself now. I was fucked, but now, I'm back. I'm fine.'

So far from fine. And yet at this conference, where the entire team met with us, the family, and reported Jhonnie's progress and projected outcome, the sleazy ad-man buried inside the brain injury patient worked the room. Somehow, he knew that if he spoke too much he'd be babbling like an idiot. He chose to agree, and even occasionally contradict, like a professional involved in his own case. Each member of the team offered that Jhonnie's insight into his own situation was remarkable for a man who'd sustained his injuries.

They all began to refer to challenges Jhonnie would face in the real world. He shouldn't ever swim alone because he runs an increased risk of seizure. He would need another brain scan after six months to check for gas in the skull and increased risk of emboli if he ever got on a plane. Clear scans would also be essential before he could think about embarking on a monocular driving course and gaining a special provisional licence. All this seemed a little ambitious for a man they suggested was not entirely safe to cross the road without a companion.

Jhonnie had to give a little presentation to all the staff about his coma experiences, and his journey through the wonderful world of rehab. It was full of tightly worked analogies, and punctuated with light one-liners. Probably only Tracey and I felt uneasy about his language choices – little short-circuits, jargon phrases that he repeated to mask the fact that he had completely lost his train of thought. To all the world he sounded like a fast-talking mobile phone salesman. Tracey and I knew it was the performance of a man desperate to sleep in his own bed on a permanent basis.

On their side, plenty of jargon pin-balled around the tiny conference room: oculomotor nerve palsy (one good eye), heel-shin ataxia (funny walk), truncal listing (funny walk on a tilt), decreased visual acuity (easily blind-sided), foreign accent syndrome (Pommy voice), double continence (house-broken), upper motor neurone facial weakness (smiles like a stroke victim) . . . In other words, he was good to go.

What? They weren't setting a date, making a plan, booking the cleaners for his room. No. He could go home with me, now. Just like that. And we packed up the station wagon, thanked one and all with bewildered, ill-prepared hugs, and buggered off back home.

Jhonnie sat next to me in the passenger seat of his not-so-new Audi and looked out the window at the mundane world of kitchen renovation, car yards and mobile phone shops. 'It's good to be back, bunny. I can't believe I get to do all of this, with you. I'm actually fine now, which is funny, because I remember thinking I was fine in Royal Men's –'

'Royal North Shore.'

'Well, yes, that was after Royal Men's. So I've really come back into myself now. Where should we go?'

'I thought, maybe, home. Then dinner and a show.'

'I might be too tired for the show.'

Jhonnie came home, went to bed and slept until the next

morning. His performance as the entirely rehabilitated renovated miracle man had done him in.

I got back on the phone to Tracey. 'Would you have let him out? Come on, Trace. Be honest.'

'It's hard to say. I don't agree with them on his high degree of insight to his own condition. There's a big part of Jhonnie that thinks he's been left in the wrong boarding school, in Ryde, and he's doing anything to get out. On the other hand, that level of cunning bodes pretty well in terms of recovery.'

'So he doesn't know he's fucked?'

'Not for a second.'

'How fucked is he?'

'I don't know . . . Those neurospych scores they're so happy about are meaningless without seeing the tests.'

'And that's his IQ?'

'No. IQ, executive skills, memory, powers of deduction, sequencing (that's logic), language. Frontal lobe damage is mostly about executive skills. He's never needed a diary or memory prompts because he's always had a brain the size of a small planet, and a secretary.'

'And now he has me. How fucked is he?'

'For a man with a Glasgow Coma Scale score of 3 and a scone the size of a watermelon on the day, he's a total miracle. I can't give you any more answers than they could. Look, they taught him how to make cheese on toast. Their work is done.'

EMAIL FROM RUTH TO JHONNIE'S LIST

My email has been down for days, so sorry for not replying. I've tried.

Very good news. After eight weeks, Jhonnie is home. I had been warned that I would have to fill the house with rails and ramps (for William to play on?). But instead I have a very cautious careful Jhonnie – who cannot pick up Patrick, or walk carrying a hot drink. But I promise, he's more capable than most of your husbands on a bad Sunday morning.

So what are we looking at? An incompetent rehab system that has him wait-listed for home care, which will kick in in six to eight weeks. Meanwhile, I've organised physio, acupuncture, massage, and had an exercise bike delivered.

Anyway, Jhonnie is savouring every moment of home and kids. We took William horse riding this morning. Jhonnie's smile was as wide as William's, for the whole lesson. William only lost concentration in the moments when he glanced away to see if his father was watching. I kept drinking in the whole picture, thinking back to recent days when no one could tell us if Jhonnie would ever leave hospital.

At Woolworths today, we ran into a friend, shopping with a trolley full of her sons. She looked as if she'd seen a ghost, or a miracle, and we all made quite a scene in Double Bay, in the nappy aisle. And I had no pictures of Patrick. Nearly bloody normal.

Jhonnie gets a haircut tomorrow. Too much vanity or good sense to get a hospital cut. Brain surgery scars and staples all grown over with that enviable thick Blampied hair. After a do – he may look more prison than rehab, but as every day passes, evidence of the-dreadful-events-of-Sept-3 pass. I'm doing fine, but I still haven't had a haircut in 2003. This is not a barber competition. Pregnancy – new baby – head injury – I'm turning into Rapunzel, but not in a good way.

For all of you who want to visit, I'm leaving the call to Jhonnie. He's called his family in the UK, America and Italy. He is so grateful for all the support and well-wishes. He just wants to find his feet (with one eye, that takes time), spend time with his kids, and literally get his head together. On Monday I subjected him to his first night of *Australian Idol*, *Queer Eye* and *Survivor*. (A TV critic has certain responsibilities, even when she's off duty.)

Continued thanks for – well – everything.

It's all coming good. Red meat, baby beetroot, Mother Mary McKillop and very great friendship cannot be underestimated in trying times. To my friends who have been going through their own extraordinary difficulties while helping us through this, I will never forget your kindness. Every card, letter and email is a shot in the arm. We are the luckiest people alive. Thank you. Very big party – in a year – when Jhonnie can drink.

more later

xrr

Day 51

WE WENT TO A MOVIE. We walked all the way from home up
to Oxford Street, me holding Jhonnie's hand because he
couldn't gauge the traffic, and we had a coffee, and met Esther,
bought sandals, and went to a movie.

After a haircut – which really scrubbed the institutional
residue from his appearance – and some lunch, Jhonnie came
home and made a few calls. Then he went to bed again, until
the next morning.

EMAIL FROM RUTH TO JHONNIE'S LIST

Dear followers of Jhonnie's progress,

We've been telling him how these emails have circled the globe,
and I have a huge file of all the amazing letters and thoughts that
have poured in over the last two months.

I really have no idea how many people have been reading
these day reports. Could you please forward this one to anybody
who has been receiving the emails, interested in Jhonnie's recovery,
and ask them to send 'Welcome Home Jhonnie' to me? It doesn't
have to be long or fancy. I'm just curious to see what comes back,
and maybe have you all online as the world's weirdest mailing list!
No urgency. My stupid email will probably jam, and the computer

will explode if they all arrive at once. But if you get a chance over the next few days, we'd appreciate it.

What a very unusual time we've all had!

xrr

Maybe no more for a while!   .

Day 57

Let's just say that perhaps Julia and the rest of the family had been right. I didn't exactly jailbreak him from Ryde. They threw him out. And that first week at home was so intense, so loaded with meaning for everybody involved, it's hard to remember in detail. It went quickly, like a wedding. It dragged slowly because Jhonnie moved so slowly, and I held his hand at every step.

Driving Jhonnie to his various appointments, making cups of tea for various overwhelmed loving friends, adjusting to the monumental invasion of home invalid life was – well, let's just say that Julia had been right.

I started smoking (I actually bought a pack, for the first time in years), and stood out by the garbage bins nursing a Scotch and ice as I burbled my sorrows on the phone to Tracey. I waited until everybody was asleep – Jhonnie, William and Patrick, all gone by 7.15 each night. Tracey wasn't giving much away. The truth was that nobody knew how much better Jhonnie would ever get, or how long that end result would take. I had to get more help. I had to say no to people who just didn't get it. I had to know that we'd get through it. We were just tired, and this is much harder than anyone thinks. Sip. Drag. She was right.

Jhonnie was blissfully happy to be home, and grateful for every kindness. Our entire tight-knit loving community was bowled over by his gentle patient philosophical approach. He appreciated all the little things so much now: the softness of our dog's ears, the colour of jacaranda, the novelty of a race-track. All the innocent wonder and joy knocked us on our arses. He was Tarzan, and Chauncy Gardener, and Gandhi, and Mork, all rolled into one. It was very inspiring, and interesting, and it could make a 10-minute trip into Woolworths feel like a none-too-entertaining Jim Jarmusch movie. It made me smoke, and drink whiskey by the garbage bins.

EMAIL FROM RUTH TO JHONNIE'S LIST

As most of you know (although I understand that email is still a mystery to some addressees) Jhonnie is home, not overnight, or for the weekend, but for good. For better and for worse!

His remarkable recovery continues. This morning he remembered the day of the accident, putting the bikes on the car. Let's hope his amnesia gives him a break from the rest of the day.

Since then, Madi has turned eight. William has won his yellow belt at karate. Connar is getting ready to go to Cranbrook (his new school). And Patrick is five months old, eating banana and sheep's milk yogurt, and still charming one and all.

Jhonnie is swimming, dog walking, getting beaten up at physio and occasionally lying down for acupuncture. His brain injury is proving convenient in its own wicked way. Jhonnie never could remember the names of people he's met at parties, and now he never has to. Yesterday he sat glued to *Naked Gun* on cable, swearing he hadn't seen it before. And on Tuesday, we went to Randwick for the Melbourne Cup. My sister Julia's responsibilities as the first female committee member of the Australian Jockey Club aren't always of paramount interest to me. But on Cup Day, after so many hospital wards, that posh committee room came into its own. We swanned through one of the racing calendar's most crowded days in VIP comfort. On inspection of the horses, and most bizarre girlie outfits in the paddock, Jhonnie was gobsmacked to find the world 'so full of sluts. Were there always so many?' See, Jhonnie really has been working too hard for too long, to only just now discover that the world is full of sluts.

So, thanks for the Welcome Home Jhonnie emails. They are amazing. I'm forwarding them to Jhonnie's (he still hasn't sat at a computer), and the list of well-wishers is already vast. If you haven't already, please forward this email to anyone who has been interested in Jhonnie's progress, and they too can send a welcome to Jhonnie.

Thanks again for everything. Miracle Man will reply, eventually. Meanwhile, I couldn't be more grateful.

Xrr

Day 70

A THOUGHTFUL FRIEND GAVE US THE name of a trainer who specialised in older, and damaged bodies. Miss Jane, as Jhonnie decided to call her, started to rebuild him from the ground up. On the first day he could only lift a one-kilo bag of rice above his head, with some difficulty. Within a few short weeks, and three visits every week, she had him cycling on a stationary bike, lunging, squatting and lifting weights. We could have underscored these workouts with the theme music from *Rocky*, so great was his effort, so profound his determination to re-inhabit his broken body. He would shout out loud, in pain, at the exhalation of difficult deep breaths. The more he shouted in the gym, the less he cried out as he rose from a chair, or the bed, or the loo. And I would forget as I watched him just walking, lumbering, smiling, that Jhonnie was in physical pain most of the time. How on earth did he do it? I take out an ad in the *Herald* when I have a paper cut.

Julia had all but disappeared. It was weird. I felt like I was walking without crutches, and mostly that was a good thing. Maybe all the nutty annoying stuff about life at home with Jhonnie was finally too much for her. Maybe we were doing so well she decided to leave the organisation, or possible lack thereof, to me. She hadn't been over for weeks.

Things were settling down, finding a new slow routine that allowed Jhonnie plenty of sleep (still 12 hours a day, minimum) and plenty of time to get everywhere late without me exploding with frustration. A half-hour physio appointment (four each week) became a three-hour return journey. That's just how long anything took. He remained positive and sweet, and all who came in contact with him remarked on his Zen attitude. Elsewhere, I was spitting enough chips for all of us.

The boys would have missed Julia more, but the novelty of this new, chilled, home Dad was fresh. For the first time in all his five years, William didn't enter a room and ask, 'Where's Dad?' There he was, every day.

When Julia called to say that she and Tracey were coming around for a cup of tea, I suspected an ambush. I hoped we could leave Meera and Jhonnie and the baby, and go shopping. Some Surry Hills coffee and girlie gossip. No, that wasn't going to happen. And I figured they were going to read me the riot act, or tell me to see a psychiatrist, or send Jhonnie back to Ryde, but I couldn't imagine what had set it off. So unlike Tracey not to say.

When Tracey and Julia arrived, Julia boiled the kettle and told Jhonnie and me to both sit down. Tracey hadn't seen Patrick, her godson, in months. She'd had that flu. Then I'd only seen her at our various hospital meetings. She held him and kissed the top of his head. With her own head bowed, her chin tucked under, I could tell she was preparing to say something very difficult, and I wasn't sure at that point, looking at her full head of dark curly hair, so thoroughly recovered from the chemotherapy, if I knew what it was.

When she looked up she looked straight at me, and didn't avert her gaze until she was through. 'The news isn't good. It's back. The cancer's back.'

'Fuck. The other breast?'

'No. This one isn't going away. It's the liver.'

We both momentarily pooled with tears, and changed our minds at the same time.

'I know. I'm sorry, little face. I was trying to work out how not to tell you. But that's just bullshit. This one isn't going away. So I can't keep it from you. The timing is just . . . I'm sorry.'

We hugged for a long time. I was determined not to cry. So much to think about. Tracey's teenage daughter, Alex, my goddaughter, would finish high school, would be alone, would . . . My mind raced. What had she said? This one isn't going away? I believe they are the exact words with which Tracey carefully chose to tell me that she was going to die.

'Any thoughts on how we're going to tell Mum?'

The idea of Tracey predeceasing my mother had a nauseating nightmarish quality to it. So that's where Julia had been. In different hospitals with different doctors. Didn't anybody go to the movies or out to dinner any more? I looked at Jhonnie, who was stunned and brimming with tears. He clambered to his feet and went over to hug Tracey.

'Oh, Nurse Brown. Miracles can happen. I promise you they can.'

She gripped his shoulders tightly and laughed. 'I know. Look who's talking. I could be killed by a speeding cyclist before the cancer gets me, so let's just . . . Really Jhonnie, you know, you should be dead.'

'I know.' He laughed a big hearty laugh. We all took deep breaths. And I thought of Tracey's own mother, my aunt, dead for five years, but a hypochondriac her entire life. She used to buy sample sizes of her make-up at the Chanel counter and explain to the salesgirls that she only needed the small size because she was dying. She did this for 20 years.

'Thank god your mother's dead. This'd fucking kill her.'

Day 80

EMAIL FROM RUTH TO JHONNIE'S LIST

Has it really been 80 days?

It's a miserable wet Saturday morning, the morning of the World Cup Final. Two straight days of rain bodes badly for our Wallabies. Jhonnie sold his finals tickets last week – A class at the front, right on the halfway line. Jhonnie was happy to forgo the crowds tonight. His one and only World Cup experience was more than enough. Perfect balmy Sydney night, 80,000 people and Jhonnie sitting with Connar, his 11-year-old son, to watch his beloved Wallabies come back from the dead and beat the All Blacks. (I know everybody said it last week, but I really did have a feeling about the Wallabies. I figured, given what we've been through, if Jhonnie could get there, the least George and the boys could do was win.)

Jhonnie was overjoyed and overwhelmed. The atmosphere here in Sydney (for the poor cold damp deluded Poms) ever since has been jubilant. As much as he loves it, he decided the Telstra Stadium pressure was a bit too much to risk again. (Having never seen it sober before, the whole experience was rather novel.) So, no matter what happens tonight, last week was total magic. If Connar doesn't realise the miracle of the experience now, he will certainly marvel when he recalls as an adult how his father nearly died, and two months later they sat together in brilliant seats for one of the greatest nights of their rugby lives.

Enough boot action.

Life at home has been a rollercoaster – mostly good, but we get great waves of exhaustion, frustration and sadness mixed with endless gratitude. The novelty of feeding Patrick or watching William laughing his arse off as he tries to master a rising trot is certainly not waning.

Lots of physiotherapy, rehab case meetings, doctors' appointments and some fairly strict swimming training from Pete. We saw the brain surgeon last week, who was very happy with Jhonnie's progress, and fascinated by his stories from the land of coma. (Really hope he writes it all down before it morphs into well-worn anecdote.) Dr Small wasn't holding out much hope for Jhonnie's eye. What is it with surgeons and that automatic well-if-you-ask-me-you're-fucked bedside manner? Amazing. He said if the eye was no better within a year, he's screwed. Marvellous. On the good side, the injury doesn't shorten Jhonnie's life expectancy, or eventually his ability to change nappies. Patrick is going to start saving some for Dad.

On Friday we arrived early at RNS for a rehab appointment so I took Jhonnie up to ward 7B – where he had lived for nearly a month. Just getting into the elevator filled me with a mixture of panic and something creepily like nostalgia.

This wretched old building – and I knew every poster, every broken elevator button. And I looked at Jhonnie and it was all new to him. Not a flicker.

And really – this Jhonnie had never been there before.

When we emerged at 7B a few things were familiar. Approaching the nurses' station – one Irish nurse nearly dropped the phone. It took her moments to recognise him – so much taller, so much fitter than the patient who arrived unconscious and left in a wheelchair.

And they came from everywhere. Just blown away. I said to

Jhonnie if anyone makes eye contact with him to just start saying thank you, and don't stop. The visit was unplanned. We're going back with flowers or cake or . . . what's appropriate? We weren't prepared, and I was shocked by the floods of emotion. So many people. There must have been more than 20 people who, in those weeks, in that place, became my everything. Associations made in life and death situations? Well I guess I've nothing to compare it to. But seeing them all again – the Kates and Helens and Sharons – I was reminded how far we've come. And now I can't believe where we were.

By the time we went down to the rehab appointment, by the time we got back in that homey old elevator, I was crying, and pretty well kept going, on and off, for the rest of the day.

So last night Pete and Nicole came over for very ordinary Thai take-away and a few standard drinks (well, two bottles of wine). Today, given the weather and the match ahead, we are happily achieving nothing. Simon and Esther will be joining us on the couch, and trust me, we sound like 80,000 once we get started.

I'm back at work, and a bit rusty on the job. Still, I'm never comfortable unless I've got a deadline to bitch about. I'm nominated for a National Comedy Award, which is judged in Melbourne next week. Yes, what the world needs is another award night. As much as I would like to go shoe shopping and then get pissed with a bunch of nervous funny people, the trip isn't practical. (Anyway – I can't win. I haven't been in print for months, and the other four nominees are famous national TV personalities, where I am only known locally – and then only for being famously unpleasant about TV personalities.)

But life goes on. Thought I'd better write today because tomorrow, if it keeps raining, just might be a bad day for the Wallabies.

Thanks again for all the Jhonnie Welcomes that continue to roll in. We are surrounded by the most amazing people. Thanks for all the time you take to read and write and think of us. I might throw a big party eventually to thank everyone. I understand Neverland is free these days, so keep your diaries open!

more later

xrr

Day 83

Jhonnie took the Wallabies' defeat remarkably well. Luck runs out. Shit happens. Teams lose. World Cups come to an end. I was relieved that this much-anticipated festival, the endless boot-talk, was now history, and Jhonnie seemed to let it go easily.

He had so many distractions. Any one job required all his energy and focus. Never one to multitask, the brain injury had rendered him domestically incompetent. Sure, he could boil water, and make toast, but not at the same time. At breakfast I would thump and bump past him to boil the kettle, to make the formula, to butter the bagel, and feed the dog, and empty the garbage, and put a new bin-liner under the sink, and the milk back in the fridge, and the teabag in the new empty bin-liner, and refill the chilled water filter, and throw the empty milk bottles into the recycling, while Jhonnie looked for a teaspoon.

I'd take deep breaths and Jhonnie would smile at me at the sink. 'Always in the way,' one of us would say affectionately, and when Jhonnie was happy and light, I meant it.

Some days, and I could tell as soon as he woke up, he would be so shut down and withdrawn that I wondered if he would ever speak. And the routine would begin. Me asking

'You okay?' Him nodding, 'Yeah, fine.' But nothing would be said for hours, unless I asked questions.

We went to Matt and Sarah's for Sunday lunch. Jo and James were there, with their kids. Esther came along, and another young family as well. It was an afternoon of delicious food, rambunctious kids and loud funny conversations. When two people spoke at once Jhonnie couldn't work out which conversation to follow. He was happy to be socialising. He told a few coma stories, but he couldn't follow the cacophony of Esther, Jo and I competing to tell the one story. As we tore apart a current news scandal I could tell Jhonnie recognised none of the names. He couldn't feign interest. When the conversation turned to the water-cooler program of the day, the first series of *Australian Idol*, he confused the contestants' names, and couldn't jump in quickly enough with an observation to get in the game. It didn't matter. It was only *Australian Idol*. But I could tell he was frustrated. At the same time I revelled in the speed and triviality of the banter. Back in the real world. Back where people were passionate about the future of tuneless teenagers and their terrible renditions of Mariah Carey songs. Back where I belonged, in the land of silly.

After lunch Jhonnie sat on the couch, away from the adoring screeching harpies, and he looked relieved. Patrick had missed his sleep, and wasn't up to a late night, so we packed up the whole caravan, and Esther, around dusk.

'Wasn't that great, to be out, to see us all together, eating Matt's incredible beef −'

'Oh yeah − I was in it for the beef!' chimed the slightly pissed vegetarian.

'Did you have fun, Jhonnie?'

'Yes. I'm very tired. I think I might have stayed too long.'

Then Patrick started to wail for a bottle I simply didn't have, and William passed out.

'Well, that makes three of you.'

Jhonnie went straight to bed, but didn't sleep. He roamed around in the dark. I got up to ask him if he was okay. He said he was fine. Perhaps I'd have more fun with my friends without him. I couldn't seem to comfort or convince Jhonnie that this assembled group, these loving friends who had been by his bedside and helped with our children when he knew no better, loved us both. Really? He couldn't feel the love. He couldn't see why I would stay with him when everybody else is so much more fun.

Chris rang to speak to Jhonnie about money, about next Friday's pick-up from school, about the lawyers, about the school fees. I told her he was asleep. She refused to discuss the children with me, ever again, thank you very much. She had put my email address in her Junk Delete file so that she wouldn't have to accept any more of my correspondence. Jhonnie could just text her from now on. I explained that Jhonnie didn't 'text' and hadn't been able to sit down at a computer to read any of her nonsense, and the only person driving her children around on weekends was me. She hung up. I didn't feel the love.

Day 84

EMAIL FROM RUTH TO JHONNIE'S LIST

Hugh and Jhonnie went back to the scene of the crime *by car* yesterday. Brilliant location for a tragedy. It really was, actually . . . when I have, well, one of those, in the middle of nowhere, doing 67 km/h, I hope I stack 20 metres from a heli-pad. Seriously!

Jhonnie remembered a lot – parking the car, getting off the bike to go up a steep hill – and then, speeding downhill, to make up some lost time for Hugh and Phil. The memories end there.

The boys had nice long talks about love and sex and fiscal policy. Nice for them. I waved them goodbye, and couldn't shake the flashes of the last time, three months ago, that they ran away to play, when hours later Hugh rang, and I said, 'What have you done with my husband?' Silence.

So yesterday, I went off to work, and came home hours later, only realising my total relief to find Jhonnie poodling around downstairs.

Some days, I used to look out the window of the Royal North Shore Hospital, even in Intensive Care, and the sky would look exactly like the sky in the credits of *The Simpsons*, and I'd think, 'That can't be right.' But then, *The Simpsons* is almost never wrong.

So Hugh is sending the pictures, because my technology is too – erhhh, details couldn't be more boring!

For those still interested – the cooking goes on. Firm believer that beetroot, cauliflower, kumera, broccolini and broad beans have a TV series coming to them. Personally, I'm missing that completely stupid stand-up food you get at parties from about Melbourne Cup until NYE. Free catered nonsense. I'd like to hire a waiter to hold a tray of duck wraps and whatever is doing the rounds this year and whip around in the distance, so I can complain that it's cold by the time it gets to me. Jhonnie is doing great. We're all buggered.

more later

xrr

Christmas 2003

I WENT BACK TO WORK, AND I went to a few parties. I had a haircut, and nice blow-dry, and discovered, as I had ceased dying my hair while pregnant then not seen a salon for the six months since Pat's birth, that I was now completely grey. All the brown was gone. I was the only woman in the eastern suburbs with my own hair colour. People hadn't seen me in a long time, and then, when they did, I guess they got the shock of their lives.

My picture in the paper (already five years old) showed a carefree girl sporting tortoiseshell earrings and a sleek brunette bob – oh, and a smile. Who the hell was she?

There was a point in Sally Field's career where she could no longer play girls. She'd kept a *Gidget*-esque lightness about her for such a long time that when she turned, somewhere around *Mrs Doubtfire*, and definitely by the time she played Forrest Gump's mother, the girl door slammed behind her, forever. And after that haircut, when I slipped into a slightly dated bit of pre-maternity eveningwear and blow-dried the new grey do, and put on lipstick, and the gorgeous earrings Jhonnie had given me at Patrick's birth, and really steep Prada heels that always made my pins look good, I looked in the mirror and saw Mrs Gump.

Even so, it was great to get out, and see colleagues, and

bitch about people I'd never met, and talk shit with journalist friends who all do the same silly party circuit before Christmas. The duck-wrap-quite-good-pinot circuit.

And if I liked standing, even awkwardly, in heels for a few hours, I loved sitting back down to the computer and writing words I knew how to spell – not a medical term on the screen. Writing about television is a completely frivolous occupation, but one that I have come to cherish. Every new mother should be paid to watch tapes of her favourite TV shows, then develop personal theories about pop culture's hidden meanings. The column, as always, was an escape, and yet I couldn't escape very far. It seemed, since the accident, that even television looked different. I had no idea Jhonnie's accident was leaking into my work.

TV Column, December 2003, *Sydney Morning Herald*

An extraordinary film clip for Coldplay's new song, 'The Scientist', is currently rolling around on Rage *(ABC, weekends). A simple device, perfectly executed, results in a totally compelling piece of storytelling and musical entertainment. For those who have not happened accidentally upon the clip, allow me to ruin it for you.*

The song begins with lead singer Chris Martin (Mr Paltrow) lying on a mattress, medium close up, singing to camera. Only when he stands up do we see that he, and everything in his world, is moving backwards, rewinding, while he sings forward, in sync.

That, in itself, is interesting enough to suck you in. He continues, backwards through a basketball game, through an open field, up into woods, singing wistfully all the time of 'going back to the start'. Great lyrics, haunting song. Martin passes a girl's body, a crashed BMW. The body flies back through the window into the passenger seat. He climbs back into the driver's seat. The BMW reverses back onto a country

*road, swerves around a truck, and the girl undoes her seatbelt
to reach back for her jacket. The couple are laughing, happily
enjoying a drive in the country.*

If only they could go back to the start.

*So many huge emotions are bound up in reflection:
remorse, regret, nostalgia, and grief. We spend a lot of time
and energy in life, and in art, looking back.*

*TV audiences are familiar with the tools of reflection. The
flashback, the sepia picture, archival footage, spinning newspapers, ripple dissolves, period music. So many of these techniques
have been well worn and finally bastardised by everyone
from Orson Welles to Walt Disney, they've lost impact.*

*The true genius of the Coldplay clip lies not in the
technical ingenuity, but its ability to give you that awful
sinking feeling. (Sorry. You may not feel it, because I've given
away the ending/beginning.) It's powerful stuff, that looking
back to the moment when everything suddenly changed,
and the simplicity of life immediately before is forever out of
reach.*

In the same piece, I managed to review *Dr Phil*, a BBC production of *Copenhagen*, and a documentary series about famous
Australian family dynasties, all from the same perspective of
personal tragic reverie. And people read my column for easy
laughs on a Saturday morning!

After that column, a lot of my colleagues emailed, pleased
to have me back on deck, and a little freaked out by my new
material. I had to reread the column to see what they were
talking about. Perhaps I was rushing things. My desperate
desire to put the whole nasty mess behind me couldn't make it
so. It was stuck to my shoes, no matter how fast I ran.

Christmas became a great, yet strange, distraction. The
whole family always came to us for Christmas Day. There were
usually 12 or 14 for lunch (depending on whether Connar and

Madison were with their mother; we swapped every year). Eleni would gravlax a whole salmon and make Christmas cassata. My mother would glaze the ham, and go to the Nut Shop for the extensive, precise Christmas selection, which began and ended with milk chocolate ginger and dark chocolate orange peel. Julia would help her with the Waldorf salad and the cucumber and dill sour cream. Tracey would bring a case of mineral water, French champagne, mustard and case of cherries, and I'd do the rest: the Christmas cake, the turkey (two different stuffings), potato salad, home-grown tomatoes and basil, and leaves.

It was a perfect division of labour. We'd have gravlax and champagne during the present opening (a festival, with six kids in the house, especially a new baby, that could go for hours). And later, the exact meal, the very same lunch my mother had been serving for 49 years, would materialise, served on the reliable, predictable bowls and platters.

We all love Christmas at our house because, although every year is a little different, we know exactly what to expect. There had only been one year, it was 1990, when we went to a restaurant and regretted it before we'd even sat down. My father had died 10 days before, and nobody, after hosting an enormous wake, felt like making potato salad. We had never needed it more.

And this particular Christmas already felt loaded. We had Patrick to celebrate, and Jhonnie's recovery, and more ominously, none of us knew if it would be Tracey's last Christmas. Nobody dared to deviate from the time-honoured Ritchie Christmas routine. Tracey and I joked about Jhonnie's enviable position at the table. He would be the only one eating it all for the first time. We pictured ourselves acknowledging to the brain injured that nearly every salad on the table was indeed white, and explaining why we would never be old enough or brave enough to change the menu.

I'd knocked off the Christmas shopping early. I had always done it on my own, as Jhonnie had been too busy. This year he wanted to come. He thought it might be an adventure. I took Jhonnie along on a few early excursions, but his slow gait and short-term memory loss made him a Westfield nightmare. At nearly every shop he'd suggest, 'That might be good for Madi.' I would explain that we'd done Madi. 'Oh good. What did we get her?' I'd tell him he was carrying it, and that would satisfy him until we stepped off another escalator and something else would catch his eye. 'That might be good for Madi.' It was easier to shop alone. One day he went for an outing with a friend and came home with armfuls of bags of elaborately wrapped presents. He'd spent hundreds. Although their sacks were already complete, he did the Christmas shopping for all four kids, all over again.

Christmas Day went well. The gravlax was particularly delicious and nobody ate or drank too much. Jhonnie was totally delighted to be alive. Some of us made speeches to that effect. Tracey decided it was important for the terminally ill to do the washing up. Her hands and feet were numb and shaky from the new treatment, but I didn't want to cross her. She took an enormous chip out of one of my favourite giant platters. Never a 'breaker', she held it out to me with a look of defeat. I thanked her for customising it, and we laughed. It's not a bad idea to get your favourite people to chip the things you love. It can keep them with you forever.

After lunch and enough champagne, I introduced a plan I'd been hatching. It might have been risky to break the spell, but I couldn't resist. The bigger kids were playing Cranium. Jhonnie and the littlies were swimming, and eating chocolate in the pool. Patrick had fallen asleep wearing his My First Christmas bib. What a happy and successful day.

We picked at cherries and chocolate, and I dived in the deep end. 'If the doctors give him the all clear, if we can pull it off, Jhonnie and I are going to go to New York to see

The Producers. In, say, two months, just for a week. If William settles in to school, and Jhonnie keeps improving, and the sky doesn't fall in.'

Julia went for her bag and her cigarettes. She stood in the doorway and smoked. The devil's advocate was on fire.

My mother looked nonplussed. 'Have you thought about New Caledonia?'

'Not for a second. Never. And I never will.'

'What about terrorists?'

'What about a brain haemorrhage!' came in with a waft of smoke.

'I really think if terrorists can manage to get us after all we've been through, then we're just not meant to be here. New Caledonia?'

'That's not funny.'

'I'm not afraid of terrorists. I'm afraid of missing Nathan Lane and Matthew Broderick.'

'They're not even doing the show anymore!' Julia knows everything, and the rest she makes up.

'No, they're back. That's the thing. When they did it two years ago, we couldn't go because I was trying to make Patrick, and having "procedures", and when I saw that documentary about it I realised that it was one of those had-to-be-there shows. It's one of my few genuine regrets. And that sounds silly, but Mum, you know what I mean.'

She did. My mother and I had trotted the globe all our lives in pursuit of theatrical high points, and still cherished programs to prove we hadn't made them up. Some of those nights number among the happiest of our lives. The opening of *La Cage Aux Folles* in San Francisco, *Equus* in London, and then there was the day we'd lucked in to two separate tickets to the matinee of Mike Nichols' production of *Waiting For Godot* with Robin Williams and Steve Martin. It's worth making the effort.

'I was sitting in the brain surgeon's office, as you do, and there it was in the *Herald* – like some kind of sign. Lane and Broderick are reprising the roles for two months. We have until the fourth of April. They're coming back just for us. What are the chances? They were gone. That moment had passed. We weren't going to get another chance *ever*, because that's the way it goes, you know, with shows. But we've got a second chance. Doesn't anybody see the symmetry in that?'

'I just think you should do a trial run to Noosa.'

'But we don't want to go to Noosa. We want to go to New York. It's the first holiday Jhonnie and I ever took together. I need new underwear, and *The Producers* isn't playing in Noosa!'

Eleni had been speechless. Julia had been blowing smoke through both nostrils. Mum was saying nothing, and finally Eleni broke the silence.

'Who are *The Producers*?'

5 months

WE BOUGHT TICKETS TO SEE *The Producers* on 30 March, and held out them as a carrot, a shining distant ultimate carrot, that kept me going because nothing about our lives was getting any easier.

The great northern Blampieds faded into the background, which was a small mercy. They all went to LA to spend Christmas with Justin. Julian was no longer speaking to anybody in Australia, and we agreed that was probably for the best. Jhonnie spoke to the others occasionally, and I managed to do little more than answer the phone and pass the receiver.

We had a few civil meetings with Chris, where we sat around a table and tried to make progress, but neither side found satisfaction, and the kids were stuck in the middle. Apparently Daddy had become a monster since his accident. He was never like this before. He'd always given Mummy everything she'd ever asked for, but now he didn't love anybody anymore and he was just angry all the time. After a weekend of that Jhonnie would sit with his heavy head in his hands and cry.

The euphoria of the homecoming passed but Jhonnie was stuck in a holding pattern. Gradually he began to see good friends and old aquaintances. Return from brain injury is so slow, there was no obvious landmark for a welcome-home party. Should we call in the caterers when he could walk up a flight of stairs without holding the wall, or when he could change Patrick's nappy? Depending on his mood or even the weather, Jhonnie would make progress, then appear to stall. He'd remain present and involved with adults at a dinner table, then sleep for great stretches of daylight without explanation.

The novelty of his story wore off for our immediate family, yet Jhonnie could muster all the wonder of survival, all the love for his kids, all the mystery of coma memories for each new audience. Perhaps the ad-man skills were resurfacing, because Jhonnie could entrance a small group at a picnic or the girl behind the counter at the dry-cleaners with his remarkable return from the dead. It was possible he had no idea how often he told his story, as a result of short-term memory loss.

While Jhonnie was honing his verbal skills I was tiring of the routine. Jhonnie would get to the part where he had a head the size of a watermelon and I would tune out. It wasn't so much that Jhonnie was milking it; I was scared he was stuck in a loop. The only place he worked, his only way to shine, was in his performance as 'the brain-injured guy'. Without a job, without the family in Europe, without any bright prospects for his future, he might have needed a new way to define himself. Unfortunately I'd been awake for all those months that Jhonnie had missed, and I was keen to move on, and redefine myself as anybody but 'the brain injury's wife'. There were some days when Jhonnie and I didn't have a lot to say to each other.

In the first week of the new school year, in February, Madison's swimming carnival was held at Homebush. Jhonnie had never been to Homebush for anything but a rugby match and the Olympics. He'd turned up sober just once, with Connar for the World Cup. He decided to make the trek by train to watch his little girl do half a lap of the pool where Ian Thorpe had broken those world records.

I was worried about him going. There was no 'special event' train. No corporate tent. He'd have to read schedules, and change platforms and get horribly confused, all on his own. And it was a long way to go on public transport in 40-degree heat.

More worrying than his potential confusion and heat exhaustion was the sad fact that he really had nothing better to do and nowhere better to go. Outside the gym, where he made great progress, I'd been unable to motivate him to any activity. So many friends had bought him paints and drawing materials that grew dusty in piles in his office. He had written thankyou letters, which people had loved, and he'd spent the whole summer with the kids, which seemed to keep him connected to the real world, but he still wouldn't open his mail, sit at a desk or sort out his finances. He had no income, a hornet's nest of debt, and a decade of filing to sort out. Daunting for the fit and conscientious. Impossible for the brain injured and often depressed.

He set out in the morning heat, and when I hadn't heard from him by four that afternoon I started to worry. Finally I rang Chris.

'Did you see Jhonnie at the swimming carnival?'

'He was there. He looked terrible. Honestly. I had no idea. He looked quite lost, as if he had no idea where he was.'

'He probably didn't. What did you do?'

'Nothing. I thought he would make Madi uncomfortable.'

'What? Did he see her race? Did she see him?'

'Only for a minute. It was very hot so I drove her home.'

'And left the brain-injured man there, dazed and confused? Seriously?'

'I didn't speak to him. I don't want to speak to him.'

'But you didn't think to even offer him a lift? Where is he now?'

'Still sitting on that stand staring into space, for all I know.

waterlemon

He said he was fine. He told Madison he was fine. Didn't he, Madi?'

'That's quite astonishing. Even for you.'

'I'm not going to have another one of these –'

'You have to. The man is brain injured. He needs help. I can't make you understand. We can barely function here and you –'

Click. Leave it to the lawyers.

Jhonnie arrived home at 6.30, purple in the face, distressed and embarrassed. His phone had died. His little girl had chosen to sit with her mother instead of her one-eyed monster father, and the trip had somehow taken nearly two hours each way. He couldn't find anything to eat and when his water bottle was empty he was too discouraged to refill it. And now he was home. He took a cold bottle of fizzy water from the fridge and went to bed.

6 months

EMAIL FROM RUTH TO JHONNIE'S LIST

Where did the time go?

Six months ago today, Jhonnie went bike riding at West Head and fell on his head. Sorry my correspondence has halted in recent months. Not so much nothing to report, as too much to do. Kids starting at new schools, me back at work, Jhonnie continuing fairly rigorous rehab and training, kids over the holidays.

Improvement has been constant and steady. Depending on which week you might ask, we are delighted or exasperated by Jhonnie's progress. Jhonnie's bung eye is opening, creating double vision, a confusing aesthetic, but hope for Jhonnie for a return to pre-September 3 health. Never going to happen. The doctors and opth – opt – people who specialise in eyes say his vision will never return to normal. While I had long ago come to terms with a one-eyed husband (easy for me – not my eye!) Jhonnie is not quite as complacent. He wears a patch over the good eye and stumbles around, slightly seasick, trying to discipline the bad one. Enough to frighten the horses, but we're used to it.

Physically, this head injury may be the key to Jhonnie's ultimate fitness. Six months off the piss, and four weight-training sessions a week are doing wonders for the broken body and occasionally drooping spirits.

The mysteries of brain injury continue to unfold. We've been warned to expect depression, anger and a sense of alienation from the lost life before the accident. Don't know if beetroot and sit-ups can ward off these evils, but we're trying.

While I am sick to my back teeth of hospitals, waiting rooms, and driving – nearly in my sleep – I can see light at the end of the long and heavily tolled tunnel. Occasionally strange and miraculous things occur and really make up for the fact that I have *still* only had one haircut in 12 months.

Connar and William started at Cranbrook. All going well so far. I felt like a traitor to Darlinghurst Public, sending William off to his posh school, when all his mates at preschool went together to Darlinghurst. All those families and kind busy women who had helped out with William when Jhonnie was in hospital. I had deserted, and found myself the worst groomed mother at Cranbrook – something new for the CV.

Just when I thought we would never fit in, something remarkable happened. One of the not-so-posh mothers – a really nice woman, with a really nice kid – stopped me one morning. She'd just heard about Jhonnie, and the accident, and said she wished I had told them at the beginning. I explained that I didn't want William to be 'that head injury kid' and anyway, we were very lucky. Jhonnie had landed on his head right next to a helicopter pad, and made it to hospital for brain surgery within the hour. Then she said, 'I think Rob Turner is a helicopter doctor.'

Whatever made her think of that? The name, I could nearly see it scribbled in my Filofax – the day of the accident, this remarkable young doctor had waited to speak to me. He'd made the call to take Jhonnie to RNS, not Gosford, because the head injury was going to kill him before the punctured lung. My mother and I remember every word he said – his frank disarming manner. And the way he apologised for his appearance. He'd been on duty for 36 hours.

Did she say Rob Turner? Was that the name? He'd written in my diary. He'd wanted to know if Jhonnie made it. I never called.

I couldn't work out when to call, and then, the 2003 diary pages went in the top drawer – buried hopefully with the rest of last year.

Yes, she said – 'That's Rob over there.'

I turned around in the playground of my son's posh new school to see a young clean-shaven man, toddler on hip. I walked over to him – prodded by the nice mum. It couldn't be. What to say?

'Excuse me – are you a helicopter doctor?'

As he replied 'West Head' I gulped a sob. He put his arms around me and I realised, at that moment, he did not know if his patient had lived or died. He remembered every detail of that day too. A keen cyclist himself, he'd remembered Jhonnie's fancy shoes. By way of understatement, he recalled, 'Your husband was very, very sick.'

So, Dr Rob Turner and I met again, six months after he had delivered Jhonnie to safety, at our sons' school. What are the chances? It's not such a big school. It was an incredible, uncanny meeting. He had come that Friday morning to see his son, Michael, get a prize at assembly. His son – not just a Cranbrook boy, but a new boy, like William. Both in kindergarten. Both in class KC, sitting at the same table at school that day. Two of 20 boys starting school together.

I feel fine about Cranbrook now.

The Turners and the Blampieds joke that in Hollywood our boys would grow up, go off to war together, and William would save Michael's life. But this is Sydney. They'll grow up, sleep with each other's girlfriends and become sworn enemies.

I can't even begin to conjecture as to what this all means. Isn't life a surprise.

Thank you all for your continued support. Jhonnie still very slow at the keyboard and, as ever, a hopeless correspondent.

So, there it is. Six months.

Not much more

Xrr

7 months

SITTING IN J ROW, IN the stalls of the St James Theatre on West 44th Street that chilly night in March, waiting for *The Producers* to begin, has forever redefined 'anticipation' for me. It had the childish excitement of Christmas and the emotional confusion that can well up just before a birth or a wedding. I was aware, almost tingling, knowing to mark every precious moment, because we would never be here again. The wonder that we had pulled it off at all was astounding. All that and more, right there, in a faded velvet theatre seat, waiting to get the pay-off for a family-sized supreme, extra-cheese order of anticipation.

I looked around at the other theatre-goers, the notes in the *Playbill*, the boys selling T-shirts and caps, and at my beautiful husband, sitting by my side, beaming, holding my hand, seeing I was close to tears. His whole body was flooded with happiness for me. This was my grail. He shared it. He wanted it, but he knew it was a prize beyond measure for me. I think I might have been shaking. I must have looked peculiar, in my new cheap-but-well-fitting Levi's from Canal Jeans, my ridiculously expensive top from Barney's, and my Eres underwear that made me feel completely pre-Gump, ever so temporarily. I looked at him, and had to look away to stop my chin from crumbling. What astounding luck to have found a man who

271

can grasp the nuances of my own particular fears and treasures, and care so much. What were the odds of coming so close to losing him, and the family we'd conjured and created, and then having him back.

He leaned over and whispered, 'It's exciting, little girl. It's like waiting for the horses at the Olympics to come thundering underneath us. I'm so glad I get to do all this with you.'

We kissed. I gulped, and sobbed, and the house lights dimmed and the show began. What does it mean to cry like a baby just before a Broadway show, yet stay arrow-straight and dry-eyed in an Emergency Room at Royal North Shore Hospital? What's that about? I stopped crying and started thinking all through the overture, first about how perfectly crisp the orchestra sounded, and then about how we'd made it here. How unlikely it was that we would ever be sitting in these perfect house seats, together, and enjoying a moment of anticipation that should have been impossible.

It hadn't just been a couple of months of planning. A lifetime, even a few generations of determination, good luck, bad luck, passion and drive had delivered us here, right here, in the impossibly exciting seats of good fortune.

My father's affection for Mel Brooks had a lot to do with it. When we were kids Dad would share Brooks' extensive wisdom on various areas of expertise and concern, whenever the mood took him. He was 47 when I was born, and maybe because he knew we wouldn't be together forever, he thought of his homilies as gifts – which often bored and annoyed us when they were badly timed. I referred to these as his 'history of the Jews' monologues. The topic was irrelevant. The fact that we'd heard it all before meant nothing. The stock market, real estate, beef, thoroughbreds, sourdough bread, oysters, jazz, fascism, history, politics, cricket, rugby, poker, retail, pastrami, exercise, newspapers and Jewish comedians. These would have been his subjects of specialty if he had ever competed on

Mastermind. British comedians were fine, and he didn't mind Benny Hill or John Cleese, but really, if you wanted to understand humour, you looked to the Jews. His argument was watertight. Three Stooges: not funny. Marx Brothers: funny. Sid Caesar, Jack Benny, Woody Allen, Lenny Bruce, Mel Brooks: funny.

He loved Mel Brooks the most because, like my father, Brooks bravely went where Jews dared not go: to Westerns and horror movies and the Holocaust. Mel Brooks took away the Nazis' power by writing *The Producers*, and I'd watched that movie with him, and we'd laughed at Zero Mostel and Gene Wilder until we'd cried.

My mother's passion for theatre, particularly musicals, had enchanted my entire childhood. She'd lived in New York in the '50s and she told us such vivid stories of the opening night of *Kismet* and of singing in bars in the Villiage with members of the chorus from *South Pacific* and *Guys and Dolls*. At home we played her heavy thick vinyl soundtracks to the shows, and pawed over the *Playbills*. After dinner, doing the washing up, we'd sing songs from *Gypsy* and *Camelot* and *West Side Story*.

Every member of our family knows every word of these songs, and at any low point we can sing ourselves into a major-key mood and just get on with it – or at least not go to bed miserable.

Mel Brooks might have cooked this show up for both of my parents. After all these years, he had written the book, the words and music, to a very great musical that had won all the Tonys and attracted the cast, one of those Ethel Merman, Mary Martin kinds of casts that I'd always longed for.

It was my mum and my dad and all of me, and it was hard to do, and they all said we couldn't. But we did. I cried as the house lights dimmed, because without all of that, I never would have hooked up with Jhonnie, and without all of that, we wouldn't have been able to get him back, get us here. It took beef and real estate, and broad beans and the Jews and the Catholics. It was a miracle (and I'm very grateful to the nuns), but in that moment, before 'another opening of another show', at the age of 43, I really knew exactly who I was. Nathan Lane came on stage, and we never looked back.

10-12 months

THAT WAS HOW IT SHOULD have ended. But Broadway musicals and new underwear can't fix everything. I don't want to give the impression that our lives were like a turgid country-and-western song without an uplifting chorus, but while everybody else moved on, Jhonnie was stuck.

We spoke to the rehab doctors, and Jhonnie's caseworker, who came to the house every few weeks, and the family psychologist we'd seen on and off over the years. They would ask Jhonnie if he was depressed, and he would say no. All he wanted to do was be there for me and the kids, he'd say. It was my turn now. He'd put me through enough, he could see that. So, he just wanted to be *in* his family, for the first time in his life, and maybe write some kids' books, but mostly just take over the load from me.

But he couldn't.

Was it brain injury or depression that stopped Jhonnie from functioning properly, I wondered; and why couldn't I make anyone understand that he wasn't getting better? One day, during the caseworker's visit, when Jhonnie explained how well everything was going, how he'd done homework with William and taken Patrick to the park so that I could write, and made shepherd's pie for the children, I cracked.

'That's not it! Jhonnie was supposed to take William to a doctor's appointment. He forgot and just came straight home. And you don't *start* making shepherd's pie at six. The kids *eat* at six. Shepherd's pie is an inedible wretched meal at the best of times, and six is not the best of times. Anyway, their dinner was already in the fridge.

'And the *park*! The park is a perfect metaphor. Jhonnie did take Pat to the park, and I asked him to get milk. I even rang and reminded him when I knew they'd be heading back for Pat's bottle, and we were still on the phone when Jhonnie went into the shop. So those little mental cues are helping, and that's all great. But Jhonnie came home and left the milk in the stroller, in the heat. So you see, it was worse than knowing I was *out* of milk and knowing I had to go *get* some. I thought I *had* milk, and I did, but I didn't . . . That's what our life's like. That's what Jhonnie's like, and I want to know what we can do to help him get better.'

After the caseworker left, Jhonnie went into a rage. How could I humiliate him like that? He'd given his entire life to make me happy, and nothing was good enough. He's not good enough. Every time we go anywhere it's plain I can't stand to be with him. I can't get away from him fast enough, and now, to shame him in front of a stranger, and make him look like an idiot . . .

That's right. I couldn't hear those stories one more time. I couldn't listen to his broken record of self-pity. I needed to speak to adults occasionally who engage with the world.

And then he didn't speak to me at all for three weeks. Silence or a brawl. I brawled back. His paranoia was becoming a self-fulfilling prophecy. Surely I had more than amply demonstrated that I was here for the long haul. I wasn't going anywhere.

He would go silently to the gym, or sit for hours at his desk, making no progress unravelling his administrative nightmare. He lost track of his investments. He started smoking, and he paced at night with insomnia. We were seeing a barrage of professionals, and they told us that if Jhonnie didn't think he was depressed, then he wasn't. And that really, considering the severity of his injuries, this morbidly moping silent stuck man was doing great.

Unfortunately, the patient who had wowed the rehab team into an early release because of his remarkable insights into his own injuries couldn't see how badly he was floundering. In one of life's cruel ironies, it appeared that Jhonnie was much easier to love in a coma.

DAY 365 EMAIL

From the head of JHONNIE BLAMPIED, 3 September 2004
My dear friends,
It has been a year since the fateful day, September 3rd, 2003. It has reframed my definition of the word 'fate'. I can hear Ray's brother in *Everybody Loves Raymond* saying, 'It was meant . . . to be.' It is strange that fate should have negative connotations? Or is it just me that has that association? Either way, there has been good stuff to come out of this. I don't want to give the impression that this has been anything but shitful and traumatic for everyone concerned. But a Phoenix doesn't rise from a bubble bath. And neither have I.

The brain injury hasn't given me delusions of grandeur. I don't actually see myself as a phoenix, but I do think I am in danger of finding true happiness. Ruth and I are more deeply in love than ever. I have more love from family & friends than is decent for any human being. I am excited by the future. I can see more possibilities in life than I have ever seen before. It *is* good to be alive. The accident may have given me the tools to live indecently well.

While I am sure I will continue getting better and stronger, I'm bloody good now. The accident has allowed me to re-evaluate many things in life, and count my many blessings. Including the many fantastic people I have in my life.

While I want to thank you individually, an open letter (or email) is a start. It is also a symbolic conclusion to Ruth's amazing emails. Your thoughts, words and love made a real difference. It helped me find my way home. I also think that making Ruth the conduit for your love and well-wishes reinforced (subconsciously) her confidence that things would be all right.

So thank you, everyone!

Your support made an enormous difference to Ruth and me. You helped us through the most challenging time of our lives.

While you got running commentary from Rufus's side of the bed, let me give you a taste of what was going on the other side. Surprisingly there was a lot happening. Ruth & Pete came into the hospital and talked 'at' 120 kg of not-so-prime, not-so-English, beef. I can remember much of my coma thoughts. They were really freaky! But in there, somewhere and somehow, Ruth found me.

I remember looking down at my body and being offered an exit from this life to the next. Whilst I asked to see my next life, it was refused. Instead I was allowed to review my current life. It was a moment of intense detachment, almost like looking through a photo album of a life of a close relative. You recognise the players but you weren't actually in the picture. Well in the darkness of this detachment, I heard Ruth's voice. The lights turned on in my head. Her voice gave me a torch to see where I was. More importantly it gave me the ability to navigate the corridors of my coma. I followed her voice, through the hallways in my head, back to reality.

Coming out of a coma was the most romantic experience of my life. Isn't it a shame that we never get to experience the rush of falling in love with the partners we marry by the time we are married? How could you fall in love with people you are already in love with? You can't.

Unless, of course, your brain has been wiped completely

clean. If your brain is rebooting itself, you get to experience a whole lot of things 'for the first time'. I got to experience that feeling of first love with Ruth all over again. It was amazing. When you are coming out of coma you can really do justice to falling in love. You know how preoccupying it can be? Well, when there is nothing else occupying your head you can do it real justice.

When I came out of the coma one of the first things I said was: 'I'll look back on this in five years' time, and see it as a gift. So much will happen because of this accident. It is a gift.' This is proving to be true. It has only been a year since the accident and already I see the positives sides.

I feel I am a 'better adjusted', 'happier and a whole-er' person after my conversation with tarmac. Who'd have thought it? It is only a near death experience that gives you a better view on living. I am rebuilding myself physically, mentally and emotionally. It looks like I will come out of this a new man.

Hopefully this note can act as a full stop to the sentence caused by my accident – end of paragraph, or is it actually the start of a new chapter? Actually, it feels like more of a fundamental shift than that. So let me leave you with how I feel a year after the accident.

It doesn't feel like I am about to start a new chapter in my life. It feels like I am about to write a new book. I am sure that it will have lots of twists and turns in it. Chapter one is proving to be a bit of a heart starter. I have no idea where the story is going. That is what makes the story interesting. About the only thing I am now certain of is that it will have a happy ending. Thank you for being part of chapter one.

In the end — it never ends

Eighteen months after the accident, anybody observing our family at a SupaCentre wouldn't have guessed we'd been through anything more sinister than a stocktaking sale. To the average onlooker, progress on every front was remarkable. We were back on track. The kids were all happy in new uniforms. Meera and Patrick played around the house and in the pool as I got back into the routines of writing my column, building our holiday house, and writing this book. We'd all become quite good at playing the irksome roles of those amazing people who had endured so much but come through it, all the same. But not the same.

Jhonnie was getting fitter every day. He looked so much younger and leaner in his gorgeous new shirts from New York. Only the bung eye gave any clue to Jhonnie's dramas, and even that he could turn to advantage. Finally free of a lifetime of business suits and ties, he forged a loud but expensive casual style that he customised with jaunty eye-patches. One day, while shopping for underwear with me at White Ivy, Jhonnie gave the lingerie queens a real challenge. Within weeks he sported a bespoke collection of patches that included fabrics from Versace to Paul Smith.

There had been nibbles from the industry, tempting him

back to the land of advertising 'consulting', and it was with mixed emotions that Jhonnie prepared to take his 'head out for a spin'. He helped Sam and a few mates out with some pitches. Sam would be discreet and constructive enough to tell Jhonnie if he lost the plot. But no, the big guy's first efforts were a success.

Jhonnie and Dr Rob appeared on *The Today Show* to promote Careflight and the lifesaving aspects of having doctors on board helicopters. With Jhonnie as exhibit A and Rob decked out as a fluoro action figure, the two men recounted their unlikely tale as their six-year-old sons played hooky from assembly and ate pastries in the green room. Such progress from West Head.

The *Australian* newspaper ran an almost full-page feature in its marketing section to celebrate the return of the industry's golden-haired boy to full health and future full employment. In the article, Jhonnie's affection for me and his vigour for life since his rude awakening were inspiring. Everybody rang or wrote emails, moved to see the whole story in print, and pleased to see Jhonnie looking so well. This was the week the Pope died. JP II's picture was actually smaller than Jhonnie's above the masthead on the *Australian* that day. There it was in black-and-white, with papal endorsement no less: Jhonnie was back.

That week Jhonnie stayed up most nights, smoking and moping. His insomnia informed his posture. The crooked stoop, the weak left side, the swollen dragging hip demanded pity, and got nothing but clench-jawed frustration in reply. He joined us for very few meals.

I went out one night for dinner with Therese. She was full of encouragement. She believed in Jhonnie, in us. This was a bad patch, she insisted, but surely nothing compared to what we'd been through. (Was I starting to sound like those women who go out for a drink and do nothing but complain about their marriage? I hate those women.) We ate Vietnamese entrées and drank Vietnamese beer. The thrill of the autumn night air, in the company of an old friend and a mountain of blue swimmer crab, improved my mood considerably. Therese was right. We could get through this.

She dropped me off at 11. Inside the gate, smoking by the garbage bins in his underwear, stood Jhonnie, lurching slightly and silently to the left.

Anyone can drop everything, every now and then, in an emergency. The broken arm, the funeral, the car accident, and especially the head injury. We can dump our plans in a hurry and swoop to the rescue. But the Blampied emergency had gone on for too long. People, a lot of people, had parked their lives to help us, because that's what you do. It's very reassuring to see. We've tested the friendships. We all know how we'll scrub up in a crisis. Very well, apparently. But there are thresholds, even in the dearest, closest relationships. And at some point I stopped reaching out for help because, other than acting as sounding boards and sympathetic ears, I couldn't see what anyone could do. Our darkest fears could no longer be relieved with babysitting or minestrone.

At certain low points it was impossible not to confide in Esther or Pete or Eleni. They seemed to have boundless patience for the topic of Jhonnie – And How to Get Him Back. But we were all stumbling around in the dark. Even with the best intentions and thoughtful consideration, without a greater understanding of brain injury, our half-arsed pop psych analysis deteriorated into kitchen-table marriage counselling.

I would often meet Esther at Parmalat straight after school drop-off to share the latest in the excruciating series of dead ends and disasters. Every new episode varied so little from the last, it's stunning that she didn't nod off into her English Break-fast . . . And then he'd . . . and then I'd . . . so he went up . . . I walked out and that was the last straw, again!

Some sagas were hilarious. Some despicable. Some I felt sure offered proof that nobody could be expected to live under these circumstances: with the silent sulking man who could set me up, let me down, hang me out to dry and then play the victim all in one day. And I learned nothing. I couldn't ignore his self-pity, or talk to somebody else during his interminable silences or laugh off an ugly fight and go shopping. I couldn't take any more but I wouldn't do anything different. We went in circles.

It's always good to be heard. I would finish my mortadella mushroom roll and Esther would leave some fruit salad for good manners and punctuate my tedious outpourings with: 'You married him!'

When people asked, 'How's Jhonnie travelling?', there was no straight answer.

'Good. It's much longer and harder than we thought. He's amazing. We're all so proud of him. Everybody's very, very tired. The kids are hanging in there. Well, it's good to get out a bit. We're moving on. It takes a while to shake that whole hospital headspace . . .'

I found a million different ways to tell our story. None of them honest. People had been so generous with us, it was unfair to give a straight answer to the question and hope they'd have the ticker or the time to hear the answer: 'After 18 months, things are worse, life is more miserable and holds less hope than it did in Intensive Care. Our lives are still fucked, but we've added 18 months of exhaustion as a special handicap to coping with brain injury.'

Hands up who wants to hear that?

I developed a palatable version of our story for public consumption, and the private truth I shared mostly with Tracey and a few close pysch friends. Before being allowed to practise, good psychologists attend a School of Meaningful Silences. Tracey was a master. I kept her updated on our regular sessions with Jhonnie's caseworker, our appointments with the brain injury doctors at the RNS clinics, and our visits with the family psychologist. I'd rabbit on, often enthusiastically, quoting the advice of one practitioner or another.

So, we checked with everybody and Jhonnie wasn't depressed. We asked them. They said no. They asked Jhonnie. 'Jhonnie, are you depressed?' 'No, doctor. I'm concentrating.' There. Not depressed. Silence.

So, the caseworker got Jhonnie to formulate a list of goals and prioritise them. Anything from writing a kids' book to taking me out to dinner. Then Jhonnie had a month to rewrite the list. I think it might have been more helpful if the caseworker had just gone downstairs and observed Jhonnie 'working' at his desk to find out how he could sit there for five hours and achieve nothing. Silence.

So, Jhonnie had made these investments and never told me how much was involved; and when I found out, during a meeting with our accountant, I was furious. When I raised it with the caseworker, Jhonnie was crushed, his cover blown. (Surely we're not here to impress the rehab team?) The caseworker wanted to look at the positive aspects of a semi-unemployed brain-injured man throwing away his nest egg. Silence.

I was asking the professionals all the right questions and feeling that my job was done because I'd asked the questions, even though I didn't really believe the answers. I was just as stuck as Jhonnie, but angry with it. And in the meaningful silences, when Tracey neither applauded nor disagreed with a 'colleague', I sensed she was holding back.

Was I crazy? I asked the doctors if I should go on antidepressants, because I cried, a lot, and if Jhonnie wouldn't go on them, perhaps one of us should. No, they said, I had a lot to cry about, and I cried appropriately. (Tick. Add 'Appropriate Crier' to CV.)

'Crazy' is not a useful or meaningful word when used in the same sentence as 'brain injury'. I could keep waiting for the brain injury to go away, but as months became years our new life, our replacement life, was far from a dream. Tracey must have held theories that she didn't want to articulate. Why? Because the news was bad, and there is no treatment/cure? Or was it true that brain injury is so unpredictable, that life would get back to normal as Jhonnie's professional confidence grew and time gave us all a necessary distance from the crisis? Silence.

Friends have told me that I have a tendency to underestimate the severity or the disastrous potential of any situation. I'm not a worrier. If my husband has a 50–50 chance of surviving an accident, those are very good odds.

I can see that this naiveté was useful in Emergency and the months that followed. We all managed to get to Ryde every day with my head firmly stuck in the sand. And pressing on with life, writing books and building houses would not have seemed sensible to somebody with a less optimistic outlook on our family. I wasn't crazy. I was just plain thick.

Two bad weeks would come to an end and one day Jhonnie would wake up, jump out of bed, initiate conversation, make plans, take action, book a babysitter, go to the butcher, have two meetings, make some jokes on the phone, pick up William from school, and help him with homework while I made a beautiful dinner; we'd then cuddle on the couch and smooch off to bed. At last, it was all coming together. Be gone, brain injury! Jhonnie's fine now. We're all fine.

Silence.

The second year after Jhonnie's accident was much harder than the first. Tracey and the meaningfully silent psych friends spoke up. There were names and phone numbers and referrals to new doctors. We fired everybody involved with Jhonnie's rehabilitation, but not before hitting our nadir after the neuropsychological exam that was intended to assess his capabilities.

The whole team found his case riveting. What an exotic specimen. So articulate. So artistic. So full of insights to his own situation.

Such a big con artist.

We assembled in the family psychologist's office for a two-hour session: the neuropsych, the caseworker, the family psychologist, Jhonnie and his angry wife.

Without the benefit of similar tests before the accident, it was hard to be sure, but Jhonnie's intellect did not seem to be impaired. He'd apparently had buckets of extra brains before the accident – so much that he could splosh most of it on the pavement and still have more than enough to hold a witty conversation and charm a roomful of professionals afterwards. His executive skills were diminished, but still in the average or acceptable zone; and interestingly he displayed a tendency to withdraw, disappearing into a hole of invisibility, periodically. He'd probably been doing it his whole life, and that may well have resulted from child abuse, as he had rickets as a toddler.

They were all enchanted. Jhonnie loved it. He wasn't fucked. He was just fascinating. Jhonnie gave the group one of his perfect little speeches about his goals, and passion for his family and his art, which he would do, one day, eventually. They nodded with him, inspired. I could feel the tears start to stream.

'This doesn't get us *anywhere*,' I cut in. 'Didn't we do this test to find out what Jhonnie's capabilities are so he can make plans? Don't these results more or less tell us he's good to go?'

'These results are very pleasing, all 'round.'

'Well, why doesn't anyone believe me when I say that Jhonnie just doesn't function? He's *not* good to go. He's not there. He doesn't initiate conversation. His desk is piled to the ceiling with serious stuff that he can't or won't face.'

The neuropsych thought she knew better. There's a certain type of straight-backed blonde that always gives me the creeps. A broom inserted way too far, a smug sense of superiority born of keeping an overly neat home in a sterile lower-north-shore suburb.

'Perhaps you're overwhelmed,' she began. 'This is the first time you've had to take care of the finances and the family. Perhaps you can do this together. What about embarking on a little financial project that you two could both undertake —'

'I've been balancing my chequebook since I was 12. I am not overwhelmed by finances. I'm telling you, *Jhonnie isn't coping*. He doesn't pay his bills. He can't keep track of his investments, and without any income this is becoming an issue.'

She turned to Jhonnie. 'Is that right, Jhonnie? Are your finances overwhelming you?'

'Well, they have in the past, because I used to work 15-hour days and travel so much. I think my own affairs were never enough of a priority, but I'm addressing that.'

'Ruth, everybody isn't going to perform to your exacting standards. Jhonnie might just need to find his own way.'

'But he isn't . . .' Jhonnie shook his head in dismay and embarrassment at my tears. 'You're not, Jhonnie. You're not coping. You have three keyboards on your desk and none of them work, and you won't finalise anything because the keyboards don't work. You can't get the computer started, yet you won't let me ring someone to come and fix it.'

'And that's how little you know. I have one of those keyboards because the K on the main board isn't functioning, and there's a K in my password, and the third one is the only keyboard that has a Send button that works. So I need all three.'

'I rest my case. This is how Jhonnie functions.'

Nobody responded. They seemed to think Jhonnie's explanation, his excuse for achieving precisely nothing, day after day, for nearly two years, was fine.

'I think you've lost sight of the big picture here, Ruth,' the neuropsych suggested, accompanying her words with a patronising toss of her perfectly highlighted mane. 'You're lucky to have Jhonnie in this room at all.'

I was unable to stop crying, abandoned and lost as I was in a roomful of very expensive, ineffectual professional help. On the way out, our psychologist told me to call up and make an appointment, as I was obviously distressed. I said nothing. The neuro-blonde faced me off at the door and made the mistake of looking into my eyes.

'It's a journey, Ruth. It's your journey.'

On the way home Jhonnie raged at me for ruining his moment and spoiling the show. That night he started chain smoking, and he didn't stop.

We were getting help, but we weren't getting anywhere. I pulled my head out of the sand, took Tracey's advice and found a new team. Jhonnie had been doing great 'for a serious head injury'. He hadn't succumbed to the violent outbursts, alcoholism or wildly inappropriate behaviour that plagues many brain-injury patients. One of his caseworker's other charges had killed himself. So, relatively speaking . . . (Now, there's an opportunity for a meaningful silence.)

Good enough for a head injury, but not good enough for Jhonnie. He had reached that point where he could use the accident as a very legitimate excuse for screwing up the rest of his life, or he could beat it.

There are probably as many different ways to rehabilitate from brain injury as there are brain injuries. With a whole new team of specialists and a huge commitment from Jhonnie, after nearly two years he turned a corner. (The clichés of human-tragedy yarns appear to be unavoidable.)

Jhonnie's slow and excruciating journey through this stage of recovery is his story to tell, not mine. Jhonnie says it is the hardest challenge he's ever faced. After months of tears, insomnia and chain smoking, Jhonnie began to emerge from the other side in one piece. Slowly, we found our way back to each other, and it seems to me that he has finally woken up from the deep. My husband has finally come out of the fog and the man I live with now is probably in much better shape than the ad exec who took his racing bike for a spin on that sunny September morning.

Jhonnie likes to refer to the accident as a gift. I think that's bollocks. I would have been much happier enjoying my new baby, William's transition from homeboy to schoolboy, and my comfortable life with my lovely family and friends. But Jhonnie would never have had to face awful truths and revisit terrible places to finally make a real go of his life.

There are highly successful, self-important, overachieving middle-aged men everywhere who are spinning too fast, not looking where they are going, not stopping long enough to care, who are just moments from a life-altering thump on the head. I might issue their wives with cricket bats to accelerate the process.

While Jhonnie's life had temporarily stalled, the rest of the world had not. All the lovely friends who had saved our lives got on with theirs, selling houses, having babies, remarrying, writing books, painting paintings, falling in and out of love, and sitting around tables of good food and wine, though never often enough for our liking.

Jhonnie has very little contact with his family in the northern hemisphere. When we were in New York, Justin flew over for the day. He was moved to tears and laughter to see his brother in one piece. Of all the Blampieds, Justin took the most merciless beating from me in those early Intensive Care days, but our day together was total joy. Justin is the only member of the family to have seen Jhonnie since the accident.

Jhonnie and Chris went back to court. Jhonnie won, but solved little more than a few contact disagreements. Communication between the two households never improved, yet Connar and Madi are growing into amazing people, and are wonderful siblings for Patrick and William.

While Jhonnie was finding his marbles, William learned to read, write, count, play soccer, surf, skateboard, collect ridiculous Japanese cards, make true friends, and play marbles. He remains the most intuitive and wise little boy I know.

Patrick, the perfect baby, grew into the prefect toddler. His inclination to make eye contact and tell long involved stories about greedy camels captivates strangers in shopping centres. (Highly unlikely he is actually my child.) After a weekend with Patrick, adults who should know better are referring to watermelons as 'waterlemons'. My fear for him is that he'll be delinquent by 10, having peaked at two.

Tracey died, but not before seeing her daughter, Alex, through the HSC, which she passed with an aggregate of 97.9, and through the first year of university with High Distinctions. We had one more Christmas together and I'll cherish my chipped platter forever.

When Jhonnie got moving again, he made giant leaps and bounds. He lost 32 kilos in the process. Women are always fascinated by this detail and want to know his secret. He tells them how he fell off his racing bike one day, went into a coma, broke all his ribs and his shoulder, and was on life support with a head the size of a waterlemon.

Surely he means *watermelon*, poor man. Perhaps that's just the brain injury talking.

No, he explains. 'Waterlemon' is his three-year-old son's

word for watermelon; but he probably wouldn't have known that if he hadn't fallen off his bike, and changed his life, because he probably wouldn't have been around Patrick at all.

We don't take Patrick and his waterlemons for granted. An accident such as Jhonnie's doesn't make you love your children more, or value your friends any better. It can sharpen your perspective and stop you from fussing over the little things, or it can cloud your judgment and lead you to exhausted irrational choices.

Even the language of brain injury is fuzzy and full of loopholes. The margin for error is also a margin for hope, or denial. A brain injury covers everything from a dizzying bump on the head to the condition that medical dramas like to refer to as 'brain death'.

Brain injury. It lacks nuance or any of the onomatopoeic impact that the uninitiated might find helpful by way of warning. It may not be a medical conspiracy but the language puts up a wall for the ignorant and optimistic. If you knew what it meant at the start, could you even begin?

The word 'miscarriage' in no way connotes the death of a baby, instead misleading us in the direction of some kind of derailment. 'Procedure' covers a multitude of invasive sins, from a DNA swab to brain surgery, as if the lucky recipient should feel equally neutral about both. And even the brain-injury 'literature' that can be found in doctors' waiting rooms everywhere but Intensive Care (where there's no room for literature real or medical) sheds no light. Those pointless pamphlets, three shiny folds, written by a roomful of nasty blonde neuropsychs, contain not a shred of truth. They don't even hint at the human endurance test that is brain injury, and their authors have the nerve to call them 'literature'.

There is no word I've found that adequately encompasses our bizarre trip. It's not 'grief', because it is not a cavernous hole that only fills with time.

'Tragedy' excludes the camaraderie and kindness, the foxhole-like quality that creates the bonds of a lifetime. What came out of the accident is a life that we would otherwise never have known, an outcome we had never bargained for. Brain injury no longer informs our every move, but we are never completely free of it. Our outcome is a hybrid of pain and ugliness, beauty and surprise. It's a disaster. It's a gift. It's a waterlemon.

Jhonnie's working again. He's 'consulting' with considerably more discipline than he displayed before the accident. Much more importantly, he's drawing. His first effort, a portrait of Pete's partner, Nicole, on the occasion of her fortieth birthday, surprised everybody. What a talented and complex man he is. Pete continues to be his best friend, brother, and godfather to half of our children.

Jhonnic is still discovering why he ever needed to ride so fast on an unknown road to almost certain self-destruction. Maybe I'm naive, but I'm more inclined to agree with my mother. Shit happens.

Acknowledgments

JHONNIE'S RECOVERY WOULD NOT HAVE been possible without the dedicated efforts of doctors, nurses, Careflight workers, ambos and the rehab teams at the Royal North Shore Hospital and Ryde Rehabilitation Centre, Sydney. They are too numerous to list individually here, but their kindness and professionalism are inspiring. Many of their names have been changed in this book to protect their privacy.

My recovery would not have been possible without my extraordinary friends and beloved family. To the Ritchies – Patricia, Julia, Anna, Michael, Angela and Cecilia – thanks for the soup and everything that comes with it.

Special thanks also to my colleagues at the *Sydney Morning Herald* for being so patient and making me laugh; and to the staff, boys and parents at Dickins House, Cranbrook, for making me cry, nearly every Friday.

Unless they fall on their heads and require quantities of invalid cooking, I will never be able to adequately thank or repay the kindness of everyone who offered our family help and support. Only a few of them are listed. In case of emergency I can strongly recommend the company and encouragement of everybody on this page. Thanks, once again, to Maggie Alderson, Nicole Anderson, Tracey Brown, Simon

Burke, Esther Clerehan, Julie Cottrell-Dormer, Richard Croall, Liz Dangar, Kate Dennis, the English family, Pete Evans, Peter FitzSimons, Mandy Foley-Quin, Helen Greenwood, Therese Hall, Hugh Hamilton, Cliff Holloway, Sarah Hopkins, Sam Hunter, Michael Kelley, Clare Koch, Meera Lawrence, Philip Le Masurier, Sally Loane, Ricardo Lopez, Kate McClymont, Georgie MacDougall, Susan McKinnon, Andrew McPhail, Matt Moran, Eleni Nakopoulos, Jane Pails, Naomi Parry, Libby Paterson, William Petley, Bob Powell, Graeme Selden, Yahoo and Lulu Serious, Katri Skala, Miriam and Les Stein, Dr Rob Turner, James Valentine and Jem Wallace.